AF422922

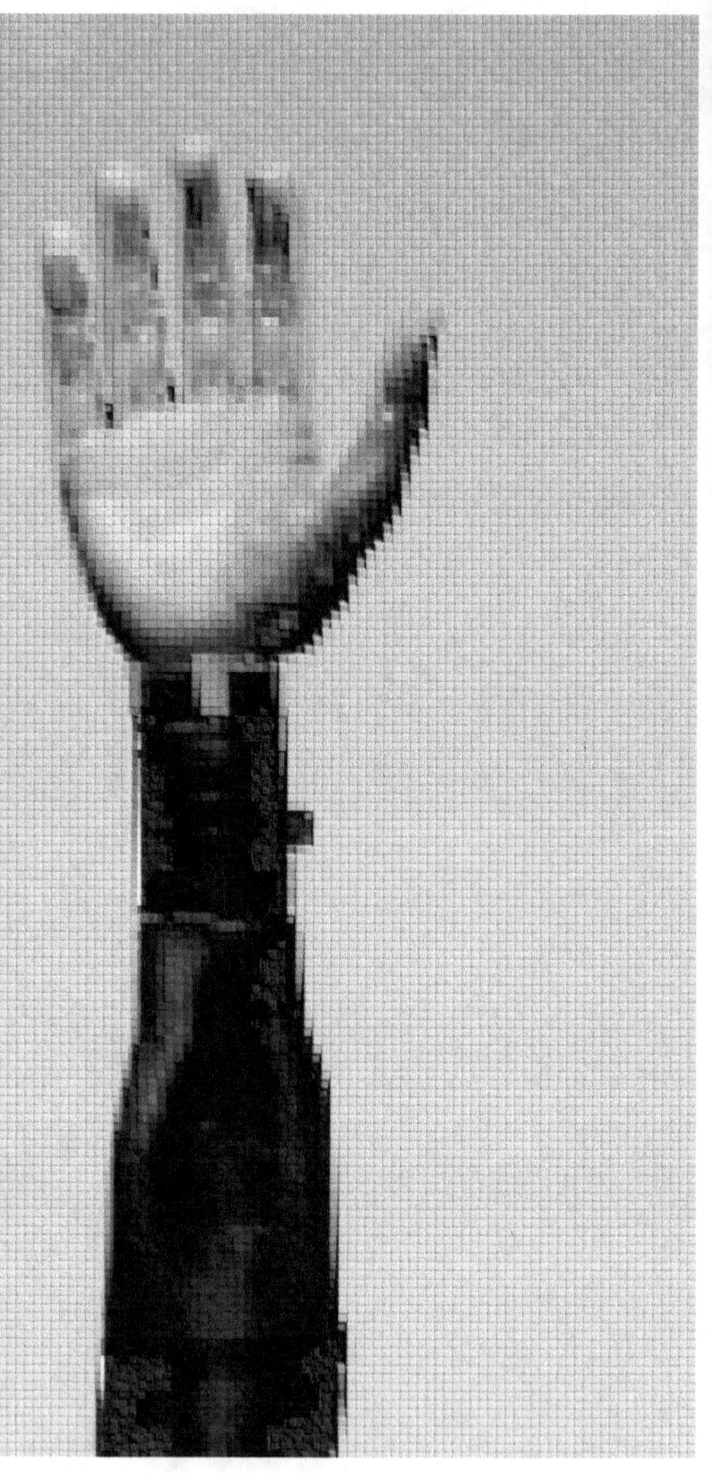

About the Author

Thomas Gresham is a visionary business strategist and renowned expert in exponential growth. With a vast amount of experience spanning several decades, he has dedicated his life to helping businesses thrive and achieve extraordinary success. Through his innovative approaches and unparalleled insights, Gresham has played a pivotal role in generating over £5 billion in revenue for businesses across industries.

As a thought leader in the field of social media marketing, Gresham recognizes the transformative power of digital platforms. He has delivered thousands of captivating lectures, captivating audiences with his deep understanding of social media's potential to revolutionize business growth. With his guidance, companies have been able to harness the power of social media, exploiting the latest techniques to achieve seemingly impossible levels of growth, regardless of their size or industry.

Gresham's expertise extends beyond social media marketing alone. His strategic acumen and groundbreaking methodologies have enabled businesses to capitalize on the latest trends and cutting-edge techniques. By working with both small startups and prestigious FTSE 500 companies, Gresham has consistently achieved remarkable results, guiding organizations to unlock unparalleled growth potential.

With a passion for sharing his knowledge, Gresham has become a highly sought-after speaker, mentor, and consultant. His captivating lectures and workshops have empowered countless individuals and businesses to reimagine their growth strategies, challenge the status quo, and embrace innovative approaches to achieve extraordinary results.

Throughout his career, Gresham has amassed a remarkable portfolio of success stories, ranging from helping small businesses skyrocket their revenue to transforming the trajectories of industry giants. His unique ability to blend strategy, creativity, and a deep understanding of market dynamics has earned him the reputation as a trusted advisor and growth catalyst.

As an author, Gresham brings his wealth of experience and insights to readers worldwide. His groundbreaking book, " Amplify 2.0: Sparking Viral Growth wIth Next-Gen Social Media, Print Disruption, Tenders, Sales Optimization, and Digital Mastery" has become a beacon of inspiration for entrepreneurs, marketers, and business leaders seeking to dominate their markets and achieve unparalleled growth.

Thomas Gresham continues to push the boundaries of what is possible, empowering businesses to amplify their presence, seize new opportunities, and achieve remarkable growth. With his unwavering commitment to excellence and his relentless pursuit of innovation, Gresham is at the forefront of the ever-evolving business landscape, guiding companies toward a future brimming with boundless possibilities.

Summary

"Amplify 2.0: Sparking Viral Growth with Next-Gen Social Media, Print Disruption, Tenders, Sales Optimization, and Digital Mastery" by Thomas Gresham is an insightful and comprehensive guide that explores the powerful strategies and techniques required to achieve exponential growth in today's dynamic digital landscape.

In this book, Gresham builds upon the concepts and ideas presented in the first edition of "Amplify" and introduces readers to the next generation of tools and tactics for maximizing the reach and impact of their brand. He emphasizes the importance of leveraging social media platforms to create viral growth, where a company's message spreads rapidly and organically through user engagement and sharing.

Gresham delves into the emerging trends in social media and offers practical advice on how to adapt to these changes to stay ahead of the competition. He discusses the potential of influencer marketing, user-generated content, and community-building strategies to foster brand loyalty and generate viral growth.

The book also addresses the disruption caused by digital technology in traditional print media. Gresham explores the shifting landscape of advertising and marketing, highlighting the importance of adapting to digital channels and exploring innovative methods to engage with consumers effectively. He provides insights into programmatic advertising, native advertising, and other cutting-edge approaches to reach target audiences efficiently.

Furthermore, "Amplify 2.0" discusses the significance of tenders and sales optimization in maximizing business growth. Gresham provides valuable tips and techniques for creating winning tenders and optimizing sales processes to enhance revenue generation. He shares real-world examples and case studies that illustrate how these strategies can lead to significant business growth and profitability.

Throughout the book, Gresham emphasizes the importance of digital mastery for businesses seeking to amplify their growth. He explores the principles of data-driven decision-making, the role of artificial intelligence and machine learning in marketing, and the integration of automation and personalization to create a seamless customer experience. By mastering these digital tools and techniques, businesses can enhance their competitive advantage and achieve substantial growth.

"Amplify 2.0" serves as a comprehensive playbook for entrepreneurs, marketers, and business leaders looking to unlock the potential of social media, print disruption, tenders, sales optimization, and digital mastery. With practical insights, actionable strategies, and compelling examples, Thomas Gresham provides a roadmap for businesses to navigate the ever-evolving digital landscape and achieve exponential growth in the modern era.

Amplify 2.0: Sparking Viral Growth with Next-Gen Social Media, Print Disruption, Tenders, Sales Optimization, and Digital Mastery

Thomas Gresham

Contents

The Power of Targeting a Specific Customer Base

Imagine you possess a secret recipe for the most delectable chocolate chip biscuits in the world. These biscuits are so scrumptious that people simply can't resist indulging in them. Now, your aim is to sell these biscuits and bring joy to people all across the country.

However, here's the catch: not everyone has the same taste preferences. Some individuals might prefer their biscuits to be crispy, while others adore a soft and chewy texture. Certain people might have allergies to certain ingredients like nuts or gluten. And believe it or not, there are even those who aren't fans of chocolate (quite surprising, isn't it?).

Instead of trying to sell your biscuits to everyone, you decide to focus on a specific group of people who will truly appreciate your baked delights. You become a master biscuit connoisseur, skilled in finding the perfect match between your biscuits and people's taste buds.

You begin by asking yourself, "Who would truly relish my mouthwatering chocolate chip biscuits?" Perhaps it's the chocolate enthusiasts who can't resist the rich and gooey chocolatey goodness. Or it could be families and children who delight in sweet treats after a long day. It may even be health-conscious individuals seeking guilt-free indulgence after a vigorous workout.

By identifying your target market, or the specific group of people you want to sell your biscuits to, you can create a marketing strategy tailored exclusively for them. You can showcase your biscuits at local food festivals, advertise in places where families and children spend their time, or collaborate with fitness centres to offer your biscuits as a reward for their clients' hard work.

When you concentrate on a specific target market, you become an expert in understanding their desires, preferences, and needs. You can enhance your biscuits even further by experimenting with new flavours or crafting gluten-free or vegan options for those with dietary restrictions. You can design packaging that appeals to your target market, such as vibrant and playful designs for children or elegant and sophisticated packaging for chocolate aficionados.

By serving a specific group of people exceptionally well, word will begin to spread. People will share their delightful biscuit experiences with their friends, families, and colleagues. They'll become your devoted customers and help expand your biscuit business. Soon enough, you'll build a community of biscuit enthusiasts who can't resist the allure of your irresistible treats.

What happens if you don't choose the right target group and narrow it down?

The General Clothing Shop: A clothing shop that attempted to cater to the fashion preferences of everyone. They stocked a wide range of clothing styles, from casual to formal, for all age groups and body types. However, this lack of focus resulted in confusion among customers. They struggled to find clothing that truly matched their style and preferences. As a result, the shop experienced low sales and couldn't sustain the costs of stocking such a diverse inventory, eventually leading to bankruptcy.

The Gourmet Vegan Restaurant: A restaurant opened with the goal of providing high-quality vegan cuisine. However, they failed to accurately identify their target market. They mistakenly believed that their main customer base would consist predominantly of vegans. Consequently, they priced their menu items at a premium to match the perceived higher spending power of the vegan demographic. However, they soon discovered that the majority of vegans in the area preferred more affordable and casual dining options. This pricing strategy alienated potential customers, resulting in low footfall and financial struggles.

The Tech Startup for Seniors: A technology startup developed a range of innovative gadgets and apps specifically designed for seniors. However, they failed to effectively target their products to the right audience. They assumed that all seniors would readily embrace their tech solutions, neglecting to consider the varying technological proficiency among different age groups within the senior demographic. As a result, they faced limited adoption of their products and struggled to generate sufficient revenue to sustain their operations.

In conclusion, business owners should remember that success lies not in selling to everyone, but in finding their unique tribe of biscuit enthusiasts who will wholeheartedly embrace and savour their biscuits. By identifying and understanding the needs, preferences, and desires of this specific group, you can create a flourishing biscuit empire that brings joy and satisfaction to your customers.

Instead of striving to cater to a broad and diverse market, focus on developing a deep connection with your target audience. Immerse yourself in their world of biscuit cravings and tailor your offerings to meet their exact expectations. From classic chocolate chip to gluten-free delights or innovative flavour combinations, craft biscuits that evoke delight and leave a lasting impression.

Remember, your tribe of biscuit enthusiasts is eagerly awaiting your delectable creations. By delivering exceptional quality, variety, and a touch of magic in every bite, you can build a loyal following that will not only satisfy their biscuit cravings but also become ambassadors of your brand.

So, let your passion for biscuits guide you on this extraordinary journey. Embrace the power of understanding your target audience, and in doing so, you will forge a successful path towards building an empire that is synonymous with scrumptious biscuits and unbridled happiness. Together, let's create a world where every bite brings a smile and where your biscuit empire reigns supreme.

Niche Domination: Effective Strategies for Growing Companies

A niche strategy is a focused approach in which a business targets a specific segment of the market with a unique product or service. It involves identifying a distinct group of customers who have specific needs, preferences, or characteristics that are not adequately addressed by mainstream offerings. By catering to this niche market, businesses can differentiate themselves and create a competitive advantage.

Niche marketing is the practice of tailoring marketing efforts specifically to the identified niche market. It involves understanding the unique needs and desires of the target audience and developing targeted marketing messages and strategies to reach and engage them effectively. Niche marketing allows businesses to stand out from the crowd, connect deeply with their customers, and build a loyal customer base.

The power of niche marketing lies in its ability to provide businesses with several advantages. Firstly, by focusing on a specific niche, businesses can become experts in that particular area, gaining in-depth knowledge and understanding of their customers' needs. This expertise enables businesses to deliver highly relevant and tailored solutions that resonate with their target market.

Additionally, niche marketing allows businesses to differentiate themselves from competitors. By offering specialised products or services, businesses can create a unique selling proposition that sets them apart. This differentiation helps attract customers who are specifically seeking solutions to their unique problems or desires, rather than being lost among the generic offerings of broader market players.

Furthermore, niche marketing can lead to increased customer loyalty. When businesses understand and cater to the specific needs of their niche audience, they can build strong emotional connections and provide exceptional value. This fosters trust, loyalty, and repeat business, as customers recognise and appreciate the specialised expertise and attention they receive.

Niche growth tactics involve expanding within the identified niche market to further capitalise on its potential. This can include developing new products or services that meet additional needs of the target audience, expanding into new geographic regions or demographic segments within the niche, or exploring strategic partnerships or collaborations to reach a wider customer base.

The power of niche growth tactics lies in their ability to maximise profitability and sustainability. By deeply understanding the niche market and its dynamics, businesses can identify untapped opportunities for growth and develop strategies to capture them. Rather than spreading resources thinly across a broad market, niche growth tactics allow businesses to focus their efforts and resources on the most promising areas, resulting in more efficient and effective growth.

Niche marketing and niche growth tactics are powerful strategies that enable businesses to thrive in competitive markets. By understanding and catering to the unique needs of a specific target audience, businesses can differentiate themselves, build customer loyalty, and achieve sustainable growth. The key lies in finding your niche, developing a deep understanding of your customers, and delivering exceptional value that sets you apart from the competition.

In the vast world of business, discovering your niche can be the key to success. But what exactly is a niche? Think of it as a specific corner within a broader category. Take, for example, the health and beauty industry. It encompasses a wide range of services, from tanning and facials to massage and cellulite treatment. Now, let's narrow it down even further. Imagine focusing solely on cellulite treatment for women who've recently had a baby. That's a tightly defined niche. But why would anyone want to limit their market like this? Let's explore the reasons:

The Power of Focus: By narrowing your focus, you can concentrate your resources and create a strong marketing message. Trying to cater to a broad audience can dilute your efforts and leave your message weak.

Relevance is Key: The goal of your advertisement is to grab the attention of your prospects and make them say, "That's exactly what I need!" If you're a new mother concerned about cellulite, wouldn't an ad targeting that specific problem catch your interest? On the other hand, a generic ad for a beauty salon listing numerous services, including cellulite treatment, might easily go unnoticed in the noise.

Think of it this way: a regular 100-watt light bulb can light up a room, but a focused 100-watt laser can cut through steel. The same principle applies to your marketing efforts. The more you narrow your focus, the more powerful and effective your message becomes.

Let's consider another example: photographers. Many photographers advertise a wide range of services, from portraits and weddings to family and commercial photography. But do you think a bride-to-be searching for a wedding photographer has the same needs as a purchasing manager looking to photograph heavy machinery for a product brochure? Of course not!

If your ad simply lists all your services without speaking directly to your target audience, it won't resonate with either group, and it will likely be ignored. That's why choosing a narrow target market for your marketing campaign is crucial.

Attempting to cater to everyone leads to marketing failure. However, this doesn't mean you can't offer a broad range of services. Instead, each category should be treated as a separate campaign.

Targeting a specific niche allows you to become a big fish in a small pond. It gives you the opportunity to dominate a particular category or geographic area in a way that would be impossible if you tried to be everything to everyone.

The ideal niches are "an inch wide and a mile deep." This means they are highly targeted subsections of a broader category, with a significant number of people actively seeking solutions to a specific problem. Once you establish dominance in one niche, you can expand your business by identifying another profitable and highly targeted niche, and continue your path to success.

By embracing the power of niche marketing, you can enjoy all the benefits of being highly focused without limiting the growth potential of your business. It's about finding your place in the market, becoming a specialist, and carving out a unique position that sets you apart from the competition.

Harnessing Niche Strategies for Pricing Power and Effective Pricing Strategies

In today's competitive business landscape, standing out from the crowd is essential for success. This is where niche marketing and niche growth tactics come into play. By focusing on a specific target market and catering to their unique needs, businesses can gain a competitive edge, control costs, charge premium prices, and secure lucrative tendering opportunities.

Imagine if you had recently experienced a heart attack. Would you prefer to receive treatment from a general practitioner or a heart specialist? Undoubtedly, you would choose the specialist. Now, in this scenario, would you expect the heart specialist to charge more for their services compared to a general practitioner? Naturally.

In such cases, the price becomes insignificant as you recognise the value of expertise. Focusing on a specific niche enables businesses to command higher prices and exercise greater control over their pricing strategies. Customers are willing to pay a premium for specialised services, acknowledging the advanced knowledge and skills possessed by specialists. Being regarded as a specialist brings admiration and respect, and clients are willing to pay handsomely for solutions to their particular needs.

The key lies in identifying the specific problem that your target market is seeking a solution for—a problem they are willing to invest in. By understanding their thoughts, concerns, and desires, you can position yourself as a trusted specialist who can address their unique needs effectively. This approach significantly enhances your business outcomes.

Contrary to popular belief, attempting to target a wide range of customers results in effectively targeting none. Casting a broad net dilutes your distinctiveness and reduces your business to a price-driven commodity. However, by narrowing down your target market and focusing on a well-defined niche, you establish yourself as a specialist with a unique value proposition. This positioning allows you to charge premium prices and gain the admiration of your customers.

It is crucial to comprehend that by narrowing your focus, you intentionally exclude certain potential customers. While it may seem counterintuitive, excluding those who do not align with your niche creates an aura of exclusivity and specialisation that attracts your ideal customers. The goal is to dominate your chosen niche, establish your authority, and then expand into other profitable niches gradually.

Remember, building a successful business takes time and strategic planning. Master one niche before moving on to the next. By becoming a specialist in each niche you conquer, you can cultivate a thriving business, strengthen your pricing power, and achieve enduring success.

Let's explore why niche strategies are so powerful and how they can transform the trajectory of a pricing.

Laser-Focused Approach: Niche marketing involves narrowing down the target market to a specific segment with distinct characteristics, preferences, and pain points. This tailored approach allows businesses to deeply understand their customers, their desires, and their challenges. By immersing themselves in the niche, businesses can develop specialised expertise and create solutions that perfectly align with the customers' needs. This deep understanding sets the foundation for building long-term relationships, fostering customer loyalty, and gaining a competitive advantage.

Targeted Communication and Marketing Efforts: With a niche strategy, businesses can fine-tune their messaging and marketing efforts to resonate directly with their target audience. By speaking their language, addressing their pain points, and showcasing how their products or services uniquely solve their problems, businesses can capture the attention and interest of their niche market. This targeted communication approach generates higher engagement, better response rates, and ultimately drives more conversions. Businesses can efficiently allocate their marketing budget to channels and tactics that are most effective in reaching their niche audience, further optimising their ROI.

Cost Control and Efficiency: Niche businesses have the advantage of focusing their resources and efforts on a specific area, allowing for better cost control and efficiency. Rather than spreading themselves thin trying to cater to a broad market, niche businesses can concentrate on perfecting their offerings within their specialised area. This focused approach reduces overhead costs, minimises wasted resources, and maximises operational efficiency. By aligning their resources precisely with their niche market's needs, businesses can operate more profitably and sustainably.

Premium Pricing and Value Proposition: One of the remarkable benefits of niche marketing is the ability to command premium prices. When businesses position themselves as experts in a specific niche, they become the go-to solution provider for customers seeking specialised offerings. Customers are willing to pay a higher price for products or services that precisely meet their unique requirements, surpass their expectations, and provide exceptional value. Niche businesses can emphasise their expertise, quality, customisation, and personalised service to justify premium pricing and differentiate themselves from more generalised competitors.

Tendering Opportunities and Competitive Advantage: In the realm of tendering, niche businesses possess a significant advantage. Tender processes often require businesses to demonstrate expertise, experience, and specialisation. Niche businesses, by virtue of their focused knowledge and tailored solutions, are ideally positioned to excel in these competitive processes. Clients looking for specific expertise and solutions within a niche market are more inclined to choose niche businesses over generalists. This opens up opportunities for securing lucrative contracts, partnerships, and long-term relationships, providing a solid foundation for sustained growth.

Conclusion: In a world where one-size-fits-all approaches are becoming less effective, niche marketing and growth tactics empower businesses to thrive by serving specific market segments with precision and excellence. By leveraging a laser-focused approach, targeted communication, cost control, premium pricing, and tendering opportunities, businesses can create a sustainable competitive advantage, establish themselves as leaders within their niche, and achieve long-term success. Embracing the power of the niche unlocks untapped potential, propelling businesses towards growth, profitability, and market dominance.

Non-Contract vs Contract Income Streams

Customers and clients can be used interchangeably (they are the same thing).

In the business world, acquiring clients can occur through various means, including winning tenders or securing contracts, as well as through informal channels without a formal tender process.

To make it easier, we differentiate between non-contract clients and contract clients.

Non-contract clients refer to customers who make direct purchases from a business. To illustrate this, let's consider a scenario where you buy an apple from a fruit vendor at a market. In this case, you become their customer and, therefore, their non-contract client.

Now if you want to win contract-clients you would have to find a tender. A tender is a process where organisations or businesses invite others to submit a formal proposal or bid for a project or contract. It's like a competition where different companies or individuals compete to win the opportunity to provide their goods or services.

Let's imagine a school needs to build a new playground. They want to find the best company to do the job. So, they create a tender and send it out to different construction companies. The tender includes all the details of the project, such as the requirements, specifications, and the deadline for submitting proposals.

The construction companies then review the tender and prepare their proposals. They showcase their experience, expertise, and cost estimates to convince the school that they are the best choice for the project. The school carefully evaluates all the proposals and selects the company that offers the most suitable solution at the best value.

Tenders can be found in all sorts of industries and markets. They are formal invitations for businesses to submit their proposals or bids to provide goods or services. Taking part in tenders allows freelancers, sole traders, and small to medium-sized businesses to compete for contracts with clients from various sectors. This ensures a fair and transparent process for choosing suppliers. By customising their proposals to meet the specific requirements of different industries, businesses can grasp opportunities and expand their presence in diverse markets.

Winning a tender can be a great opportunity for anyone. It allows them to work on exciting projects, gain new clients, and grow their reputation. It gives them a chance to showcase their skills and win contracts that they might not have access to otherwise.

So, think of a tender as a way for organisations to find the best match for their needs, and for businesses to showcase their abilities and secure exciting opportunities.

Understanding the differences between contract clients and non-contract clients is crucial for businesses to make informed decisions about their customer acquisition strategies.

Let's delve into the advantages and disadvantages of each approach:

<u>Contract Clients:</u>

Contract clients are customers that a business acquires by successfully winning tenders or securing formal contracts. Here are some key points to consider:

Advantages:

Stability: Contract clients offer a predictable revenue stream since they are committed to a specified contract period.

Higher Revenue Potential: Contracts often involve larger projects or ongoing service agreements, which can lead to higher revenue compared to non-contract clients.

Long-Term Relationships: Working on contracts allows for the development of long-term relationships, fostering trust and potentially leading to repeat business.

Disadvantages:

Competitive Bidding: Winning tenders requires competing against other businesses, which can be challenging and time-consuming.

Compliance Requirements: Contract clients may have specific compliance and reporting requirements that businesses need to meet.

Limited Flexibility: Once committed to a contract, businesses may have limited flexibility to adjust terms or pricing during the contract period.

<u>Non-Contract Clients</u>

Non-contract clients are customers acquired through informal channels without a formal tender process. These customers may approach the business directly or be won through networking, referrals, or marketing efforts. Consider the following aspects:

Advantages:

Greater Flexibility: With non-contract clients, businesses have more flexibility to set pricing, terms, and adjust services according to customer needs.

Quick Decision-Making: Acquiring non-contract clients often involves faster decision-making processes, allowing businesses to respond swiftly to customer demands.

Lower Administrative Burden: Unlike contract clients, non-contract clients may have fewer compliance requirements and administrative obligations.

Disadvantages:

Revenue Uncertainty: Non-contract clients may not provide the same level of stability and predictability as contract clients, leading to fluctuating revenue streams.

Increased Competition: Without a formal tender process, businesses may face higher competition in acquiring non-contract clients due to the wider market.

Limited Customer Loyalty: Non-contract clients may have less commitment to a specific business, making it easier for them to switch to competitors.

<u>Choosing Focus</u>

Advantages and disadvantages deciding whether to focus on contract clients or non-contract clients depends on various factors, including business goals, industry dynamics, and resource availability.

Understanding the differences between contract clients and non-contract clients enables businesses to make informed decisions about their customer acquisition strategies. While contract clients offer stability and revenue potential, non-contract clients provide flexibility and agility. Ultimately, businesses should assess their goals, resources, and industry landscape to determine the most suitable approach that aligns with their long-term growth and profitability objectives.

Anyone, including sole traders, micro-businesses, and small companies, can benefit from both acquiring contract clients and non-contract clients, and it is possible to pursue both approaches even when working solo or as a small business entity. Let's explore why this is the case and the advantages it offers:

<u>1. Contract Clients:</u>

Small businesses, including sole traders and micro-businesses, can actively participate in tender processes or respond to requests for proposals (RFPs) to secure contract clients. Here's why they can benefit from contract clients:

- Stable Revenue and Growth: Acquiring contract clients provides small businesses with a stable revenue stream and opportunities for business growth. Contracts offer predictable income over the contract period, allowing small businesses to plan and invest in their operations.

- Credibility and Professionalism: Winning contracts and delivering successful projects enhance the credibility and professionalism of small businesses. It builds a positive reputation in the market, leading to more opportunities and potential partnerships.

- Long-Term Relationships: Contract clients often require ongoing services, allowing small businesses to build long-term relationships. This helps in developing a loyal client base, fostering repeat business, and generating referrals.

<u>2. Non-Contract Clients:</u>

Small businesses can also acquire non-contract clients through various channels, such as direct marketing, networking, referrals, or online platforms. Here's why they can benefit from non-contract clients:

- Flexibility and Customisation: Working with non-contract clients provides small businesses with flexibility in pricing, terms, and project scope. They can tailor their services to meet the specific needs and budgets of individual clients.

- Quick Turnaround and Agility: Non-contract clients often have shorter decision-making processes, allowing small businesses to start projects quickly and deliver results in a shorter timeframe. This agility helps in meeting client expectations and securing positive testimonials.

- Diversification and Learning Opportunities: Serving non-contract clients exposes small businesses to a diverse range of projects and clients. It expands their skillset, industry knowledge, and professional network. This diversity can lead to new business opportunities and collaborations.

Why Pursue Both Approaches?

Small businesses, including sole traders, micro-businesses, and small companies, can benefit from pursuing both contract clients and non-contract clients.

Here's why it is advantageous:

- Income Stability and Growth Potential: By combining contract clients and non-contract clients, small businesses create a more stable and diversified revenue stream. This helps in managing financial fluctuations and achieving sustainable growth.

- Adaptability to Market Dynamics: Having a mix of contract clients and non-contract clients allows small businesses to adapt to changing market conditions and client demands. They can pivot their offerings and approach based on the needs of different client segments.

- Professional Development and Expansion: Working with a variety of clients through both contract and non-contract arrangements facilitates professional development and expands the small business's capabilities. It helps in refining skills, gaining industry expertise, and broadening the client base.

- Enhanced Business Reputation: Successfully serving both contract clients and non-contract clients builds a strong reputation in the market. It fosters trust, credibility, and positive word-of-mouth, leading to increased brand recognition and more opportunities for growth.

In conclusion, small businesses, including sole traders, micro-businesses, and small companies, can benefit from acquiring both contract clients and non-contract clients. The combination of stable income, long-term relationships, and growth potential from contract clients, along with the flexibility, agility, and learning opportunities gained from non-contract clients, contributes to the overall success and resilience of small businesses.

Striking a balance between the two approaches enables small businesses to maximise opportunities, expand their reach, and build a strong foundation for sustainable growth.

Revealing the Best Money Targets

Discovering your ideal client is a transformative journey that unlocks the true potential of your business. By narrowing down and understanding your target market, you can tailor your offerings, create meaningful connections, and achieve remarkable success. Let's delve deeper into the process of identifying your ideal client and explore how this strategic approach can revolutionise your business.

<u>Non-Contract Clients</u>

The PVP Index: To identify your ideal client, we utilise the powerful PVP Index, which encompasses three key factors: Personal Fulfilment, Value to the Marketplace, and Profitability. By evaluating each market segment based on these criteria, you can pinpoint the segment that aligns most closely with your business goals and strengths.

Personal Fulfilment: Consider how much joy and satisfaction you derive from serving a particular market segment. Reflect on your passion, expertise, and natural inclination towards certain clients. Remember, when you genuinely enjoy working with your clients, your enthusiasm shines through, leading to greater success and fulfilment.

Value to the Marketplace: Evaluate the market segment's perception of your products or services. Are they willing to invest significantly in what you offer? Analyse their purchasing patterns, willingness to pay a premium, and recognition of the unique value you provide. Understanding the value your ideal client places on your offerings allows you to position yourself effectively and command higher prices.

Profitability: Profitability is more than just revenue. Evaluate the costs associated with serving each market segment and the resulting profit margins. Consider the resources, time, and effort required to deliver exceptional value. By focusing on segments that yield higher profitability, you can optimise your resources and maximise your returns.

To use the PVP Index, you can start by thinking about all the different things you're good at or enjoy doing. It could be drawing, playing an instrument, playing sports, or anything else you're passionate about.

Once you have a list of activities or skills, it's time to give them a score from 1 to 10 in each category of the PVP Index. Imagine a scale where 1 means you don't enjoy it much or others might not find it valuable, and 10 means you absolutely love it and others would find it really useful.

After you've given each activity or skill a score, you can add up the numbers to find out which ones have the highest total score. These are the activities or skills that you're most likely to enjoy, others will find valuable, and they could even help you make money in the future.

Think of it like a game where you're trying to find the perfect combination of things you love and things that others need. The PVP Index is like a treasure map that guides you towards your true passions and helps you discover how they can bring you happiness and success.

So, let your imagination run wild, explore different activities, and use the PVP Index to unlock the hidden potential within you. Who knows, you might just find your own unique path to a fulfilling and prosperous future.

Remember, the PVP Index is a fun way to explore your interests, think about what others might need, and find ways to turn your passions into something that can bring you happiness and success in the future.

Example: The Videographer's Journey: Let's explore the journey of a videographer to illustrate the power of identifying an ideal client. Initially, the videographer might serve various market segments such as weddings, corporate events, documentaries, and music videos. Using the PVP Index, they evaluate each segment and assign ratings:

Weddings: P - 8, V - 7, P - 9

Corporate Events: P - 7, V - 6, P - 8

Documentaries: P - 9, V - 8, P - 7

Music Videos: P - 6, V - 7, P - 6

Based on these ratings, the videographer identifies documentaries as their ideal market segment. It offers high personal fulfilment, significant value to the marketplace, and profitable opportunities. By focusing their marketing efforts on this specific segment, they can establish themselves as the go-to videographer for documentaries, attract more clients, and command higher prices.

The Power of Niche Growth: Narrowing down your target market provides several advantages:

Differentiation: By specialising in a specific niche, you differentiate yourself from competitors. You become the expert, the go-to provider in your chosen domain, setting yourself apart from generalists.

Relevance: A focused marketing strategy allows you to create tailored messages and offerings that resonate deeply with your ideal clients. They feel understood and valued, increasing their connection with your brand.

Higher Prices: By positioning yourself as a specialist, you can charge premium prices. Clients are willing to pay more for specialised expertise and exceptional value.

Cost Efficiency: With a well-defined target market, you can optimise your marketing efforts, concentrating resources where they yield the highest return on investment. This precision reduces wasteful spending and enhances cost efficiency.

Example: The Adventure Destination Wedding Planner's Triumph: Imagine a wedding planner who decides to specialise in planning destination weddings for adventurous couples seeking unique experiences. By focusing on this niche, the planner can offer tailored services

<u>Contract Clients</u>

Let's imagine you have a special talent for creating beautiful artwork, and you want to sell your artwork to people who will appreciate it the most. One way to do that is by participating in an art competition where people can bid on your artwork.

When you see an opportunity to participate in a competition or tender, you need to decide if it's a good fit for your artwork. Think about what they're looking for and what they're willing to pay. You also need to consider if you have the right skills and style to meet their requirements.

Before you decide to submit your artwork, it's important to learn more about the competition or tender. You can research and ask others if they've participated before and if it's a fair and reputable event. You want to make sure you choose competitions or tenders that will be fair and give you a chance to showcase your talent.

You should also think about the benefits of participating. Is it a well-known competition that will give you a chance to gain recognition and exposure for your artwork? Will it provide you with an opportunity to learn from other artists and grow your skills?

Sometimes, you might find that a competition or tender is not a good fit for your artwork. Maybe they are looking for a different style or theme that doesn't match your artistic vision. In those cases, it's okay to skip that particular opportunity and wait for a better one.

By carefully selecting the competitions and tenders you participate in, you can make sure that your artwork is seen and appreciated by people who value it. It's important to be patient and wait for the right opportunities because they can help you grow as an artist and open doors to new possibilities in your artistic journey.

In the business world, tenders play a vital role in securing contracts and opportunities. To enhance your chances of winning tenders, it's essential to understand and align with the needs and expectations of the tendering party. One powerful tool that can help you achieve this is the PVP Index, which allows you to evaluate tenders based on Personal Fulfilment, Value to the Marketplace, and Profitability. Let's explore how the PVP Index can be utilised to maximise your success in tendering processes.

Personal Fulfilment: Consider how well the tender aligns with your business's mission, expertise, and core values. Evaluate whether the project genuinely excites and inspires you, as this enthusiasm will be reflected in the quality of your proposal. When you find tenders that resonate with your passion and purpose, you can approach them with genuine dedication and deliver outstanding results.

Value to the Marketplace: Examine the tender's potential impact on your business and its perceived value to the marketplace. Assess the significance of the project, the potential for future opportunities or partnerships, and the prestige associated with winning the tender. By targeting tenders that offer substantial value, you position yourself as a valuable and sought-after provider.

Profitability: While tenders are not solely about profitability, it is crucial to evaluate the financial viability of the project. Consider the resources, time, and effort required to complete the tender successfully. Assess whether the potential rewards outweigh the costs and ensure that the financial aspects align with your business goals. Striking a balance between profitability and value will help you make informed decisions.

Example: The Construction Company's Tender Success: Let's explore how a construction company can leverage the PVP Index to evaluate and prioritise tenders. Suppose the company is presented with three potential tenders:

Tender A: Personal Fulfilment - 9, Value to the Marketplace - 8, Profitability - 7

Tender B: Personal Fulfilment - 7, Value to the Marketplace - 9, Profitability - 8

Tender C: Personal Fulfilment - 8, Value to the Marketplace - 7, Profitability - 9

Based on the ratings, the company identifies Tender B as the ideal opportunity. It offers significant personal fulfilment, high value to the marketplace, and strong profitability. By focusing their efforts on crafting a compelling proposal for Tender B, the company increases its chances of securing the contract and achieving long-term success.

Utilising the PVP Index for Tender Success:

Targeted Proposal Development: By aligning tenders with your business's passions and expertise, you can tailor your proposals to address the specific needs and goals of the tendering party. This targeted approach enhances your chances of standing out among competitors.

Value-Centric Offerings: Understanding the perceived value of the tender to the marketplace allows you to position your proposal as a valuable and indispensable solution. By highlighting the unique value you bring to the table, you increase your competitiveness and demonstrate your commitment to delivering exceptional outcomes.

Strategic Resource Allocation: Evaluating the profitability of a tender ensures that you allocate your resources efficiently. Assessing the potential return on investment helps you make informed decisions and avoid pursuing tenders that may not yield desirable financial outcomes.

Whether you are target customers directly or acquire them through tenders, you should unlock the power of your ideal client by honing in on a specific market segment. By targeting a narrow market, you can differentiate yourself, charge higher prices, and deliver unmatched value. Embrace the art of niche marketing, connect with your ideal clients on a profound level, and watch your business thrive.

The Power of Personas

Personas are fictional representations of your ideal customers. They are detailed profiles that capture the characteristics, needs, motivations, and behaviours of your target audience. Think of personas as "typical customers" who embody the traits and preferences of a specific segment of your market.

Creating personas involves conducting research, gathering data, and gaining insights into your customers' demographics, psychographics, and purchasing behaviours. This information helps you understand who your customers are, what they want, and how you can best meet their needs.

Personas typically include information such as age, gender, occupation, goals, challenges, hobbies, and preferences. They go beyond mere demographics and delve into the psychological and emotional aspects that drive customer behaviour.

By developing personas, businesses gain a deeper understanding of their target audience and can tailor their marketing and sales strategies accordingly. Personas help businesses:

Target the Right Audience: Personas help you identify and focus on the specific groups of people who are most likely to be interested in your products or services. By understanding their unique needs and preferences, you can tailor your messaging and communication to resonate with them effectively.

Improve Customer Engagement: Personas allow you to create content, products, and experiences that directly address the pain points and desires of your target audience. This helps you build stronger connections with your customers and increase engagement with your brand.

Enhance Product Development: Personas provide valuable insights into the features, functionalities, and improvements that would be most appealing to your customers. By aligning your product development efforts with their needs, you can create offerings that better meet their expectations.

Guide Marketing and Sales Efforts: Personas help you craft targeted marketing campaigns and sales strategies that are tailored to the specific needs and preferences of different customer segments. This leads to more effective communication, higher conversion rates, and increased customer satisfaction.

Remember, personas are not meant to represent every individual customer, but rather serve as a representative archetype that captures the key traits and behaviours of a specific segment. They provide a framework for understanding and empathising with your customers, allowing you to deliver more relevant and compelling experiences.

Let's dive deeper into the world of personas and explore how they can be used by marketing and sales staff to grow businesses. Imagine you're embarking on a thrilling adventure to understand your customers and meet their needs. Personas are like treasure maps that guide you towards success.

Uncovering Customer Insights: To create personas, you embark on a journey of discovery. You gather data from various sources, such as customer surveys, interviews, and market research. You become a detective, unraveling the mysteries of your target audience. You discover their aspirations, challenges, and what makes them tick.

For example, let's imagine you have a small bakery. Through your detective work, you uncover that some of your customers are health-conscious individuals seeking gluten-free options, while others are indulgent dessert lovers looking for decadent treats.

Painting Vivid Pictures: Once you have gathered the necessary clues, you create vivid portraits of your personas. These portraits are like works of art that capture the essence of your customers. You give them names, faces, and unique characteristics that make them come alive.

Imagine meeting "Gluten-Free Grace," a fitness enthusiast who loves your bakery for its delicious yet healthy gluten-free offerings. On the other hand, there's "Sweet Tooth Sam," a dessert connoisseur who can't resist your mouthwatering pastries and cakes.

Empathy and Understanding: Personas help you step into your customers' shoes and understand their world. You become an empathetic storyteller, crafting marketing messages and sales pitches that resonate with their desires, fears, and dreams.

With "Gluten-Free Grace," you showcase your commitment to providing nutritious and delicious gluten-free treats. You speak her language, understanding her quest for a guilt-free indulgence. Meanwhile, with "Sweet Tooth Sam," you tempt him with tantalising descriptions of your decadent creations, sparking his imagination and cravings.

Tailoring the Customer Journey: Personas act as guides along the customer journey. You map out the various touchpoints and interactions your customers have with your business, ensuring each step is tailored to their needs and preferences.

For "Gluten-Free Grace," you create a seamless online ordering experience for her busy lifestyle. You provide detailed ingredient information and share testimonials from satisfied gluten-free customers. For "Sweet Tooth Sam," you create an enticing in-store atmosphere, complete with mouthwatering displays and a friendly, knowledgeable staff to guide him through his dessert selection.

Channeling Superpowers: Personas help you channel your marketing and sales superpowers in the right direction. Armed with the knowledge of who your customers are, you can focus your resources on the channels that matter most to them.

For "Gluten-Free Grace," you optimise your social media presence, targeting health and wellness communities. You create engaging content and collaborate with influencers who align with her values. For "Sweet Tooth Sam," you showcase your creations through visually appealing posts on platforms like Instagram and partner with local food bloggers who can spread the word about your delectable treats.

Building Lasting Relationships: With personas as your compass, you foster meaningful relationships with your customers. You become their trusted guide, providing tailored experiences and anticipating their needs. This builds loyalty and turns them into advocates for your business.

"Gluten-Free Grace" becomes a regular customer, recommending your bakery to her health-conscious friends. "Sweet Tooth Sam" eagerly awaits your new creations, sharing photos on social media and generating buzz among his dessert-loving peers.

Remember, personas are like secret weapons that give you a competitive edge. They enable you to understand your customers deeply and tailor your marketing and sales efforts to their specific needs. By using personas, you embark on an adventure of customer-centricity, forging connections, and unlocking the treasure trove of business growth.

So, put on your detective hat, wield your creativity, and let the power of personas guide you to marketing and sales success. Adventure awaits!

Persona marketing is a powerful strategy that involves creating detailed profiles or personas of your ideal customers. These personas are fictional representations of real people who align with your target market. By understanding their characteristics, needs, preferences, and behaviours, you can tailor your marketing and growth strategies to effectively reach and engage them.

Let's dive deeper into how persona marketing can drive business growth:

1. Targeted Messaging: By creating personas, you can develop highly targeted and personalised marketing messages. Each persona represents a specific segment of your target market, allowing you to address their unique pain points, desires, and interests. This tailored approach helps you resonate with your audience, capturing their attention and building strong connections.

For example, if one of your personas is a young, tech-savvy professional seeking convenience, you can craft marketing messages that highlight how your product or service simplifies their life and saves them time.

2. Better Product Development: Personas guide product development by providing insights into what your target customers truly want. Understanding their goals, challenges, and preferences helps you create offerings that meet their specific needs. By aligning your products or services with your personas' desires, you increase customer satisfaction and loyalty, leading to long-term growth.

For instance, if one of your personas is a fitness enthusiast seeking sustainable and eco-friendly products, you can develop an eco-friendly line of fitness apparel that aligns with their values.

3. Precise Targeting: Persona marketing allows you to focus your resources and efforts on the most relevant audience. Rather than casting a wide net and hoping for random success, you can identify the specific segments that are most likely to convert into loyal customers. This focused targeting helps you optimise your marketing budget and achieve higher conversion rates.

For example, if one of your personas is a middle-aged professional looking for luxury travel experiences, you can direct your advertising budget towards platforms and publications that cater to affluent travellers.

4. Enhanced Customer Experience: By understanding your personas' preferences and behaviours, you can deliver a tailored customer experience that exceeds their expectations. From website design and content to customer support and after-sales service, every touchpoint can be optimised to meet their unique needs. This personalised experience fosters customer loyalty, positive word-of-mouth, and repeat business.

For instance, if one of your personas values prompt customer support, you can implement a live chat feature on your website to provide instant assistance.

Remember, persona marketing is an ongoing process. As your business grows and evolves, so should your personas. Regularly update and refine your personas based on market research, customer feedback, and emerging trends to ensure your marketing and growth strategies remain effective.

By embracing persona marketing, you can create a strong connection with your target audience, drive customer engagement, and ultimately achieve sustainable business growth.

Let's use two examples:

Meet Emily Clark, the Successful Graphic Designer:

Emily is 35 years old.

She runs her own graphic design business, which has grown steadily over the past five years.

Before starting her business, she gained experience working for well-known design agencies.

She has a degree in graphic design and is always staying updated with the latest design trends.

Emily is married and has a young daughter.

She lives in a vibrant city neighbourhood in a cosy flat.

Her design studio is located in a shared co-working space, which she finds inspiring.

Emily's business primarily focuses on branding and marketing materials for small businesses.

She is passionate about creating eye-catching visuals and helping her clients stand out.

In her free time, Emily enjoys painting, exploring art galleries, and attending design conferences.

She follows design blogs, reads design magazines, and connects with other designers on social media.

Emily uses a high-performance laptop and professional design software to bring her ideas to life.

She values collaboration and often meets clients in person to understand their design needs.

Now let's meet James Smith, the Savvy Marketing Manager:

James is 42 years old.

He works as a marketing manager for a well-established software company.

He has over 15 years of experience in the marketing industry, working with various technology companies.

James holds a bachelor's degree in marketing and has attended numerous marketing conferences and workshops.

He is married with two teenage sons and lives in a suburban area close to his workplace.

James' responsibilities include developing marketing strategies, managing advertising campaigns, and analysing market trends.

He thrives on staying ahead of the competition and finding innovative ways to promote his company's products.

In his spare time, James enjoys playing guitar, going on hiking trips, and spending quality time with his family.

He keeps himself updated on the latest marketing trends by reading marketing books and subscribing to industry newsletters.

James uses a range of marketing tools and analytics software to track the success of his campaigns and make data-driven decisions.

He values networking and attends industry events to connect with other marketing professionals.

By creating these personas, we gain valuable insights into the lives, interests, and motivations of our target customers. This helps us tailor our marketing and sales strategies to resonate with them effectively. Remember, understanding your customers is like having a secret superpower that can drive the success of your business.

Let's delve into how this information can be used as part of a customer or growth strategy:

Targeted Marketing Campaigns: Armed with the knowledge of Emily and James, you can create targeted marketing campaigns that speak directly to their needs and interests. For Emily, you could design visually stunning adverts that showcase your design expertise and emphasise the value of professional branding. For James, you could develop informative content that highlights the benefits of your software solutions and how they can drive marketing success. By tailoring your messaging and channels to each persona, you increase the likelihood of capturing their attention and generating leads.

Product Development and Enhancements: With Emily's persona in mind, you can refine your graphic design services to cater specifically to the branding needs of small businesses. You can develop packages or add-ons that address common pain points she may face, such as logo design, social media graphics, or website visuals. For James, you can gather insights from his perspective to identify potential software features or integrations that would enhance marketing campaign management and analytics. By aligning your offerings with their specific needs, you position yourself as the go-to solution provider in their respective industries.

Customer Experience Optimisation: By understanding Emily and James, you can optimise the customer experience at every touchpoint. From the initial website visit to post-purchase support, you can tailor the experience to their preferences. For example, you can design a user-friendly website with a portfolio of your design work that resonates with Emily's aesthetics. For James, you can provide comprehensive product demos and ongoing customer support to ensure a seamless experience with your software solutions. This personalised approach fosters customer satisfaction, builds trust, and encourages repeat business.

Partnership Opportunities: Identifying personas like Emily and James can open doors to collaboration and partnership opportunities. For Emily, you can reach out to small business networks or local entrepreneur communities to offer design workshops or guest speaking engagements. This positions you as an expert in your field and expands your reach within her network. For James, you can explore partnerships with marketing agencies or industry associations to offer joint webinars or co-branded content. This exposes your software solutions to a wider audience and strengthens your credibility.

Remember, these personas are just the beginning. As you gather more insights and customer feedback, you can continuously refine and expand your personas to capture the nuances of your target market. The key is to use these personas as a guiding compass throughout your marketing, sales, and growth strategies, allowing you to connect on a deeper level with your customers and drive business success

How can we optimise this further and tailor it tenders?

Persona marketing is relevant for tenders because it helps businesses understand the needs, preferences, and pain points of the decision-makers involved in the tender process. By developing personas for key stakeholders, businesses can tailor their tender submissions to effectively address the specific concerns and requirements of each persona.

Here's how persona marketing can be relevant for tenders:

Targeted Messaging: Personas provide insights into the motivations, priorities, and challenges of different decision-makers involved in the tender process. With this understanding, businesses can craft targeted messages that resonate with each persona, showcasing how their products or services meet their unique needs.

For example, if one persona is concerned about cost-efficiency, the tender submission can highlight the cost-saving benefits of the proposed solution. Another persona might prioritise environmental sustainability, so the submission can emphasise the eco-friendly aspects of the offering.

Tailored Solutions: By understanding the specific pain points and requirements of each persona, businesses can tailor their tender proposals to offer solutions that address those needs directly. This demonstrates a deep understanding of the stakeholders' concerns and positions the business as the ideal provider to meet their requirements.

For instance, if a persona is seeking a solution that integrates with existing systems, the tender submission can showcase how the proposed solution seamlessly integrates with their current infrastructure, saving time and resources.

Competitive Advantage: Persona marketing allows businesses to differentiate themselves from competitors by highlighting their unique value proposition. By aligning the tender submission with the priorities and preferences of the personas, businesses can position themselves as the most suitable choice, gaining a competitive edge.

For example, if a persona values exceptional customer service, the tender submission can emphasise the company's commitment to providing dedicated support throughout the implementation process and beyond.

Improved Evaluation: Personas provide evaluators with a clear understanding of how the proposed solution aligns with their needs and priorities. This facilitates the evaluation process, as the tender submission directly addresses the evaluators' concerns and makes it easier for them to assess the value of the offering.

By incorporating persona-driven insights into tender submissions, businesses can increase their chances of success by demonstrating a deep understanding of the stakeholders' needs, offering tailored solutions, and effectively positioning themselves as the best fit for the project.

Persona marketing in the context of tenders allows businesses to create targeted and tailored tender submissions that address the specific needs and preferences of decision-makers and the organisation. By aligning their proposals with the concerns and requirements of each persona, businesses can increase their competitiveness and improve their chances of winning tenders.

Each decision-maker in the procurement team represents the needs/likes of the buyer (potential client), but the decision-maker will also have their own thoughts/needs. Persona marketing enables you to target both. Here are some real examples of how persona marketing can be applied in the bidding or tender world:

Infrastructure Development Project:

Persona: Sarah, the Government Decision-Maker

Sarah is a government official responsible for overseeing infrastructure development projects. She prioritises projects that are cost-effective, environmentally sustainable, and have a positive impact on the local community.

Bidding Strategy: The bidding company develops a persona-driven tender submission that highlights their expertise in delivering infrastructure projects that align with Sarah's priorities. They showcase their track record of completing projects within budget, incorporating green initiatives, and engaging with local stakeholders to ensure community benefits. By directly addressing Sarah's concerns, the company stands out as a suitable choice for the project.

IT Services Contract:

Persona: Mark, the IT Manager

Mark is an IT Manager in a large corporation. He is looking for an IT services provider that offers reliable support, seamless integration with existing systems, and data security measures.

Bidding Strategy: The bidding company develops a persona-driven tender submission that focuses on the specific needs of Mark. They highlight their expertise in providing round-the-clock technical support, their experience in successfully integrating complex IT systems, and their robust data protection measures. By addressing Mark's concerns directly, the company positions themselves as the ideal partner for the IT services contract.

Healthcare Equipment Tender:

Persona: Dr. Lisa, the Hospital Procurement Officer

Dr. Lisa is responsible for procuring medical equipment for a hospital. She values high-quality, reliable equipment that enhances patient care and improves operational efficiency.

Bidding Strategy: The bidding company develops a persona-driven tender submission that emphasises the superior quality, durability, and advanced features of their healthcare equipment. They highlight case studies and testimonials from other hospitals where their equipment has resulted in improved patient outcomes and streamlined workflows. By aligning their submission with Dr. Lisa's priorities, the company demonstrates their understanding of her needs and positions themselves as a trusted provider.

In each of these examples, persona marketing is used to tailor the bidding strategy to the specific needs and preferences of the decision-makers and the buying organisation involved in the tender process. By addressing their concerns, showcasing relevant expertise, and aligning with their priorities, businesses can increase their chances of success and stand out among competitors.

Know Where To Find Them

Understanding where to find and how to reach your target group and customers is like having a secret map to success. It allows you to navigate the vast landscape of marketing with precision and purpose. Here's why it's crucial and some intriguing examples to illustrate its importance:

Efficient Marketing Expeditions: Imagine you're a tech startup targeting young professionals. Knowing that they spend a significant amount of time on platforms like LinkedIn, you can tailor your marketing campaigns to reach them precisely where they are. By crafting engaging content, participating in industry groups, and running targeted adverts on LinkedIn, you can efficiently capture their attention and generate quality leads.

Social Media Safari: Social media platforms offer an expansive savannah of potential customers. If you have a trendy clothing brand aimed at fashion-conscious millennials, platforms like Instagram and TikTok are fertile hunting grounds. By collaborating with influential fashion bloggers, creating eye-catching visual content, and using relevant hashtags, you can cultivate a vibrant online community and attract a loyal following.

Trade Show Treasures: Trade shows and industry conferences are like hidden treasure troves teeming with potential customers. For a B2B software company, attending relevant trade shows in your industry gives you a prime opportunity to showcase your product, network with decision-makers, and form valuable partnerships. By strategically positioning your stand, delivering captivating presentations, and offering exclusive promotions, you can capture the attention and interest of potential clients.

Content Quests: Content marketing is a powerful way to engage and attract customers. For a home improvement company, creating a blog filled with informative articles on DIY projects, interior design tips, and renovation guides can draw in homeowners seeking inspiration and guidance. By optimising your content for search engines, sharing it on social media, and encouraging reader interaction, you can establish yourself as a trusted authority and convert visitors into loyal customers.

Local Expeditions: If you have a brick-and-mortar business, such as a boutique coffee shop, understanding the local community is vital. Engaging in community events, sponsoring local sports teams, and collaborating with nearby businesses can create a buzz and make your establishment a go-to spot for residents. By offering personalised promotions, hosting local artist showcases, and actively participating in neighbourhood initiatives, you can forge deep connections and foster customer loyalty.

Email Excursions: Email marketing remains a potent tool for reaching customers directly. Building a targeted email list allows you to send tailored messages and offers to those who have already shown interest in your products or services. For an e-commerce store specialising in organic skincare products, offering exclusive discounts, sharing educational content on natural ingredients, and nurturing customer relationships through personalised emails can drive repeat purchases and word-of-mouth referrals.

Understanding where to find and how to reach your target group and customers is like having a secret map to success. It allows you to navigate the vast landscape of marketing with precision and purpose. Here's why it's crucial and some intriguing examples to illustrate its importance:

Efficient Marketing Expeditions: Imagine you're a tech startup targeting young professionals. Knowing that they spend a significant amount of time on platforms like LinkedIn, you can tailor your marketing campaigns to reach them precisely where they are. By crafting engaging content, participating in industry groups, and running targeted adverts on LinkedIn, you can efficiently capture their attention and generate quality leads.

Social Media Safari: Social media platforms offer an expansive savannah of potential customers. If you have a trendy clothing brand aimed at fashion-conscious millennials, platforms like Instagram and TikTok are fertile hunting grounds. By collaborating with influential fashion bloggers, creating eye-catching visual content, and using relevant hashtags, you can cultivate a vibrant online community and attract a loyal following.

Trade Show Treasures: Trade shows and industry conferences are like hidden treasure troves teeming with potential customers. For a B2B software company, attending relevant trade shows in your industry gives you a prime opportunity to showcase your product, network with decision-makers, and form valuable partnerships. By strategically positioning your stand, delivering captivating presentations, and offering exclusive promotions, you can capture the attention and interest of potential clients.

Content Quests: Content marketing is a powerful way to engage and attract customers. For a home improvement company, creating a blog filled with informative articles on DIY projects, interior design tips, and renovation guides can draw in homeowners seeking inspiration and guidance. By optimising your content for search engines, sharing it on social media, and encouraging reader interaction, you can establish yourself as a trusted authority and convert visitors into loyal customers.

Local Expeditions: If you have a brick-and-mortar business, such as a boutique coffee shop, understanding the local community is vital. Engaging in community events, sponsoring local sports teams, and collaborating with nearby businesses can create a buzz and make your establishment a go-to spot for residents. By offering personalised promotions, hosting local artist showcases, and actively participating in neighbourhood initiatives, you can forge deep connections and foster customer loyalty.

Email Excursions: Email marketing remains a potent tool for reaching customers directly. Building a targeted email list allows you to send tailored messages and offers to those who have already shown interest in your products or services. For an e-commerce store specialising in organic skincare products, offering exclusive discounts, sharing educational content on natural ingredients, and nurturing customer relationships through personalised emails can drive repeat purchases and word-of-mouth referrals.

Being strategic in sourcing prospects is crucial for effective customer acquisition. Here are some steps to help you be strategic in finding and reaching customers, along with 15 examples of methods you can employ:

Define your target audience: Clearly identify the characteristics and demographics of your ideal customers to focus your efforts effectively.

Conduct market research: Gain insights into your target market's preferences, behaviours, and needs to tailor your approach.

Utilise customer personas: Create detailed profiles of your target customers to understand their motivations and pain points.

Develop a value proposition: Clearly articulate the unique value your product or service offers to attract and engage potential customers.

Leverage online platforms: Establish a strong online presence through your website, social media platforms, and online directories.

Content marketing: Create valuable and engaging content such as blog articles, videos, and infographics to attract and educate your target audience.

Search engine optimisation (SEO): Optimise your website and content to rank higher in search engine results and increase visibility.

Pay-per-click (PPC) advertising: Run targeted adverts on platforms like Google Ads or social media channels to reach potential customers.

Email marketing: Build an email list and send targeted campaigns to nurture leads and drive conversions.

Referral programmes: Encourage your existing customers to refer your business to their network by offering incentives or rewards.

Networking events: Attend industry conferences, trade shows, and networking events to connect with potential customers and industry professionals.

Partnerships and collaborations: Form partnerships with complementary businesses to tap into their customer base and expand your reach.

Influencer marketing: Collaborate with influencers or industry experts who have a significant following and can promote your products or services.

Customer reviews and testimonials: Encourage satisfied customers to leave positive reviews and testimonials that can build trust and attract new customers.

Direct mail campaigns: Send targeted, personalised mailers or brochures to a specific audience to grab their attention and generate leads.

Local advertising: Utilise local newspapers, radio stations, or community notice boards to target customers within your geographical area.

Mobile marketing: Utilise mobile apps, SMS marketing, or location-based targeting to reach customers on their smartphones.

Social media contests and giveaways: Run contests or giveaways on social media platforms to engage your audience and attract new followers and potential customers.

Customer loyalty programmes: Implement loyalty programmes to reward repeat customers and incentivise them to continue doing business with you.

Online customer reviews and directories: Ensure your business is listed and actively managed on review platforms like Google My Business, Yelp, and industry-specific directories.

By adopting a strategic approach and employing a combination of these methods, you can effectively reach and find customers who align with your target audience, increase brand awareness, and drive business growth.

Depending on the type of business you operate or the services/products you offer, the sources where you can meet prospects and customers can change. Here is a list of sources where you can find customers for your business:

Online Marketplaces:

Amazon

eBay

Etsy

Alibaba

Shopify

Walmart Marketplace

Target Plus

Rakuten

Newegg

Wish

Social Media Platforms:

Facebook

Instagram

Twitter

LinkedIn

Pinterest

TikTok

Snapchat

YouTube

Reddit

Quora

Search Engines:

Google

Bing

Yahoo

DuckDuckGo

Baidu (China)

Yandex (Russia)

Business Directories:

Yelp

Yellow Pages

Google My Business

Bing Places for Business

Yahoo Local

TripAdvisor

Foursquare

Angie's List

Houzz

Thumbtack

Industry-Specific Directories:

Upwork (Freelancers and Remote Work)

Zocdoc (Medical Professionals)

Houzz (Home Improvement and Interior Design)

Behance (Creative Professionals)

HomeAdvisor (Home Services)

Angie's List (Home Services)

Thumbtack (Local Services)

Houzz Pro (Home Improvement Professionals)

WeddingWire (Wedding Services)

Houfy (Vacation Rentals)

Networking Events and Trade Shows:

Industry conferences

Trade shows and exhibitions

Business networking events

Meetup groups

Chamber of Commerce events

Professional association meetings

Referrals and Word-of-Mouth:

Encourage satisfied customers to refer others

Offer referral incentives or discounts

Establish a referral programme

Ask for testimonials and reviews

Email Marketing:

Build an email list and send targeted campaigns

Offer exclusive promotions or discounts via email

Provide valuable content in newsletters

Content Marketing:

Create a business blog

Publish articles and guides on your website

Guest post on industry blogs

Create informative videos or podcasts

Share content on social media platforms

Advertising:

Google Ads

Facebook Ads

Instagram Ads

LinkedIn Ads

Twitter Ads

Pinterest Ads

YouTube Ads

Display advertising on relevant websites

Sponsored content on industry publications

Local Community Engagement:

Sponsor local events or teams

Participate in community fundraisers

Collaborate with other local businesses

Support local charities or causes

Host or sponsor local workshops or seminars

Partnerships and Affiliates:

Establish strategic partnerships with complementary businesses

Create an affiliate programme to incentivise referrals

Collaborate on joint marketing initiatives

Direct Mail:

Send targeted direct mail campaigns to potential customers

Use postcards, flyers, or catalogues to showcase your products or services

Online Forums and Communities:

Participate in relevant online forums and communities

Answer questions and provide value to establish yourself as an expert

Share your business offerings when appropriate

Trade Publications and Industry Magazines:

Advertise in trade publications and magazines

Contribute guest articles or expert opinions

Attend industry events advertised in these publications

The effectiveness of these sources may vary depending on your specific industry, target audience, and business objectives. It's important

Here's a breakdown of free and paid sources to find tenders or contracts for your business:

Free Sources:

Government Procurement Websites:

The Official Journal of the European Union (OJEU)

Public Contracts Scotland

Sell2Wales

eTenders Ireland

Local Government and Municipal Websites:

City, county, or state government websites

Local council websites

Municipal purchasing departments

Industry-Specific Platforms:

Constructionline (Construction industry)

TED Tenders Electronic Daily (European Union)

eTendersNI (Northern Ireland)

Business Support Organisations:

Local business support organisations

Small Business Development Centres (SBDCs)

Economic development agencies

Networking and Industry Events:

Attend industry conferences and trade shows

Network with potential clients and partners

Subcontracting Opportunities:

Explore subcontracting opportunities with larger companies

Reach out to prime contractors for potential collaborations

Social Media and Online Platforms:

LinkedIn groups and communities

Social media hashtags related to tenders and contracts

Online forums and communities related to your industry

Paid Sources:

Commercial Tendering Platforms:

ProContract (UK)

Supply2Gov (UK)

BidNet (USA)

Tenders Electronic Daily (TED)

Bidding Source (Global)

International Development and Aid Agencies:

United Nations Development Programme (UNDP)

World Bank Group (WBG)

European Bank for Reconstruction and Development (EBRD)

Industry-Specific Platforms:

Achilles (Various industries)

SEAP (Utilities and energy sector)

FBO.gov (US Federal contracts)

Tender Aggregator Websites:

Tenders Direct (UK)

TenderSearch (Australia and New Zealand)

Tender247 (India)

Tenderio (Global)

Newspaper and Media Publications:

Industry-specific publications

Online Business Directories:

Industry-specific directories

Trade Associations and Professional Networks:

Industry-specific trade associations

Chambers of commerce

Professional networking platforms

Corporate Supplier Diversity Programmes:

Large corporations with supplier diversity initiatives

It's important to note that the availability and pricing of sources may vary over time. Some sources may offer a combination of free and paid options, with additional features and benefits for paid subscriptions or memberships. Consider your business needs, budget, and the value you expect to derive from each source to make informed decisions on whether to utilise free or paid options.

Remember, the key is to research and understand your target group and customers. Stay updated on emerging trends, test different marketing channels, and adapt your strategies accordingly. By mastering the art of finding and reaching your audience, you can forge powerful connections, drive growth, and unlock the true potential of your business. Happy hunting!

2.0 Social Media

In the era of social media 2.0, businesses have an array of powerful platforms at their disposal to perform marketing and unlock unparalleled success. Let's delve deeper into the latest platforms and how they can be leveraged to drive impactful marketing strategies.

Instagram, with its visually-driven nature, has emerged as a frontrunner in social media 2.0. It offers a visually captivating environment where businesses can showcase their products or services through high-quality images, engaging stories, and immersive videos. Brands can curate an aesthetically pleasing feed that resonates with their target audience, using clever storytelling and creative visuals to build a strong brand identity. Moreover, Instagram's interactive features, such as polls, question stickers, and shoppable tags, enable businesses to foster two-way communication, gather feedback, and facilitate seamless purchasing experiences.

Pinterest, another image-centric platform, provides a unique opportunity for businesses to tap into the power of inspiration and aspiration. By creating visually appealing boards and pins, brands can inspire their audience, offering ideas, tips, and solutions related to their niche. Users often turn to Pinterest to discover new products, plan their lifestyles, or seek creative inspiration. By optimizing content for searchability, businesses can ensure their pins appear in relevant searches, driving organic traffic to their websites and increasing brand visibility.

Video-based platforms have witnessed a meteoric rise in social media 2.0, offering dynamic and immersive experiences. YouTube, the world's largest video-sharing platform, presents a vast landscape for businesses to demonstrate their expertise, showcase product demonstrations, or provide educational content. The platform's recommendation algorithms allow businesses to reach a broader audience, and monetization options provide additional revenue streams. Short-form video platforms like TikTok and Instagram Reels have captivated the attention of younger demographics, providing businesses with an opportunity to create engaging, snackable content that quickly grabs attention and goes viral. Brands can collaborate with influencers or leverage trending challenges to amplify their reach and brand awareness.

Social media 2.0 also emphasizes the power of user-generated content (UGC) and community-building. Encouraging customers to share their experiences, reviews, and creative content generates social proof and fosters authentic connections. By featuring UGC on their social media channels, brands demonstrate that they value and appreciate their customers, strengthening loyalty and advocacy. Online communities, such as Facebook Groups or LinkedIn communities, provide spaces for businesses to interact with their audience, answer questions, and provide valuable insights. These communities foster engagement, allow businesses to gather feedback, and establish themselves as trusted industry leaders.

Influencer marketing has become a prominent strategy within social media 2.0. Influencers, with their dedicated followings and niche expertise, possess the ability to sway consumer opinions and drive purchasing decisions. Businesses can collaborate with influencers whose values align with their brand, leveraging their authenticity and credibility to reach a highly targeted and engaged audience. Through influencer partnerships, brands can tap into new markets, increase brand exposure, and generate buzz around their products or services.

Data-driven decision-making and personalization are integral components of social media 2.0 marketing strategies. Advanced analytics and tracking tools provided by platforms offer valuable insights into audience demographics, preferences, and behaviors. Businesses can use this data to refine their targeting, tailor content, and deliver personalized ad campaigns that resonate with specific customer segments. By delivering relevant and tailored experiences, businesses can forge deeper connections with their audience and maximize the impact of their marketing efforts.

ocial media 2.0 is not limited to individual platforms; it encompasses a holistic approach to marketing that involves integration and synergy across multiple channels. Businesses can create cross-platform strategies that leverage the strengths of each platform to achieve maximum impact. By maintaining a consistent brand voice and visual identity across platforms, businesses can reinforce their messaging and create a cohesive brand experience for their audience.

To succeed in social media 2.0, businesses need to stay updated with the latest trends, features, and algorithms of each platform. This requires continuous learning and adaptability to leverage new opportunities as they arise. It's crucial to monitor industry best practices, engage with thought leaders, and attend relevant conferences or webinars to stay at the forefront of social media marketing.

Additionally, businesses should prioritize engagement and authentic connections with their audience. Social media 2.0 thrives on meaningful interactions, and brands that actively engage with their followers build trust, loyalty, and advocacy. Responding to comments, messages, and reviews in a timely and genuine manner shows customers that their opinions matter and strengthens the brand-customer relationship.

A comprehensive social media strategy in the era of 2.0 should also include paid advertising. Platforms offer robust targeting options that allow businesses to reach their desired audience with precision. By investing in targeted ads, businesses can amplify their reach, increase brand visibility, and drive conversions. It's important to monitor ad performance, analyze data, and optimize campaigns regularly to ensure maximum return on investment (ROI).

Social media 2.0 is not solely about broadcasting marketing messages but also about fostering a sense of community. Businesses can create dedicated hashtags, host live events, or run contests to encourage user participation and engagement. By building an active and engaged community, businesses can tap into the power of user-generated content, generate buzz, and create a network of loyal brand advocates.

Lastly, social media 2.0 is an ever-evolving landscape, and businesses should continuously evaluate and refine their strategies. Regularly analyzing metrics, tracking conversions, and conducting A/B testing allows businesses to identify what works best for their target audience and make data-driven decisions. Staying agile and adaptable is key to staying ahead of the curve and maintaining a competitive edge in the fast-paced world of social media.

Here are a few examples of how businesses have leveraged the latest social media platforms to achieve marketing success:

Gymshark (Instagram and TikTok): Gymshark, a fitness apparel brand, effectively utilized Instagram and TikTok to build a strong online community. They collaborated with fitness influencers on Instagram, leveraging their reach and credibility to promote their products. Gymshark also created engaging content on TikTok, including workout challenges and behind-the-scenes glimpses, which quickly gained traction and attracted a younger audience.

Glossier (Pinterest): Glossier, a beauty and skincare brand, harnessed the power of Pinterest to drive brand awareness and inspire their audience. They created visually appealing boards with makeup tutorials, skincare tips, and user-generated content. By optimizing their pins for search, Glossier appeared in relevant searches, leading to increased website traffic and conversions.

Wendy's (Twitter): Wendy's, a fast-food chain, developed a unique and engaging Twitter presence with a humorous and witty brand voice. They leveraged trending topics and engaged in humorous banter with followers, resulting in increased brand awareness, viral tweets, and a strong online following. Wendy's effectively used Twitter as a platform for timely and entertaining customer interactions.

Airbnb (Instagram and Facebook): Airbnb, an online marketplace for accommodations, utilized Instagram and Facebook to showcase unique properties and inspire travel enthusiasts. They collaborated with travel influencers to share captivating visuals and stories from different destinations. Airbnb also used Facebook to encourage user-generated content by creating contests and campaigns, amplifying their reach and fostering a sense of community among their users.

Chipotle (TikTok and Snapchat): Chipotle, a fast-casual restaurant chain, embraced TikTok and Snapchat to connect with younger demographics. They created engaging and humorous content on TikTok, participating in trending challenges and leveraging user-generated content. Chipotle also used Snapchat to launch exclusive promotions, leveraging the platform's disappearing content feature to create a sense of urgency among their audience.

Here's a step-by-step guide get started:

Step 1: Set Clear Goals and Define Your Target Audience Identify your marketing objectives and define your target audience. Understand their demographics, interests, and pain points to tailor your messaging effectively.

Step 2: Choose the Right Platforms Research and select the social media platforms that align with your target audience and business goals. Consider platforms like Instagram, YouTube, TikTok, LinkedIn, or Facebook, based on the nature of your business and the content you want to create.

Step 3: Develop a Content Strategy Create a content strategy that aligns with your brand identity and resonates with your target audience. Determine the types of content (images, videos, stories, etc.) that will best convey your message and engage your audience. Plan a content calendar to ensure consistent posting.

Step 4: Optimize Your Profiles Optimize your social media profiles by using relevant keywords in your bio, providing a compelling description of your business, and incorporating high-quality visuals. Include links to your website or landing pages to drive traffic.

Step 5: Create Engaging Visual Content Leverage the power of visuals to captivate your audience. Develop eye-catching images, videos, and stories that showcase your products or services in an appealing and creative way. Maintain a consistent visual aesthetic that aligns with your brand.

Step 6: Foster Engagement and Build Community Actively engage with your audience by responding to comments, messages, and mentions. Encourage conversations, ask questions, and seek feedback to foster a sense of community. Create and participate in relevant groups or communities to establish yourself as an industry leader.

Step 7: Collaborate with Influencers Identify influencers who align with your brand values and have a dedicated following in your niche. Collaborate with them to amplify your reach and gain credibility. Develop mutually beneficial partnerships that promote your products or services to their engaged audience.

Step 8: Leverage Paid Advertising Consider allocating a portion of your marketing budget to paid advertising on social media platforms. Utilize advanced targeting options to reach your specific audience segments. Continuously monitor and optimize your ad campaigns to maximize their effectiveness.

Step 9: Analyze and Adapt Regularly track and analyze your social media metrics to measure the success of your efforts. Evaluate engagement rates, follower growth, click-through rates, and conversions. Use this data to refine your strategies, identify trends, and make data-driven decisions.

Step 10: Stay Updated and Evolve Keep up with the latest social media trends, algorithm changes, and emerging platforms. Experiment with new features, formats, and content types to stay ahead of the competition. Continuously adapt your strategies to meet the evolving needs and preferences of your target audience.

By following these steps and consistently refining your social media 2.0 marketing strategies, you can leverage the power of these platforms to amplify your brand, engage your audience, and achieve remarkable marketing success.

Arsenal of Content: Unleashing the Power of Words

Content is like ammunition in the world of marketing, sales, and bidding—it has the power to make a significant impact when effectively loaded and fired. Just as a skilled marksman carefully selects the right bullets for different targets, businesses must craft and deliver the right content to engage and influence their audience.

In marketing, content is the fuel that drives brand awareness and customer engagement. Through blog articles, social media posts, and informative videos, businesses can educate their audience, showcase their expertise, and establish themselves as industry leaders. By consistently delivering valuable and relevant content, businesses can build trust, attract a loyal following, and ultimately drive sales.

When it comes to sales, content becomes a vital tool in the arsenal of the sales team. Well-crafted sales collateral, such as persuasive presentations, case studies, and product demos, can effectively communicate the unique value proposition of a product or service. Compelling content helps sales professionals address customer objections, showcase the benefits of their offering, and guide prospects through the buying journey.

In the competitive world of bidding and tenders, content plays a crucial role in making a strong impression and winning contracts. A thoughtfully written proposal, supported by compelling visuals, can effectively communicate a business's capabilities, experience, and approach to solving the client's challenges. Detailed case studies and success stories can demonstrate previous achievements and build confidence in the bidder's ability to deliver.

To illustrate the power of content, consider some noteworthy examples. The emotional storytelling in Coca-Cola's "Share a Coke" campaign, the informative and entertaining blog posts by HubSpot, and the visually captivating product videos from Apple—all of these examples showcase the power of content to capture attention, inspire action, and create lasting impressions.

Ultimately, the success of content lies in its ability to connect with the target audience, address their pain points, and provide valuable solutions. By understanding the needs and preferences of the audience, businesses can tailor their content to resonate on a deeper level. This personalisation creates a sense of connection and relevance, leading to increased engagement, customer loyalty, and business growth.

So, businesses should treat content as their ammunition—their strategic tool to captivate, persuade, and win over their audience. By continuously refining and delivering high-quality content, businesses can stand out from the crowd, build strong relationships, and achieve their marketing, sales, and bidding goals.

Imagine soaring above the competition, even in industries where products or services may seem ordinary. I'm about to unveil mystifying strategies that will elevate you to the status of a true industry luminary, leaving your competitors scratching their heads in wonder. Farewell to the days of solely competing on price – it's time to unlock a world where differentiation and value reign supreme.

But hold on tight, because there's more excitement to come. I'll arm you with a treasure trove of tools to forge irresistible offers that your target market simply cannot resist. Prepare to uncover legendary examples of the most mesmerising advertising headlines in history, dissecting their enigmatic allure and extracting their essence of power. Get ready to tap into the minds of the marketing greats and unleash a whirlwind of persuasion.

And that's just the beginning. We're about to embark on an awe-inspiring expedition into the deepest corners of your prospects' minds, unravelling their innermost desires, fears, and aspirations. By stepping into their world and engaging in the conversations already taking place in their minds, you'll become their trusted confidant and the ultimate solution to their needs.

But wait, there's a sprinkle of magic yet to be unveiled. I'll reveal the secret art of naming that will ignite sparks of curiosity and excitement. Prepare to master the craft of creating names that dance on the tip of tongues and resonate deep within the souls of your audience.

So fasten your seatbelt, for I am about to revolutionise your marketing approach and embark on a remarkable journey that will etch your brand into the annals of greatness. Get ready to unleash the power of captivating messages and propel your business to unprecedented heights of success.

Studying Content

In a vast sea of content that inundates our digital landscape, standing out and capturing the attention of your target audience has become an art form. Whether you're aiming to attract contract clients or entice non-contract customers, the key lies in crafting compelling and captivating messaging that distinguishes itself from the crowd.

To make a real impact, it's crucial to develop a unique brand identity and messaging that deeply resonates with your audience. Think of it as creating your own distinct voice amidst a chorus of voices. Your messaging should clearly communicate the value you bring, the problems you solve, and the benefits you offer.

When targeting contract clients, direct and personalised messaging is of utmost importance. Delve deep into understanding their pain points, desires, and goals. Craft your messages to address their specific challenges and position yourself as the solution they've been seeking. By demonstrating a profound understanding of their needs and offering tailored solutions, you establish credibility and trust, thereby increasing your chances of winning their business.

However, don't underestimate the power of indirect targeting for non-contract customers. Even if they're not actively seeking your products or services, you can still capture their attention and sow the seeds of interest. Engaging content that educates, entertains, or sparks curiosity can help build brand awareness, foster a positive perception, and nurture potential leads over time. By consistently delivering valuable content that aligns with their interests, you stay top of mind and position yourself as a reliable source of information.

To maximise impact, a strategic multi-channel approach is essential. Combine the power of social media, blog posts, videos, podcasts, and other content formats to amplify your message across various platforms. Experiment with different formats and engage with your audience to create a two-way conversation. Remember, it's not just about talking at them, but also listening and responding to their needs.

As you embark on this journey, continuously monitor and analyse the performance of your content. Keep a close eye on engagement metrics, conversion rates, and customer feedback to gauge the effectiveness of your messaging. Adapt and refine your approach based on these insights, fine-tuning your content strategy to achieve even greater impact.

The battle for attention in today's content-saturated world requires strategic and compelling messaging. By developing a unique brand voice, tailoring your messages to contract clients and non-contract customers, and delivering engaging content across multiple channels, you can rise above the noise and leave a lasting impression. Embrace the power of storytelling, captivate your audience's imagination, and witness your impact soar to new heights.

So, we delve into the realm of content marketing and bidding, where the majority of messages fall short in capturing attention and inspiring action. However, fear not, for we humbly present to you the key to crafting compelling and impactful content that truly resonates with your target audience.

Imagine a vast digital landscape, brimming with content from countless businesses, all vying for attention. Many rely on the traditional approach of sharing generic information or self-promotion, hoping that by chance, someone will stumble upon their content. Yet, the results often leave much to be desired, leaving businesses yearning for more.

But what if there is a better way? A purpose-driven approach that breaks free from the norm and creates meaningful connections with your audience. Let us humbly unveil the secrets of persuasive content that captivate hearts and minds.

To embark on this transformative journey, we must address two fundamental elements that will revolutionise your content marketing strategies:

Clarify the Objective of Your Content: Instead of attempting to achieve multiple objectives with a single piece of content, let us focus on a singular goal that aligns with your business objectives. By honing in on a specific objective, we can craft content that speaks directly to the hearts and minds of your audience, inspiring them to take meaningful action.

For example, if your objective is to generate leads, let us create content that offers valuable insights or presents a compelling solution to a common problem. By providing actionable information or addressing a pressing concern, we can build trust and credibility with your audience, fostering meaningful engagement.

Shift the Focus to Your Audience: Instead of overwhelming your audience with self-promotion, let us strive to truly understand their needs, desires, and pain points. By empathising with your target audience, we can tailor our content to address their specific concerns and provide solutions that truly resonate.

For instance, if you are creating content for a fitness brand, let us focus on the benefits it offers to individuals seeking to improve their health and well-being. By sharing inspiring stories, practical tips, and expert advice, we can establish ourselves as a trusted resource in the industry, fostering a loyal following.

With a humble and audience-centric approach, we can break free from the noise and make a genuine impact. Our content will stand out amidst the sea of self-centered messages, capturing attention and driving meaningful engagement.

Let us leave behind the outdated notion of chance encounters and embrace the power of purposeful content marketing. By defining our objectives and focusing on our audience's needs, we can create content that inspires action and delivers tangible results. Together, we can unlock the untapped potential of persuasive content, leaving a lasting impression on your target market.

Get ready to embark on this exciting journey and grasp the opportunity to transform your content marketing strategies. Let the power of persuasion guide our every move, as we humbly captivate hearts and minds with compelling content that deeply resonates. The path to success awaits, and we are honored to be your guide.

Unique Selling Points (USP) and Value Propositions (VP)

USPs and VPs are extremely important to attract attention and persuade. In the world of marketing, two heavyweight contenders vie for attention: the Unique Selling Proposition (USP) and the Value Proposition (VP). These strategic concepts pack a punch and can make or break a business's success. Let's step into the ring and explore the distinction between these powerhouses.

In the red corner, we have the USP! Imagine a dazzling product or business that shines brighter than its competitors. The USP is the secret ingredient that makes it stand out in a crowded marketplace. It's like a superhero's special power, a unique feature or benefit that captures the hearts of customers. Why should they choose you? The USP holds the answer and delivers a knockout blow of differentiation.

But don't count out the blue corner just yet! Here comes the VP, armed with the promise of value and benefits. Picture a savvy customer who wants to make a smart choice. The VP swoops in, highlighting the irresistible advantages and rewards of choosing a particular product or business. What's in it for them? The VP unveils the enticing reasons to jump on board and experience the value-packed journey.

In this clash of titans, the USP appeals to the emotions, capturing the hearts of customers with its unique charm. It's like a magician's spell, weaving a story that sets a product or business apart from the crowd. On the other hand, the VP takes a rational approach, appealing to customers' practical side. It's like a brilliant strategist, presenting a clear roadmap of benefits, cost savings, or convenience.

But wait, there's more! These contenders are not mutually exclusive. In fact, they can join forces and create a dynamic duo. Picture the USP drawing customers in with its unique allure, and then the VP stepping up to seal the deal with its undeniable value. It's a one-two punch that leaves competitors in awe and customers craving more.

So, whether you're in the corner of the USP or cheering for the VP, remember that both are essential players in the marketing game. They bring their own strengths and strategies to the ring, ready to captivate customers and secure victory. Embrace the power of your unique qualities and deliver an unbeatable value proposition. That's how you can conquer the market and become a champion in your industry. Let the battle begin!

The Distinction Between Unique Selling Proposition (USP) and Value Proposition (VP)

Unique Selling Proposition (USP):

A USP concentrates on what distinguishes a product, service, or business from its competitors.

It highlights the unique features, benefits, or qualities that make a product or business stand out in the market.

A USP answers the question, "Why should customers choose your product/business over others?"

It helps differentiate a product/business and establish a distinct identity in the minds of consumers.

A USP often appeals to customers' emotions, needs, or desires to create a compelling reason to purchase.

Value Proposition (VP):

A VP focuses on the value and benefits that a product, service, or business offers to customers.

It emphasises the unique value or advantages that customers gain by choosing a particular product or business.

A VP answers the question, "What value or benefit does the customer receive from using your product/service?"

It communicates the specific problem-solving capabilities, outcomes, or advantages that customers can expect.

A VP often appeals to customers' rational decision-making by highlighting the tangible benefits, cost savings, or convenience provided.

While both the USP and VP are important marketing concepts, they differ in their focus. The USP primarily highlights what makes a product/business unique and distinctive, while the VP emphasises the value and benefits that customers derive from using the product/service. Both aspects are essential for effective marketing and creating a compelling offering in the competitive business landscape.

USP

Crafting a Unique Selling Proposition (USP) In the vast sea of businesses, many small enterprises find themselves without a true purpose. Take away their name and logo from their website or other marketing materials, and their identity becomes indistinguishable from others in their industry. Their existence boils down to mere survival and paying the bills, with little more to show.

From a customer's perspective, there is no compelling reason to choose them over competitors. Any sales they manage to secure are purely coincidental, relying on chance encounters rather than intentional selection. This scenario is all too common in retail, where businesses receive sales from random walk-in traffic but fail to attract customers seeking their specific offerings. Harsh, but an unfortunate reality.

The root of the problem lies in these businesses being "me too" entities. Their pricing, products, and marketing strategies are typically determined by mimicking their closest rivals, with slight modifications at best. While emulating successful models is not inherently flawed, it often results in copying competitors who are themselves struggling to stand out. These decisions are based on guesswork and lack a clear direction. It's like a case of the blind leading the blind.

After a while, many of these businesses, after surviving on meager profits, decide to venture into marketing. However, they approach it with the same uninspiring "me too" mindset, resulting in equally lackluster messages. Predictably, these efforts yield little return on investment, failing to cover the costs incurred.

Here's the reality: Achieving marketing success from the outset is incredibly rare. Even seasoned marketers will attest that hitting a home run on the first try is a lofty goal. It takes numerous iterations, testing, and careful measurement to refine your message, find the right target market, and select the most effective channels.

Unfortunately, these struggling businesses cannot afford the time, money, or effort required to navigate this trial-and-error process. Moreover, their generic offerings leave them with little hope of making significant strides.

Think of marketing as an amplifier for your message. Imagine telling one person about your business, and they show no excitement. Now imagine sharing your message with ten people, yet the response remains underwhelming. If you amplify this message to reach 10,000 individuals through marketing efforts, why would the outcome be any different?

To overcome these challenges, it is imperative to develop a Unique Selling Proposition (USP). This is often where businesses stumble. They believe there is nothing unique about their offerings, accepting their fate as just another face in the crowd.

But consider this: If selling coffee were solely about the product itself, why do people willingly queue up and spend significantly more on a cup of coffee from a hipster cafe? It's not just the commodity they seek—it's the experience, the atmosphere, and the story behind it. The same can be said for other industries, where the circumstances and presentation surrounding a commodity make all the difference.

The goal of your USP is to answer one crucial question: Why should customers choose your business over your closest competitor? It's about creating differentiation and highlighting the unique qualities that make you stand out.

A valuable test is to remove your company name and logo from your website. Does your website still convey a distinctive identity, or could it easily be mistaken for any other company in your industry? If it lacks individuality, it's time to rethink your USP.

Avoid falling into the common trap of claiming "quality" or "great service" as your USP. While these are important aspects of any business, they are expected and not inherently unique. Your USP should captivate potential customers before they make a purchasing decision, showcasing what sets you apart from the competition.

Positioning your business as a commodity driven solely by price is a precarious path. It leads to a race to the bottom, undermining your profitability and devaluing your offerings. Instead, by developing a robust USP, you position yourself in a way that forces customers to make a discerning choice, comparing apples to oranges and recognising your superiority.

Always remember that someone will always be willing to sell at a lower price. However, by establishing a compelling and unique USP, you rise above the price wars and provide customers with a genuine reason to choose your business over the rest.

My dear friend Alex had always dreamed of venturing into the world of entrepreneurship. Armed with passion and a vision, they took the leap and founded their own digital marketing agency, SparkDigital Solutions. However, they soon realised that standing out in the fiercely competitive industry was no easy feat.

Driven by their determination to make a mark, Alex embarked on a remarkable journey of discovery. They spent countless hours researching, engaging with potential clients, and delving deep into understanding their needs and challenges. It was through this dedicated effort that Alex truly began to unlock the secrets of creating a compelling value proposition.

With a keen eye for identifying opportunities, Alex carefully examined the unique features and strengths of SparkDigital Solutions. They realised that one area where businesses struggled the most was lead generation. Many were desperately seeking ways to stand out in the crowded digital landscape and attract qualified prospects.

Inspired by this insight, Alex set out to develop a revolutionary lead generation system that would address these challenges head-on. They meticulously designed and implemented a comprehensive strategy, leveraging cutting-edge technologies and data-driven approaches to identify and engage with the most promising prospects.

As the lead generation system began to yield remarkable results, Alex crafted a compelling value proposition that highlighted the incredible impact it had on our clients' businesses. They passionately shared stories of how the system generated a staggering 46% increase in qualified prospects within just one month.

With the value proposition at the core of their communication strategies, Alex and the team at SparkDigital Solutions set out to spread the word. They revamped their website, launched captivating social media campaigns, and confidently presented the value proposition in client meetings and pitches.

The response was overwhelming. Prospects were captivated by the promise of tangible results and eagerly reached out to learn more about SparkDigital Solutions' innovative approach. Within a short span of time, the agency experienced an unprecedented surge in qualified leads, with the remarkable 46% increase becoming a testament to the power of their value proposition.

The news of SparkDigital Solutions' success quickly spread throughout the industry, establishing them as pioneers in lead generation and digital marketing expertise. Colleagues and clients alike marvelled at the impact that Alex's unwavering dedication and customer-centric mindset had on their business.

Alex's journey is a testament to their tenacity, analytical acumen, and unwavering belief in the power of a compelling value proposition. Their story serves as an inspiration to all aspiring entrepreneurs, reminding us of the incredible rewards that come with investing time and effort into understanding customer needs and crafting a value proposition that truly resonates.

Their success stands as a shining example of the transformative power that lies within developing a strong value proposition and using it as a guiding light in our entrepreneurial endeavours.

As you can see, a value proposition is like a secret weapon that helps businesses secure the loyalty and attention of customers. It's a unique combination of features, benefits, and promises that make your product or service irresistible to your target audience. Creating an engaging value proposition requires strategic thinking and a touch of creativity. Let's dive into the process with enthusiasm!

Uncover Hidden Desires: Picture yourself as a detective on a mission to understand your target audience. Conduct thorough research, listen to their needs, and identify their deepest desires. For instance, if you're selling fitness equipment, you might discover that your audience craves convenience, quick results, and a sense of accomplishment.

Craft Your Winning Formula: Armed with valuable insights, it's time to formulate your unique selling points. What sets your offering apart from the competition? Let's say you've developed a smart fitness device that combines cutting-edge technology with personalised workout plans and real-time performance tracking. These features are the key ingredients to your success.

Create a Captivating Story: Every hero needs a captivating story, and your value proposition is no different. Weave a narrative that resonates with your audience, highlighting how your offering can transform their lives. Imagine this: "Unleash your inner superhero with our smart fitness device. Crush your fitness goals with personalised workouts, track your progress in real-time, and unlock your true potential. Join the fitness revolution!"

Paint a Picture of Benefits: To captivate your audience, paint a vivid picture of the benefits they'll experience. Show them how your offering solves their problems, fulfills their desires, or makes their lives easier. For example, "Say goodbye to monotonous workouts and hello to a fitness experience tailored just for you. Our smart device makes exercising enjoyable, efficient, and addictive. Get ready to embrace the thrill of reaching new heights of fitness!"

Ignite Curiosity and Desire: Spark curiosity and create a sense of urgency by highlighting what makes you stand out. Emphasise limited-time offers, exclusive bonuses, or unique features that leave your audience wanting more. For instance, "Join our fitness community and unlock exclusive access to expert trainers, virtual challenges, and a supportive network of like-minded individuals. Don't miss out on this limited opportunity to elevate your fitness game!"

Test and Refine: Like a skilled alchemist, continuously test and refine your value proposition. Gather feedback, run A/B tests, and make improvements based on the response of your target audience. Pay attention to what resonates, generates excitement, and compels them to take action. Adapt and refine your value proposition until it shines brilliantly.

Remember, an exceptional value proposition speaks directly to the hearts and minds of your audience. It's the enchanting spell that captures their attention, ignites their desires, and compels them to choose your offering above others. So, gear up, unleash your creativity, and craft a value proposition that leaves your competitors in awe. The quest for customer loyalty begins now!

What about tenders (contract clients)?

Winning tenders is like embarking on an epic quest in the business world, where a well-crafted value proposition (VP) or unique selling proposition (USP) can be your secret weapon. Picture this: You're a valiant knight in shining armour, ready to battle it out against a fierce army of competitors. Your VP or USP is the mighty sword that sets you apart and helps you emerge victorious.

In the land of tenders, every bidder is vying for attention, but only those with a compelling VP or USP can capture the buyer's heart and secure the coveted contract. Imagine you're a wizard, wielding the power of differentiation. With a flick of your wand, you conjure a spellbinding proposition that showcases your unique abilities, expertise, and irresistible charm.

But it's not just about dazzling the buyer with magic words. Your VP or USP must address their deepest desires and vanquish their pain points. Just like a skilled archer aiming for the bullseye, you take aim at the buyer's challenges and shoot arrows of value, demonstrating how your solution will slay their problems and bring them glory.

Numbers hold great power in the realm of tenders. You're a master of alchemy, transforming abstract benefits into tangible value. You sprinkle your proposal with metrics and statistics, revealing the potential cost savings, efficiency gains, or competitive advantages that await the buyer. Your magical potion of benefits leaves them spellbound, unable to resist the allure of what you offer.

The beauty of a well-crafted VP or USP is its ability to shape-shift and adapt to each tender's unique requirements. Like a skilled shape-shifter, you seamlessly transform your offering to match the buyer's needs. Whether it's a government agency seeking sustainability or a corporate entity yearning for innovation, you tailor your proposition to fit their desires perfectly.

Trust is the knight's armour in this battle. Your VP or USP acts as a shield, protecting you from doubt and uncertainty. You parade your past victories, displaying a trophy room of successful projects, glowing testimonials, and accolades from satisfied clients. Your reputation precedes you, instilling confidence in the buyer that you are the chosen one, destined to deliver greatness.

So, fellow adventurer, as you set out on your quest for tender triumph, remember the power of a captivating VP or USP. It's the spell that enchants the buyer, the potion that quenches their thirst for a remarkable solution, and the armour that shields you from competitors. With your proposition as your trusty companion, victory will be within your grasp, and the spoils of a successful tender will be yours to claim.

Therefore, Value propositions (VPs) and unique selling propositions (USPs) play a vital role in winning tenders by helping businesses differentiate themselves and demonstrate their value to the buyer. Here are some additional insights and examples on how VPs and USPs contribute to tender success:

Emphasising Differentiation: Tenders attract a multitude of bidders, and it's crucial for businesses to stand out from the competition. A well-crafted VP or USP enables a bidder to clearly articulate what sets them apart and why they are the best choice for the project. For instance, a construction company bidding for a government infrastructure project may emphasise their expertise in sustainable building practices and commitment to timely delivery as their unique selling point.

Addressing Buyer's Pain Points: Successful tenders address the specific pain points or challenges faced by the buyer. By aligning their VP or USP with these pain points, businesses can position themselves as the solution provider. For example, a software development company bidding for an IT project may highlight their experience in developing customised solutions that streamline processes and improve efficiency, addressing the buyer's need for optimisation.

Demonstrating Value and Benefits: VPs and USPs allow businesses to clearly communicate the value and benefits their proposal offers to the buyer. This can be done by quantifying the potential cost savings, time efficiencies, or performance improvements that their solution brings. For example, a logistics company bidding for a transportation contract may showcase their advanced tracking systems, optimised routes, and proven track record of punctual deliveries, highlighting the potential cost savings and reliability benefits for the buyer.

Tailoring the Proposal: A well-defined VP or USP enables businesses to customise their tender proposal to meet the specific needs of the buyer. This involves aligning the features, benefits, and outcomes of their offering with the buyer's requirements. For instance, a marketing agency bidding for a branding project may tailor their VP to highlight their expertise in brand strategy, creative storytelling, and digital marketing channels, addressing the buyer's need for a comprehensive and impactful brand campaign.

Building Trust and Confidence: VPs and USPs help build trust and confidence with the buyer by showcasing the bidder's expertise, experience, and track record. By presenting a compelling VP or USP, businesses can demonstrate their capabilities and establish themselves as a reliable and trustworthy partner. This can be achieved through case studies, client testimonials, or highlighting relevant certifications and industry recognition.

Successful tender submissions often incorporate a strong VP or USP that effectively communicates the bidder's unique value, addresses the buyer's needs, and stands out from the competition. By crafting a compelling proposition and tailoring the proposal accordingly, businesses can increase their chances of winning tenders and securing lucrative contracts.

Turn Boring Concepts Into New Features

In a world saturated with businesses offering similar products and services, you may find yourself pondering, "How can I possibly stand out? Is there anything unique about my business?" Fret not, my dear friend, for I'm here to guide you on the path to developing an extraordinary Unique Selling Proposition (USP) and a captivating Value Proposition (VP) that will distinguish your business and capture the hearts of your audience.

To create a truly compelling USP, it's essential to delve into the minds and desires of your customers, asking yourself a series of thought-provoking questions:

• What pain points do my customers experience that remain unaddressed?

• How can my business provide an innovative solution to these pain points?

• What sets my business apart from the competition, making it the obvious choice for customers?

By carefully considering these questions, you'll uncover insights that will shape both your USP and VP, propelling your business forward. Let's delve deeper into the process, with some inspiring examples to fuel your imagination:

Imagine you're in the fiercely competitive fashion industry. Whilst many clothing brands focus solely on style and trends, your USP could revolve around inclusivity and body positivity. By offering an extensive range of sizes and promoting diverse representation in your marketing campaigns, you create a welcoming and empowering environment for customers who have felt overlooked by traditional fashion brands. This unique offering becomes your USP, while the value and benefits it brings to customers form the core of your VP.

Similarly, let's explore the tech industry, where groundbreaking gadgets flood the market. Your USP could be centred around user-friendly design and exceptional customer support. By providing comprehensive tutorials, easily accessible customer service, and a seamless user experience, you differentiate yourself as a company that genuinely cares about its customers' success and satisfaction. This focus on user experience becomes your USP, while the tangible value it brings to customers becomes your VP.

Now, imagine the hospitality industry, where hotels are abundant. Your USP could focus on creating a personalised and unforgettable guest experience. By offering bespoke services, tailored recommendations, and unique amenities that cater to each guest's preferences, you transform a simple hotel stay into a memorable journey that leaves an indelible impression. This emphasis on personalised experience becomes your USP, while the unique benefits and value it brings to guests form your VP.

A robust USP and VP go beyond catchy marketing slogans or empty promises. They require delivering on your commitments and consistently surpassing customer expectations. They entail providing tangible value and solving customers' problems in a way that no one else can.

Even the oldest and seemingly most mundane content can be transformed into new ideas and captivating features that ignite interest and drive sales. It's about taking a creative approach to repurposing and reinventing your existing content, breathing new life into it and capturing the attention of your audience.

Here are a few strategies to rejuvenate your content and infuse it with a fresh spark that boosts sales:

1. Revamp and Revitalise: Take your old content, such as blog posts or articles, and give them a makeover. Update the information, inject fresh insights, and reformat them into visually appealing and easily digestible formats. Consider transforming a blog post into a captivating infographic, an engaging podcast episode, or an enticing video tutorial. By presenting your content in different formats, you can broaden your reach and engage your audience in exciting new ways.

2. Uncover Unique Perspectives: Look at your existing content from different angles or viewpoints. Seek out unique perspectives that haven't been explored before. For instance, if you have a blog post about the benefits of a particular product, consider creating a new piece that focuses on great customer success stories or expert tips on maximising the product's potential. By offering fresh perspectives, you can generate a sense of novelty and captivate your audience's interest.

3. Incorporate Interactive Elements: Transform your content into interactive experiences that actively engage your audience. This could involve incorporating quizzes, polls, calculators, or interactive videos. By involving your audience in the content, you not only capture their attention but also create a memorable and immersive experience that deepens their connection with your brand.

4. Embrace User-Generated Content: Encourage your customers to share their experiences, testimonials, and reviews. User-generated content adds authenticity and social proof to your marketing efforts. Feature customer stories or testimonials to showcase the benefits of your products or services, building trust and credibility with your audience.

5. Collaborate with Influencers: Forge partnerships with influencers or industry experts to infuse your content with a fresh perspective. Invite them to contribute guest blog posts, participate in interviews, or collaborate on content creation. Their unique insights and expertise will bring a fresh voice and attract their followers to your brand, increasing exposure and driving potential sales.

The key lies in continuously innovating and finding ways to present your content in a manner that resonates with your audience. By breathing new life into old content, you can ignite interest, create excitement, and ultimately drive sales. Embrace your creativity, experiment with different approaches, and remain open to feedback from your audience. With a fresh and engaging content strategy, your business will thrive and stand out in a crowded marketplace.

So, invest time in understanding your customers intimately, thoroughly analyse your market, and allow your creativity to flourish as you craft a USP and VP that truly set your business apart. Embrace your uniqueness, infuse it into every facet of your brand, and let it radiate through all your communication strategies. With a well-crafted USP and VP, you'll attract a loyal following, grasp new opportunities, and leave an indelible mark on your industry.

Prospect Psychology

Let us embark on a captivating exploration through additional examples and delve deeper into the realm of understanding our prospects' true desires. By doing so, we can shape our unique selling proposition (USP) and value proposition (VP) to create a powerful and compelling message that resonates with our target audience.

In the world of fashion, consider a clothing brand that targets environmentally conscious consumers. Whilst prospects may be initially drawn to sustainable and ethical fashion choices, their motivations extend beyond simply purchasing eco-friendly garments. They aspire to make a positive impact on the planet, contribute to a more sustainable future, and align their values with the brands they choose to support. By crafting a USP and VP that emphasise not only the use of organic materials and ethical production practices but also the brand's commitment to social and environmental causes, this clothing brand can attract customers who are deeply passionate about making a difference through their fashion choices.

Now, let's shift our focus to the world of technology and software solutions. Suppose you run a software development company. Whilst prospects may approach you for a specific software application, their underlying desires often revolve around improving efficiency, streamlining processes, and enhancing productivity. By crafting a USP and VP that emphasise the seamless integration, user-friendly interface, and customisable features of your software solutions, you can position yourself as a partner who understands their unique needs and provides tailored solutions that empower their businesses to thrive.

Moving into the realm of personal development and coaching, imagine you offer life coaching services. Whilst clients may seek guidance to overcome specific challenges or achieve personal goals, their deeper motivations often involve personal growth, self-discovery, and a desire to live a fulfilled and purposeful life. By crafting a USP and VP that emphasise your expertise, proven methodologies, and personalised approach to coaching, you can attract individuals who are committed to personal transformation and position yourself as the catalyst for their journey towards a more meaningful and fulfilling life.

These examples illustrate the power of understanding our prospects' underlying motivations and desires. By aligning our USP and VP with these deeper aspirations, we transcend transactional exchanges and create meaningful connections that resonate with our target audience. By clearly communicating the value we offer and the unique benefits our products or services bring, we differentiate ourselves in the marketplace and become the go-to choice for customers seeking solutions that go beyond their immediate needs.

So, let us embrace the art of understanding, immerse ourselves in the minds of our prospects, and uncover the secret desires that drive their choices. By crafting compelling narratives, delivering exceptional experiences, and continuously evolving to meet their evolving needs, we can differentiate ourselves, forge lasting customer relationships, and elevate our businesses to new heights of success. The adventure awaits, my fellow explorers of prospect psychology!

Keep It Simple

I have a friend named David who faced a significant challenge in generating sales for his business consulting service. Despite implementing various growth tactics and investing considerable time and effort into his marketing strategies, David struggled to see tangible results.

After conducting a thorough analysis of his marketing approach, David realised that the complexity and overwhelming number of options he presented to potential clients were creating confusion and hindering their decision-making process. His consulting service offered a wide range of specialised solutions tailored to different industries and business needs. However, this extensive array of choices often left his target audience feeling overwhelmed and uncertain about the best option for their specific requirements.

Recognising the need for a change, David embarked on a journey to simplify his messaging across all his marketing channels. He carefully examined each consulting service he offered, identifying the most common pain points and challenges faced by his target clients. Armed with this valuable insight, David streamlined his service offerings into three comprehensive packages that catered to different business sizes and objectives.

David then dedicated himself to revamping his website, refining his social media posts, and crafting compelling email campaigns. He focused on communicating the clear benefits and unique value of each package, using plain and straightforward language to ensure maximum clarity. By reducing complexity and eliminating unnecessary options, David aimed to empower potential clients to easily understand his services and make informed decisions without feeling overwhelmed.

The results of David's revamped messaging strategy were nothing short of remarkable. Within a mere three weeks, he witnessed an astounding 223% increase in sales. The simplified and focused messages resonated with his target audience, allowing them to swiftly grasp the value of his consulting services and make confident choices. By alleviating the burden of choice overload, David had successfully removed the barriers that had previously hindered his sales efforts.

Not only did the simplified messaging yield impressive sales figures, but it also fostered trust and enhanced customer satisfaction. Clients appreciated the straightforward and transparent approach, which instilled a sense of confidence in David's expertise and reliability. This newfound trust translated into positive word-of-mouth referrals and repeat business, further fuelling his success.

Inspired by this transformative experience, David remained committed to refining and optimising his marketing messages. He continuously sought ways to simplify and clarify his communication across all channels, ensuring that potential clients could effortlessly navigate the available options and find the perfect solution for their specific needs. This unwavering dedication to transparency and simplicity became the foundation of David's marketing strategy, driving ongoing growth and solidifying his reputation as a trustworthy and results-oriented business consultant.

When people are confronted with a plethora of options, it often leads to decision paralysis or choice overload. This occurs when individuals are overwhelmed by the sheer number of choices available, making it arduous for them to make a decision or take action.

One reason for this phenomenon is that having an abundance of options increases the cognitive load on individuals. The more choices they have to consider, the greater the mental effort and time required to evaluate each option. This can result in decision fatigue, wherein individuals become mentally exhausted from the decision-making process.

Furthermore, a surplus of options can create a sense of uncertainty and apprehension about making the wrong choice. When people are presented with numerous alternatives, they may harbour concerns about missing out on a superior option or making a suboptimal decision. This fear of regret can impede them from taking any action at all.

Additionally, the availability of copious options can lead to information overload. People may feel inundated by the volume of information they need to process in order to make an informed decision. This can render decision-making a daunting and time-consuming task, prompting individuals to defer or avoid making a choice altogether.

In such situations, individuals often resort to simplifying strategies, such as relying on heuristics or seeking recommendations from others, to cope with the complexity of the decision-making process. They may also be more inclined to choose familiar options or default to the status quo, as these choices feel safer and require less cognitive effort.

To effectively engage and motivate individuals in the face of numerous options, businesses and marketers need to simplify the decision-making process for their target audience. This can be achieved by providing clear and concise information, highlighting the key benefits and differentiators of their offerings, and offering guidance or recommendations based on the specific needs and preferences of their customers.

By reducing complexity, providing relevant information, and guiding customers towards the best option for their needs, businesses can help individuals overcome decision paralysis and take action. Creating a sense of urgency, offering limited-time promotions or discounts, and providing social proof can also aid in motivating individuals to make a decision in a timely manner.

When people encounter an excessive number of options, it can lead to decision paralysis, decision fatigue, and information overload. The overwhelming array of choices can make it challenging for individuals to take action. To address this, businesses need to simplify the decision-making process, provide pertinent information, and guide customers towards the optimal choice. By doing so, they can help individuals surmount the challenges posed by choice overload and increase the likelihood of action and conversion.

In today's fast-paced world, where we are bombarded with countless messages and options, capturing the attention and interest of our prospects has become more challenging than ever. The key lies in clarity and simplicity - if you confuse them, you lose them.

Consider the example of a mobile phone company launching a new model. They could craft a clear and impactful message by highlighting the unique benefit of their product in a single sentence: "Experience the fastest processing speed and the most advanced camera technology in our latest mobile phone."

This succinct message immediately communicates the key selling points of the product, capturing the interest of potential customers who are seeking a fast and powerful mobile phone with excellent camera capabilities. By avoiding confusion and delivering a clear value proposition, the mobile phone company stands a better chance of attracting customers in a saturated market.

Now let's take a look at the hospitality industry. Imagine a luxury hotel that wants to differentiate itself from the competition. Instead of confusing potential guests with a lengthy description of all their amenities and services, they could focus on a single compelling statement: "Indulge in the epitome of luxury and personalised service at our award-winning boutique hotel."

This concise and impactful message conveys the unique selling point of the hotel - an unrivalled luxury experience coupled with exceptional personalised service. It appeals to discerning travellers who are seeking a truly exceptional and memorable stay. By avoiding confusion and providing a clear value proposition, the hotel increases the likelihood of attracting guests who are willing to pay a premium for an extraordinary experience.

The underlying principle here is that in a world filled with options and information overload, simplicity and clarity are paramount. When crafting your message, whether it's for a product, service, or brand, strive for immediate understandability and impact. Avoid overwhelming your prospects with complex explanations or convoluted descriptions. Instead, focus on succinctly communicating the unique benefit and value you offer.

Remember, confusion leads to lost sales. Your prospects are unlikely to invest the time and effort to decipher a muddled message when they have numerous alternatives vying for their attention. By delivering a clear and concise value proposition, you cut through the noise, engage your prospects, and increase the chances of converting them into loyal customers.

So, take a step back, assess your message, and ensure that it is crystal clear, compelling, and easily understood. Embrace the power of simplicity and watch as your prospects become captivated by your offering in a sea of confusion.

Creating Competitive Advantages

Let's say we have a new player in the fitness industry named James. James noticed that the market was saturated with traditional gyms offering the same equipment and generic workout routines. He knew that to succeed, he needed a competitive advantage that would set his fitness business apart.

After careful research and understanding his target audience, James identified a common pain point among gym-goers—an overwhelming feeling of isolation and lack of support during their fitness journey. Recognising the opportunity to address this need, James decided to build a fitness community centred around camaraderie, motivation, and personalised guidance.

James transformed his gym into a welcoming and inclusive space where members not only had access to state-of-the-art equipment but also received individualised attention from expert trainers. He fostered a sense of community by organising group workout sessions, social events, and fitness challenges that encouraged interaction and mutual support among members. Additionally, James leveraged technology to provide members with personalised workout plans, progress tracking, and virtual support, ensuring that they felt connected and motivated even outside the gym walls.

This unique approach created a competitive advantage for James's fitness business. It wasn't just about offering exercise equipment and training; it was about providing a holistic fitness experience that addressed the emotional and social needs of his members. Word quickly spread about James's gym, attracting individuals who were looking for a supportive environment that went beyond the traditional gym model.

By recognising and capitalising on a specific pain point and differentiating himself through a community-focused approach, James gained a competitive advantage in the fitness industry. His gym became the go-to destination for individuals seeking a sense of belonging, personalised guidance, and a supportive community to help them achieve their fitness goals.

This example showcases the power of creating a competitive advantage by identifying unmet needs and developing a unique offering that resonates with your target audience. By understanding what sets you apart and leveraging that as a competitive edge, you can carve out a distinctive position in the market and attract loyal customers who value the differentiated experience you provide.

When it comes to selling a product or service in a crowded market, standing out can feel like an uphill battle. You might find yourself wondering, "How can I possibly make an impact when my offerings are similar to others?" The key lies in being remarkable.

Allow me to share the inspiring story of Sarah, an ambitious small business owner in the baking industry. With countless bakeries scattered throughout the town, Sarah faced the daunting challenge of carving out a unique space for herself. She knew that relying solely on taste would be a tough game to win. Determined to leave her mark, Sarah unleashed her boundless creativity and elevated her cakes to a whole new level of artistry.

Rather than baking ordinary cakes, Sarah focused on creating edible masterpieces that were as visually stunning as they were delectable. She honed her skills in crafting intricate sugar flower decorations that transformed her cakes into breathtaking works of edible art. Each cake became a bespoke creation, showcasing meticulous craftsmanship and an unparalleled attention to detail. News of Sarah's remarkable creations quickly spread, and customers flocked to her bakery, eager to experience the awe-inspiring beauty and unparalleled artistry. Despite commanding higher prices than her competitors, customers were more than willing to pay a premium for the extraordinary experience and unparalleled craftsmanship that Sarah offered.

Now, let's shift our attention to Mark, a visionary entrepreneur in the pet grooming industry. Recognising the common struggles faced by pet owners when it came to grooming their beloved companions, Mark saw an opportunity to make a real difference. He understood that pet owners often endured the stress of transporting their furry friends to a grooming salon, which could be a daunting experience for both pets and their owners.

To tackle this problem head-on, Mark conceived a brilliant idea. He ingeniously transformed a regular van into a cutting-edge mobile grooming salon. The van was meticulously outfitted with all the essential tools and amenities, but it also offered something truly extraordinary—a tranquil and soothing environment for pets. Mark designed plush and comfortable seating, played calming melodies, and employed gentle handling techniques that put pets at ease. The convenience of having the grooming service come directly to their doorstep, coupled with the unparalleled care provided, made Mark's mobile grooming service an instant hit. Pet owners gladly paid a premium for the convenience and peace of mind, knowing that their cherished companions were receiving top-notch care.

These captivating examples vividly illustrate that being remarkable does not require reinventing the wheel or creating something entirely novel. It is about finding innovative ways to enhance the customer experience and address unmet needs. By going above and beyond, you create a sense of value and differentiation that sets you apart from your competitors.

As the esteemed marketing expert Seth Godin astutely said, "Don't be afraid to be different. Be afraid to be the same as everyone else." This timeless quote resonates deeply in today's fiercely competitive landscape. Customers are irresistibly drawn to businesses that offer something truly unique, something that stands out from the vast sea of similarity.

To create a truly remarkable business, begin by immersing yourself in a thorough understanding of your target audience. Dive deep into their pain points, desires, and unfulfilled needs. Then, unleash your creative spirit and find ways to address those needs in unexpected and captivating ways. Whether it's through awe-inspiring packaging that delights customers, personalised customer service that goes above and beyond, or an unforgettable brand story that resonates on an emotional level, every interaction with your business should leave an indelible impression.

Remember, the pursuit of remarkability is an ongoing journey. It requires unwavering dedication and a commitment to delivering excellence at every turn. However, the rewards that await are truly worth the effort. When you consistently exceed customer expectations and provide an unparalleled experience, you not only attract loyal customers but also inspire them to become

The Art of Optimal Pricing: Balancing Value and Profitability

When it comes to pricing your products or services, taking a one-size-fits-all approach can lead to missed opportunities and suboptimal results.

To truly maximise your revenue and connect with your target audience, it's essential to develop pricing strategies that align with specific scenarios and cater to different customer personas.

Let's explore three pricing tiers - low, medium, and high - and examine how they can be adapted based on various scenarios and target groups.

Low Prices: The Value Proposition

In certain situations, offering competitive pricing can be an effective way to attract a broad customer base. This strategy works particularly well when you want to position your business as the go-to option for affordability and accessibility. By keeping your prices competitive, you can tap into the market of price-sensitive customers who prioritise cost savings. This approach is especially advantageous if you operate in a highly competitive market or if your business model relies on generating high volume sales.

Low prices can be an effective strategy in certain scenarios, particularly when targeting price-sensitive customers or when you're in a highly competitive market. This approach aims to capture a larger customer base by offering affordable options. However, it's crucial to emphasise the value proposition alongside the low prices to avoid positioning your brand as merely cheap or low-quality. Instead, focus on delivering exceptional value and cost savings.

For example, imagine you're running an online clothing store targeting budget-conscious shoppers. Your low-price strategy could revolve around offering discounted items, budget-friendly bundles, or regular sales and promotions. Highlight the affordability of your products while showcasing the quality, durability, and style that sets your brand apart. By clearly communicating the value customers will receive at an affordable price, you can attract a wide range of customers who appreciate the combination of affordability and quality.

Medium Prices: The Balanced Choice

Medium prices offer a balance between affordability and perceived value. This strategy works well when targeting customers who value quality and are willing to pay a slightly higher price for superior products or services. It allows you to position your brand as a trusted provider, offering a step up from the low-price options without entering the premium pricing territory.

Choosing a middle-ground pricing strategy allows you to strike a balance between affordability and value. By offering competitive prices without compromising on quality, you can cater to a broader range of customers. This approach is ideal if you aim to differentiate your business based on a combination of factors, such as product features, customer service, or unique selling points. The goal is to position your business as offering great value for the price, attracting customers who appreciate a balance between quality and affordability.

Consider a scenario where you're running a skincare brand targeting health-conscious consumers. Your medium-price strategy could involve offering a range of natural and organic skincare products. Emphasise the benefits of using high-quality ingredients, highlight the effectiveness of your products, and provide educational content to showcase your expertise. By pricing your products in the mid-range, you appeal to customers who value quality, sustainability, and conscious consumerism. This pricing strategy enables you to strike a balance between affordability and perceived value.

High Prices: The Luxury Experience

In certain cases, pricing your products or services at a premium level can create an aura of exclusivity and luxury. This strategy works when you offer unique and high-end offerings that cater to a specific target audience. By charging higher prices, you can convey a sense of prestige, craftsmanship, or exceptional service. This approach appeals to customers who value exclusivity, superior quality, and are willing to pay a premium for a premium experience.

High prices can be justified when targeting customers who seek exclusivity, luxury, or a premium experience. This strategy positions your brand as a premium provider, focusing on exceptional quality, unique features, and impeccable customer service. It's important to understand that high prices alone are not enough; customers need to perceive the value and be willing to pay a premium for the elevated experience you offer.

Imagine you're running a boutique hotel targeting luxury travellers. Your high-price strategy could revolve around providing luxurious amenities, personalised services, and bespoke experiences. Showcase the exquisite attention to detail, the breathtaking views, and the world-class facilities available to your guests. By positioning your hotel as a haven of exclusivity and indulgence, you can attract affluent travellers who appreciate and are willing to pay for the elevated experience you provide.

Persona-Based Pricing: Adapting to Different Target Groups

In addition to tailoring your pricing strategies to specific scenarios, it's important to consider the unique needs and preferences of different customer personas. By understanding your target audience, their motivations, and their willingness to pay, you can fine-tune your pricing to appeal directly to each persona.

For example, if you're targeting price-conscious families, you could offer discounted family packages, loyalty programmes, or seasonal promotions that cater specifically to their needs. On the other hand, if you're targeting professionals seeking efficiency and convenience, you might introduce premium membership tiers or subscription-based pricing models that provide added benefits and priority access to services.

By creating persona-based pricing, you can customise your offerings, communicate value effectively, and resonate with each target group. This approach enhances customer satisfaction, loyalty, and willingness to pay for the specific benefits and experiences that matter most to them.

Price Performance

It's a common misconception that high prices always equate to high performance, and vice versa.

However, the relationship between price and performance is not as straightforward as it may seem.

Let's delve deeper into this relationship and debunk some common myths:

High Price, High Performance: Whilst it's true that certain premium products or services command higher prices due to their superior quality, craftsmanship, or exclusive features, this is not always the case. Price alone does not guarantee exceptional performance. Customers have become savvy and are no longer willing to pay exorbitant prices without tangible value. It's crucial for businesses to deliver on their promise and provide a truly outstanding product or service to justify the higher price point.

Low Price, Low Performance: Similarly, assuming that low-priced products or services always indicate lower quality or performance is an oversimplification. There are instances where businesses can offer competitive prices whilst still maintaining a high level of value. Cost-efficient operations, streamlined processes, and strategic sourcing can enable businesses to deliver value without compromising on quality. In fact, offering affordable options can be a deliberate strategy to reach a broader customer base and gain a competitive edge.

Value is Key: The key factor in the price-performance equation is value. Customers seek products or services that provide the right balance of quality, features, and benefits at a fair price. It's the perceived value that drives purchasing decisions. Businesses that understand their target audience and deliver exceptional value, whether through high-end offerings or affordable alternatives, are the ones that thrive in the market.

Aligning Price and Performance: The challenge for businesses lies in finding the sweet spot where price and performance align to meet customer expectations and create a competitive advantage. It requires understanding your target market, conducting market research, and continuously assessing customer feedback to refine your offering. By providing a product or service that consistently exceeds customer expectations at a fair price, you can create a positive perception of value and build customer loyalty.

Price performance outlines the value that demonstrates the difference between quality and price. A product with a low price tag may deliver a high price performance because it offers a level of quality that is unmatched at that price point. Conversely, a product with a high price may provide a low price performance if its quality is subpar and the high price is merely a ploy to create a perception of luxury.

In evaluating price performance, it is important to consider the alignment between price and value. A product or service can command a higher price if it genuinely delivers exceptional quality and unique features that justify the premium. Similarly, a lower-priced option can offer excellent value if it meets or exceeds customer expectations.

Nowadays, customers are better informed and trained to assess price performance by considering factors such as quality, durability, functionality, customer support, and overall satisfaction. The vast amounts of options and similar products/services enabled them to understanding the relationship between price and performance, so customers can determine whether a product or service offers the desired value and make choices that align with their needs and preferences more effectively than ever before.

For businesses, it is crucial to be more intelligent about their prices because it can damage brand and reputation. So, it becomes more important to strike a balance between pricing and performance.

The art of pricing lies in crafting strategies that align with different scenarios and target groups. Whether you opt for low, medium, or high prices, it's essential to communicate the value proposition, emphasise quality, and cater to the specific needs of each customer persona. By understanding the nuances of pricing and continuously refining your strategies, you can optimise revenue, build strong customer relationships, and drive long-term business success.

Setting the appropriate price that reflects the quality and value of your offerings is key to attracting and retaining customers. It is not simply about offering the lowest or highest price, but about providing exceptional value that surpasses customer expectations.

The relationship between price and performance is nuanced. High prices don't always guarantee high performance, and low prices don't necessarily indicate low performance. Value is the key factor that drives customer satisfaction and loyalty. Businesses that focus on delivering exceptional value, regardless of their pricing strategy, are the ones that succeed in the long run. By delivering a high price performance, businesses can establish a strong reputation, foster customer loyalty, and drive long-term success in the market.

So, don't be swayed by those who claim that low prices are foolish or consultants who adamantly believe that high prices always work without exception. You possess the intelligence to see beyond these simplistic notions.

Concise Communication: The Power of Clear Content

The ability to captivate and engage potential clients is a skill that sets successful entrepreneurs apart. For instance, elevator pitches, with their concise and impactful nature, have the potential to revolutionise a business person's fortunes. In this report, we delve into an extraordinary tale of how an elevator pitch became the catalyst for a business person to secure a client partnership that shattered all previous records.

Meet Sarah, a tenacious business professional with a flair for marketing consultancy. Despite her expertise, Sarah yearned for a breakthrough that would catapult her career to new heights. Recognising the power of an elevator pitch, she set out on a quest to craft a message that would resonate with her target audience and leave a lasting impression.

Sarah dedicated tireless hours to perfecting her elevator pitch, weaving together the essence of her unique value proposition. She infused her message with passion and charisma, emphasising the transformative impact her consultancy had on businesses' fortunes. Through careful refinement and rehearsals, Sarah honed a pitch that would leave her audience spellbound and hungry for more.

Sarah's moment of truth arrived at an exclusive industry conference, where serendipity intervened. As she stepped into the lift, she found herself sharing a ride with a high-powered executive from a global corporation. Sensing an extraordinary opportunity, Sarah grasped the moment and initiated a conversation that would change the trajectory of her career.

With mere seconds to make an indelible impression, Sarah unleashed her meticulously crafted elevator pitch. Her words danced in the air, painting a vivid picture of the remarkable success her consultancy had achieved for its clients. She effortlessly conveyed case studies of businesses skyrocketing to unprecedented heights, underpinned by her strategic guidance and innovative marketing solutions.

The executive, intrigued by Sarah's pitch, couldn't help but be drawn into the electrifying energy of her words. A spark ignited, and the executive recognised the potential for a mutually beneficial collaboration. Eager to explore further, they requested a follow-up meeting to delve deeper into the possibilities of partnering with Sarah's consultancy.

Subsequent meetings allowed Sarah to delve into the specific challenges faced by the executive's corporation. Armed with her elevator pitch as a foundation, she tailored her proposal, showcasing how her consultancy could overcome obstacles, drive exponential growth, and reshape their industry landscape. Her magnetic presence and unwavering belief in her expertise solidified the executive's conviction that Sarah was the missing piece they had been searching for.

In a breathtaking turn of events, Sarah secured a client partnership that surpassed all expectations. The collaborative agreement reached with the executive's corporation surpassed any previous engagement in terms of financial investment and long-term commitment. The partnership promised to be a game-changer, propelling Sarah's consultancy into uncharted territories of success.

The power of an exceptional elevator pitch cannot be underestimated. Sarah's remarkable journey serves as a testament to the transformative impact of crafting a compelling and magnetic message. Through the artful delivery of her pitch, Sarah secured a groundbreaking client partnership that defied industry norms and shattered all previous records. Elevator pitches continue to be a formidable tool, capable of unlocking unprecedented opportunities and catapulting ambitious entrepreneurs to the pinnacle of success. With a captivating elevator pitch in their arsenal, business professionals can embark on extraordinary journeys, leaving an indelible mark on their industry and reaping the rewards of their unwavering determination and brilliance.

The ability to communicate your unique value proposition is an art form, particularly in complex industries. To distil your business essence into a powerful message, the creation of an "elevator pitch" can be your secret weapon. This succinct and well-rehearsed summary of your business and its value proposition is designed to be delivered within the time it takes for an elevator ride, typically lasting 30-90 seconds.

While the concept of an elevator pitch may seem cliché, don't dismiss its significance. Even if you rarely find yourself delivering it in an actual elevator, the elevator pitch serves as a valuable tool for clarifying your message and defining your unique selling proposition (USP). It plays a vital role when crafting your offer to prospective clients.

While some people may judge others based on job titles or industries, there is a more effective way to respond. It doesn't involve inflating or obfuscating the true nature of your work.

Next time you are asked about your occupation, grasp the opportunity to deliver an elevator pitch. This concise and carefully crafted message allows you to consistently convey your marketing message in various settings, capturing attention and leaving a lasting impression.

However, it is important to strike a balance between being assertive and coming across as pushy or arrogant. Structuring your elevator pitch effectively is crucial. Far too many elevator pitches suffer from the same problem as inflated job titles—they leave the listener confused or thinking, "What a show-off," rather than creating the intended impact.

Effective marketing always focuses on the customer and addresses their problems and needs. Your elevator pitch should follow this principle, highlighting the problem you solve, the solution you offer, and the evidence to support your claims.

To effectively communicate these three components within a 30-second timeframe, consider the following examples:

In the realm of digital marketing: "You're familiar with the struggle many businesses face in attracting customers online, right? Well, what I do is help businesses increase their online visibility and reach their target audience through strategic digital marketing campaigns. In fact, one of my recent clients experienced a 50% increase in website traffic and a remarkable 30% boost in conversions after implementing my strategies."

In the field of personal fitness training: "You know how challenging it can be for individuals to achieve their fitness goals on their own. That's why I provide personalised fitness training programs that empower individuals to transform their bodies and improve their overall well-being. In fact, one of my clients lost an impressive 20 pounds and gained significant strength within just three months of training with me."

Within the realm of interior design: "You're familiar with the struggle many homeowners face when it comes to creating a space that truly reflects their style and personality. That's where I come in with my customised interior design services, turning houses into beautiful and functional homes. In fact, one of my recent projects received accolades for its unique design and was featured in a prominent home decor magazine."

These examples showcase the formula for crafting an effective elevator pitch that focuses on the customer and the problem you solve. Remember, your elevator pitch is an opportunity to make a memorable impression and demonstrate the value you bring to the table.

When you want to tell people about the amazing things you do, there's a special way to do it called an elevator pitch. It's like a short and exciting summary of what you do and why it's special. Even though it's called an elevator pitch, you don't have to say it in an actual lift.

An elevator pitch is important because it helps you explain your business or skills in a clear and interesting way. Sometimes, when people ask you what you do, you might give an answer that doesn't really make them remember you. But with an elevator pitch, you can make them interested and excited about what you do!

Here is a step-by-step guide to help you create an effective elevator pitch:

Identify Your Objective: Start by clarifying your objective. What do you want to achieve with your elevator pitch? Is it to introduce yourself, promote your business, or showcase your skills? Knowing your objective will guide the content and tone of your pitch.

Define Your Target Audience: Consider who you will be delivering your elevator pitch to. Is it potential clients, employers, or investors? Understanding your audience will help you tailor your pitch to their specific needs and interests.

Identify Your Unique Value Proposition: Determine what makes you or your business unique. What problem do you solve or what value do you offer? This is the core message of your elevator pitch and should be compelling and memorable.

Craft a Hook: Start your pitch with a captivating opening line that grabs the listener's attention. This could be a thought-provoking question, a surprising fact, or a compelling statement related to your industry or field.

Describe the Problem: Clearly and concisely describe the problem or pain point that your target audience faces. Make it relatable and emphasise the significance of the problem.

Present Your Solution: Introduce your solution or how you address the problem. Highlight the benefits and advantages of your approach, emphasising what sets you apart from competitors.

Provide Evidence or Examples: Support your pitch with evidence or examples to demonstrate your credibility and expertise. This could be in the form of success stories, testimonials, or specific achievements that showcase your track record.

Keep it Simple and Clear: Use clear and simple language that anyone can understand. Avoid jargon or technical terms that might confuse your audience. The goal is to convey your message in a concise and easily digestible manner.

Practice and Refine: Practice delivering your elevator pitch until it flows smoothly and sounds natural. Pay attention to your tone, pace, and body language. Seek feedback from others and make adjustments to improve the pitch over time.

Tailor to Different Situations: Adapt your elevator pitch to different contexts or audiences. Customise it based on the specific needs and interests of the person or group you are addressing.

Let's walk through an example of how a business owner named Emma applied the steps to create her elevator pitch:

Identify Your Objective: Emma's objective was to promote her website design services and attract potential clients.

Define Your Target Audience: Emma identified her target audience as small businesses and startups in need of professional website design.

Identify Your Unique Value Proposition: Emma's unique value proposition was her expertise in creating visually stunning and user-friendly websites that help businesses establish a strong online presence and attract more customers.

Craft a Hook: Emma began her elevator pitch with an attention-grabbing opening line: "Did you know that a well-designed website can be a game-changer for your business?"

Describe the Problem: Emma explained the common problem her target audience faces: "Many small businesses struggle to create an impactful online presence that truly reflects the quality of their products or services."

Present Your Solution: Emma introduced her solution: "That's where I come in. I specialise in designing bespoke websites that not only captivate visitors but also drive results for businesses."

Provide Evidence or Examples: To showcase her expertise, Emma shared specific examples of successful projects she had worked on. She mentioned how one of her clients experienced a significant increase in website traffic and sales after she redesigned their website.

Keep it Simple and Clear: Emma used plain and simple language to explain her services, avoiding technical jargon that could confuse her audience.

Practice and Refine: Emma practised her elevator pitch in front of a mirror and with friends. She paid attention to her delivery, ensuring she sounded confident and engaging.

Tailor to Different Situations: Emma adapted her elevator pitch depending on the situation. For networking events, she highlighted the benefits of her services to potential clients. For industry conferences, she focused on her expertise in website design trends and technologies.

By following these steps, Emma was able to create an impactful elevator pitch that effectively communicated her unique value proposition and helped her attract new clients for her website design business.

<u>How to apply this to all content marketing activities</u>

Alex is a professional photographer specialising in capturing breathtaking landscapes. He wanted to expand his client base and establish himself as a reputable landscape photographer.

Here's how he applied the elevator pitch principles to his content marketing strategy:

Objective: Alex's objective was to position himself as a sought-after landscape photographer, attracting clients who appreciate his unique artistic style and expertise in capturing stunning natural scenery.

Target Audience: He identified his target audience as travel enthusiasts, nature lovers, and individuals in need of captivating visual content for their publications or websites.

Craft a Hook: Alex created compelling blog titles like "Discover the Magic of Landscapes: Unveiling the Beauty of Nature through Photography" and "Journey into the Wilderness: Capturing Nature's Majesty in Every Frame."

Define the Problem: Alex emphasised the challenge that many people face in capturing the true essence and beauty of landscapes in their photographs, whether due to technical limitations or a lack of artistic vision.

Present the Solution: He introduced his solution as a professional landscape photographer who possesses the technical skills, artistic eye, and passion for capturing breathtaking landscapes that evoke emotions and tell captivating stories.

Provide Evidence or Examples: Alex showcased a portfolio of his most stunning landscape photographs on his website and social media channels. He shared images accompanied by stories and descriptions that highlighted the beauty and significance of each location, allowing potential clients to see the quality and style of his work.

Keep it Simple and Engaging: Alex used simple language to describe his photography process, techniques, and the emotions he aims to evoke through his images. He also incorporated storytelling elements to engage readers and make them feel connected to the landscapes he captures.

Call to Action: At the end of each blog post or social media caption, Alex included a clear call to action, inviting readers to explore more of his portfolio, book a session, or follow his photography journey for regular updates and inspiration.

Tailor to Different Formats: Alex repurposed his photography content into visually appealing blog posts, social media posts, and even short videos that showcased his process and behind-the-scenes moments. This allowed him to reach a wider audience and cater to different content consumption preferences.

Measure and Refine: Alex monitored the performance of his content by tracking website analytics, social media engagement, and inquiries for photography services.

Based on the insights gained, he refined his content strategy, focusing on the landscapes that resonated the most with his audience and adjusting his messaging to better communicate his unique value proposition. By applying the elevator pitch principles to his content marketing strategy, Alex successfully positioned himself as a sought-after landscape photographer. He attracted clients who valued his artistic vision, expanded his online presence, and achieved recognition in the photography community.

<u>How to apply this to tenders</u>

John, a construction project manager, applied the principles of an elevator pitch to a tender proposal and ultimately won the project.

The objective of the tender proposal was to secure a contract for a large-scale commercial construction project.

John's company had extensive experience in commercial construction projects and was known for delivering high-quality results on time and within budget.

Understand the Client: John thoroughly researched the client's requirements, project specifications, and their key priorities for selecting a contractor. He identified that the client valued cost-effectiveness, timely delivery, and a strong track record in similar projects.

Craft a Hook: John started the tender proposal with a captivating introduction that captured the client's attention. His opening line was, "Building Brilliance: Transforming Visions into Reality for Your Commercial Project."

Define the Problem: John identified the challenges the client faced, including the need for a construction partner with expertise in managing complex projects, strict adherence to budget, and maintaining open communication throughout the process.

Present the Solution: John highlighted his company's unique selling points, emphasising their experience in delivering large-scale commercial projects on time and within budget. He showcased their comprehensive project management approach, quality assurance processes, and commitment to client satisfaction.

Provide Evidence or Examples: John included case studies of previous commercial projects his company had successfully completed, highlighting their ability to overcome challenges, deliver exceptional results, and exceed client expectations. He also included testimonials from satisfied clients who praised the company's professionalism and attention to detail.

Keep it Clear and Concise: John presented the proposal in a clear and organised format, using headings, bullet points, and visuals to enhance readability. He avoided jargon and technical terms, ensuring the proposal was easily understandable by the client.

Call to Action: John concluded the proposal with a clear call to action, inviting the client to schedule a meeting to discuss the project further and address any questions or concerns they may have.

Tailor to the Client: John tailored the proposal to address the specific needs and priorities of the client. He highlighted how his company's approach aligned with the client's goals, emphasising their commitment to cost-effectiveness, timely delivery, and open communication throughout the project.

Proofread and Review: Before submitting the proposal, John carefully proofread the document to eliminate any errors or inconsistencies. He also reviewed the proposal from the client's perspective, ensuring it effectively addressed their needs and showcased his company's value proposition.

Thanks to John's well-crafted tender proposal that effectively communicated his company's value proposition and demonstrated their expertise, they successfully won the contract for the commercial construction project.

The client appreciated the clarity, professionalism, and alignment of the proposal with their project requirements, ultimately choosing John's company as their trusted construction partner. By applying the principles of an elevator pitch to the tender proposal, John effectively conveyed his company's strengths, addressed the client's needs, and showcased their ability to deliver exceptional results. This helped them stand out amongst the competition and secure the contract for the project.

Unveiling the Power of Irresistible Offers

Creating irresistible offers is a strategic approach that businesses can employ to captivate their target audience and achieve remarkable success. An irresistible offer is one that compels customers to take immediate action, leading to increased sales, customer loyalty, and overall business growth. In this article, we will explore how businesses can craft irresistible offers and provide valuable insights to enhance your understanding.

Understand Your Target Audience: Before crafting an irresistible offer, it is crucial to have a deep understanding of your target audience. For example, if you are a fitness brand targeting busy professionals, you may offer a time-saving workout programme specifically designed for their hectic schedules.

Highlight Unique Value Propositions: To make your offer irresistible, you must clearly communicate the unique value it brings to customers. For instance, a furniture store might emphasise its high-quality craftsmanship, durable materials, and exclusive designs that cannot be found elsewhere.

Offer Compelling Benefits: Craft your offer in a way that highlights the compelling benefits customers will receive. For example, a skincare brand may offer a limited-time promotion with the benefit of a free full-size product with any purchase, enticing customers to stock up on their favourite items.

Create a Sense of Scarcity or Exclusivity: Utilise scarcity or exclusivity elements to make your offer even more irresistible. For instance, a travel agency might offer a limited number of discounted holiday packages, creating a sense of urgency and encouraging customers to book quickly.

Offer Guarantees and Risk Reversals: Reduce customer concerns and barriers to purchase by offering guarantees and risk reversals. For example, a software company may offer a 30-day money-back guarantee, allowing customers to try the product without any risk.

Personalise Your Offers: Tailor your offers to individual customer segments whenever possible. For instance, an online clothing retailer may send personalised discount codes to customers based on their previous purchase history or preferences.

Utilise Compelling Copy and Visuals: Craft persuasive and captivating copy that effectively communicates the value and benefits of your offer. For example, a food delivery service may use enticing phrases like "Delicious meals delivered to your doorstep in minutes" to capture the attention of hungry customers.

Test and Iterate: Continuously test and refine your offers to optimise their effectiveness. For instance, an e-commerce store may test different pricing strategies or incentives to see which generates the highest conversion rates. Customer feedback and data analysis can guide further iterations.

Here are some additional examples of irresistible offers across different industries:

A clothing retailer offers a "Buy One, Get One Free" promotion on selected items, encouraging customers to purchase more and take advantage of the deal.

A beauty salon offers a "Pamper Package" that includes a facial, massage, and manicure at a discounted price, providing customers with a luxurious and comprehensive spa experience.

A software company offers a limited-time free trial of their premium software, allowing potential customers to experience its full capabilities before committing to a purchase.

A restaurant offers a loyalty programme where customers earn points for every visit and receive exclusive rewards, such as free appetisers or discounts, incentivising repeat business.

An online course provider offers a money-back guarantee if students are not satisfied with their learning experience, giving them peace of mind and boosting trust in the programme.

By applying these strategies and principles and incorporating creative examples, businesses can create irresistible offers that captivate their target audience and drive remarkable results. Remember, an irresistible offer not only attracts customers but also builds long-term relationships and fosters customer loyalty. Embrace the power of irresistible offers and unlock the full potential of your business.

Most professionals miss the mark by presenting something lacklustre, resorting to run-of-the-mill discounts, or simply following the crowd.

Imagine this: You're at a bustling fairground, torn between two game stalls. One stall offers a plain old teddy bear as a prise, while the other tempts you with an extraordinary, one-of-a-kind colossal unicorn plush. A showstopper that's sure to turn heads! Which game would you eagerly step up to? Exactly! It's the offer that makes all the difference.

To concoct an offer that stands out and mesmerises your target market, let's ponder over some thought-provoking questions:

The Confidence Booster: Amidst all your impressive products and services, which one fills you with unwavering confidence? If you were only rewarded when your client achieved their desired result, which gem would you choose to showcase? Picture the sheer certainty that you possess in solving a problem for your target market, almost like having a secret superpower.

For instance, let's say you're a fitness guru, witnessing jaw-dropping transformations in clients who embrace your bespoke fitness programmes. You could boldly extend a "Results Guaranteed" package, where clients only part with their money if they achieve their fitness aspirations.

The Passion Project: Within your delightful repertoire of offerings, which one stirs your soul, bringing you boundless joy and fulfilment? It's that remarkable service that lights up your eyes each morning, ready to be shared with the world.

For instance, imagine being a chef with an unquenchable love for crafting divine desserts. You might present an irresistible "Indulgence Extravaganza" where clients are whisked away on a delectable journey through a personalised dessert tasting menu, guaranteed to leave them in awe of your culinary prowess.

Now, let's sprinkle some pizzazz and excitement onto your offer by addressing these supplementary questions:

What truly motivates your target market's purchase? Are they yearning for convenience, status, peace of mind, or perhaps something altogether extraordinary? For instance, it's not just about selling cars; it's about unlocking a world of freedom and exhilaration on the open road.

What's the juiciest benefit your offer delivers? Does it save time, skyrocket productivity, or create an utterly transformative experience? Highlight the most captivating aspect that sets your offer miles apart from the competition.

What evocative words and phrases will grasp and hold your target market's attention? Infuse your language with a touch of excitement, curiosity, or a dash of urgency. Think "Unleash Your Inner Brilliance" or "Unveiling the Gateway to Extraordinary Success."

What pesky objections might your prospects raise, and how can you expertly tackle them head-on? Anticipate their concerns and provide crystal-clear solutions or rock-solid guarantees that build unshakable trust and confidence.

Does your offer harbour an alluring tale? Share the enchanting journey that led you to concoct this exceptional service or product. Stories create profound connections and infuse a personal touch that resonates deeply with your audience.

Who else might be offering something similar, and how can you tantalisingly differentiate yourself? Study your competitors and seek that extraordinary angle that sets you apart. Whether it's unrivalled customer service, a groundbreaking feature, or an unforgettable brand personality.

Learn from others' follies. Dive into the annals of past attempts by competitors or industry players who ventured into similar offers but stumbled along the way. Unearth their shortcomings and weave them into invaluable lessons to sidestep the same pitfalls.

One of the main culprits behind failed marketing campaigns is a lacklustre and half-hearted offer. It's time to cast off the shackles of mediocrity and create an offer that sparks excitement, ignites curiosity, and compels your target market to take action.

Let's explore an example of how Emily, a business owner, applied the previously mentioned techniques to create irresistible offers.

Emily runs a boutique skincare brand called "GlowOrganics." She wanted to attract more customers and increase sales by creating compelling offers that would set her brand apart from competitors. Here's how she embarked on her journey:

Understanding the Target Market: Emily conducted market research and identified her target market as health-conscious individuals, primarily women aged 25-45, who prioritise natural and sustainable skincare products.

Identifying the Problems: Emily discovered that her target market faced several skincare challenges, such as dryness, dullness, and sensitivity. Many struggled to find effective products that were both natural and delivered visible results.

Crafting the Irresistible Offer: Emily developed a range of irresistible offers that addressed the problems faced by her target market. Here are a few examples:

"The Radiant Skin Collection": This offer included a bundle of GlowOrganics' best-selling products, specifically formulated to nourish and revitalise dull skin. Emily emphasised the use of natural and organic ingredients that deliver a radiant and healthy complexion.

"Soothe & Restore Skincare Set": Recognising the struggles of individuals with sensitive skin, Emily curated a set of gentle and hypoallergenic products designed to soothe and restore balance. She highlighted the absence of harsh chemicals and fragrances in these formulations.

"Intense Hydration Trio": Understanding the prevalence of dry skin concerns, Emily created a trio of products that provided intense hydration and long-lasting moisture. She emphasised the use of potent hydrating ingredients, such as hyaluronic acid and plant-based oils.

Demonstrating Results: To prove the effectiveness of her products, Emily incorporated before-and-after photos, testimonials, and customer success stories into her marketing materials. She showcased the visible improvements achieved by using GlowOrganics products, highlighting the transformation in skin texture, radiance, and overall health.

Solving Customer Objections: Emily anticipated potential objections from her target market, such as concerns about product safety, compatibility with sensitive skin, or the effectiveness of natural ingredients. She addressed these objections proactively by providing detailed product information, third-party certifications, and reassuring testimonials from customers with similar concerns.

Offering Additional Value: Emily went beyond the products themselves and added value to her offers. She included free skincare consultations, personalised skincare routines, and educational resources on her website and social media platforms. This extra support and guidance enhanced the overall customer experience.

Creating Limited-Time Promotions: Emily introduced limited-time promotions, such as exclusive discounts, gift-with-purchase offers, and loyalty rewards programmes. These incentives created a sense of urgency and encouraged customers to take advantage of the irresistible offers.

Emily was successful because she identified and addressed the problems faced by her target market, offering solutions that were both effective and aligned with their needs and values. Here are the problems she initially faced and how she overcame them:

Lack of Differentiation: Emily's skincare brand initially struggled to stand out in a crowded market. There were numerous competitors offering similar products, making it challenging for her brand to gain attention.

Solution: Emily conducted thorough market research to understand her target market's pain points and preferences. She identified the need for natural, sustainable skincare products that deliver visible results. By emphasising the use of organic ingredients, highlighting product efficacy, and showcasing customer testimonials, she differentiated GlowOrganics as a trustworthy and effective skincare brand.

Customer Concerns about Natural Skincare: Some potential customers were skeptical about the effectiveness of natural skincare products. They questioned whether these products could deliver the desired results without synthetic ingredients or harsh chemicals.

Solution: Emily proactively addressed these concerns by providing scientific evidence, studies, and testimonials that highlighted the effectiveness of natural ingredients in skincare. She educated her target market about the benefits of natural skincare, explaining how the carefully selected ingredients in GlowOrganics' products work synergistically to deliver visible results.

Sensitive Skin Concerns: Many individuals with sensitive skin were hesitant to try new skincare products due to the fear of irritation or allergic reactions. They needed reassurance that GlowOrganics' products were safe and gentle on their skin.

Solution: Emily invested in product development, formulating hypoallergenic and gentle skincare products specifically designed for sensitive skin. She obtained certifications and third-party testing to validate the safety and efficacy of her products. By highlighting these features and sharing customer testimonials from individuals with sensitive skin, she alleviated concerns and built trust among her target market.

Market Saturation and Price Sensitivity: The skincare market was saturated with various brands offering products at different price points. Emily needed to navigate the challenge of price sensitivity while maintaining the perceived value of her offerings.

Solution: Emily focused on creating value-driven offers rather than engaging in price competition. She bundled her products into curated sets, offering additional benefits, such as free consultations, personalised skincare routines, and educational resources. By emphasising the overall experience and value customers would receive from GlowOrganics, she justified the pricing and positioned her brand as a premium option worth investing in.

By addressing these initial challenges and providing solutions that resonated with her target market, Emily was able to overcome customer objections, build trust, and establish GlowOrganics as a successful and differentiated skincare brand. Her strategic approach, customer-centric focus, and commitment to delivering effective and natural skincare solutions were key factors in her success.

Research: Illuminating the Path to Success

To truly create irresistible offers, you need to go beyond surface-level insights and uncover the unspoken desires of your target market. By employing a mix of strategies and tapping into your creativity, you can gain a deeper understanding of what truly captivates your audience. Here are some additional techniques and captivating examples to inspire you:

Immersive Customer Experiences: Go beyond traditional surveys and market research by immersing yourself in your customers' experiences. Join relevant online communities, attend industry events, or even become a customer of your competitors to gain firsthand insights. By walking in their shoes, you can uncover hidden desires and pain points that shape their decision-making.

For example, let's say you're in the travel industry. By immersing yourself in travel enthusiast forums and online communities, you might discover a growing desire for off-the-beaten-path adventures. Armed with this knowledge, you can craft offers that highlight unique, undiscovered destinations and provide extraordinary travel experiences.

Harness the Power of Storytelling: Stories have the ability to connect with people on a deeper level and tap into their desires. Use storytelling techniques in your market research and customer interactions to uncover the emotional drivers behind purchasing decisions. Encourage customers to share their experiences, aspirations, and dreams, allowing you to gain insights that numbers alone cannot provide.

For instance, let's say you run a fashion brand. By inviting customers to share their personal style stories and the emotions they associate with their favourite outfits, you can uncover their desire for self-expression and the confidence that comes with wearing something truly unique. This insight can inform your offers, showcasing how your brand enables customers to embrace their individuality.

Collaborative Co-Creation: Engage your target market in the creation process by seeking their input and involving them in product development or service design. Conduct focus groups, host brainstorming sessions, or launch beta-testing programs to gather feedback and co-create solutions that truly resonate.

For example, imagine you're a software developer. By involving users in the early stages of product development and collecting their insights on functionality, user interface, and features, you can create software that meets their specific needs and desires. This collaborative approach not only leads to more tailored offers but also fosters a sense of ownership and loyalty among your customers.

Explore Non-Traditional Channels: Look beyond traditional market research methods and explore unconventional channels to gain fresh perspectives. Engage with influencers in your industry, follow niche blogs or podcasts, or even conduct ethnographic research by observing your target market in their natural environments. These alternative approaches can uncover unique insights and reveal untapped desires.

For instance, let's say you're in the wellness industry. By following wellness influencers on social media and analysing their content, you may discover a rising interest in holistic wellness approaches, such as mindfulness and self-care rituals. Incorporating these insights into your offers can position your brand as a leader in the evolving wellness landscape.

Remember, uncovering your market's desires is an ongoing journey of discovery. Embrace curiosity, explore creative research methods, and maintain an open mindset. By understanding the unspoken desires of your audience, you can create truly irresistible offers that resonate deeply and drive your business to new heights.

Let's explore the journey of Sarah, a passionate entrepreneur. Sarah started her own online fitness coaching business and was determined to create a programme that truly resonated with her audience. Here's how her journey unfolded:

1. The Initial Struggle: At the beginning of her venture, Sarah found it challenging to gather reliable data about her target group's needs and desires. She realised that she needed a deeper understanding of her audience's pain points and aspirations to create an irresistible offer.

2. Creative Solutions: Undeterred by the lack of readily available data, Sarah decided to take matters into her own hands. She began engaging with her audience through social media platforms, hosting live Q&A sessions, and actively participating in fitness-related online communities. By directly interacting with her potential clients, Sarah gained valuable insights into their desires, challenges, and motivations.

3. Building Authentic Connections: Sarah understood the importance of building genuine relationships with her target group. She created surveys and questionnaires to gather specific information about their fitness goals, preferences, and obstacles. Through these personal connections, Sarah not only obtained valuable data but also built trust and loyalty with her audience.

4. Leveraging Online Tools: Recognising the power of technology, Sarah utilised various online tools to gain deeper insights into her target group's needs and wants. She conducted keyword research using tools like Google's Keyword Planner and explored trending topics and discussions on fitness-related forums and social media platforms. This allowed her to tap into the collective consciousness of her audience and identify emerging trends and interests.

5. Analysing Competitors: Sarah didn't shy away from learning from her competitors. She analysed the strategies and offerings of successful fitness coaches who catered to a similar target group. By studying their customer testimonials, social media engagement, and programme offerings, Sarah gained valuable insights into what her target group found most appealing.

6. Iterating and Refining: Armed with a wealth of information, Sarah meticulously analysed the data she gathered and made iterative adjustments to her programme offerings. She fine-tuned her coaching approach, developed tailored workout plans, and created engaging content that addressed her audience's specific needs and desires.

7. Transformation and Success: As Sarah implemented her newfound knowledge and insights, her business began to flourish. Her programme resonated deeply with her target group, and word of

mouth spread. The increased engagement, positive testimonials, and growing client base were a testament to the power of market research in shaping a successful business.

In addition to the steps mentioned earlier, Sarah took further actions to uncover her target group's needs and wants. Let's explore these additional points in her journey:

1. Interviewing Potential Customers: Sarah recognised the value of one-on-one interviews with potential customers. She reached out to individuals who fit her target group profile and conducted in-depth interviews to gain deeper insights. By asking open-ended questions and actively listening, Sarah discovered nuanced preferences, pain points, and desires that she wouldn't have uncovered through surveys alone.

Example: During an interview, Sarah discovered that many of her potential customers struggled with maintaining motivation to exercise regularly due to their busy lifestyles. Armed with this insight, she developed a personalised coaching approach that included daily reminders, tailored workout plans, and ongoing support to keep clients motivated.

2. Recording Behavioural Data: Sarah understood the importance of tracking and analysing customer behaviours to better understand their preferences and habits. She used analytics tools to gather data on website visits, engagement with online content, and conversion rates. This data provided valuable insights into which aspects of her programme resonated the most with her target group.

Example: By tracking user engagement on her website, Sarah noticed a high bounce rate on her nutrition-focused blog posts. Digging deeper, she discovered that her audience was more interested in workout routines and fitness tips. Armed with this knowledge, she pivoted her content strategy to focus more on workout-related topics, which led to increased engagement and a higher conversion rate.

3. Leveraging Social Listening: Sarah harnessed the power of social listening to gain real-time insights into her target group's conversations, opinions, and challenges. She monitored relevant hashtags, joined online communities, and actively engaged with her audience on social media platforms. This helped her uncover emerging trends, address specific pain points, and tailor her content to resonate with her target group.

Example: Through social listening, Sarah noticed a growing interest in home-based workouts and fitness equipment due to the COVID-19 pandemic. Recognising the opportunity, she developed a series of home workout programmes and provided recommendations for affordable fitness equipment. This timely response to her audience's needs resulted in increased engagement and a surge in new clients.

4. Analysing Customer Support Interactions: Sarah paid close attention to customer support interactions, whether through emails, phone calls, or online chat. These interactions provided valuable insights into the challenges and questions her target group faced, allowing her to refine her programme offerings and improve the customer experience.

Example: After noticing a recurring question about modifying workouts for individuals with physical limitations, Sarah developed specialised programmes and resources that catered to these specific needs. This proactive approach not only addressed her audience's concerns but also positioned her as a knowledgeable and caring coach.

Through her perseverance and resourcefulness, Sarah overcame the initial struggle of gathering data and transformed her understanding of her target group's needs and wants. This pivotal journey allowed her to create an irresistible offer that genuinely resonated with her audience, propelling her business to new heights of success. By incorporating these points into her market research efforts, Sarah gained a comprehensive understanding of her target group's needs and wants. Through interviews, behavioural data analysis, social listening, and customer support insights, she gathered valuable information that informed her programme offerings, content strategy, and customer interactions. This commitment to understanding her audience on a deeper level allowed Sarah to create an irresistible offer that truly met their needs, leading to sustained business growth and customer satisfaction.

The actions described in Sarah's journey are not restricted to any particular group of individuals and can be embraced by anyone, including children, with a little guidance and support. Here's why these actions are both accessible and worth investing time in:

Engagement and Communication: Engaging with others and effectively communicating with your target audience can be as straightforward as initiating conversations, posing thought-provoking questions, and actively listening to their responses. Children can easily learn to interact and communicate with people around them, while adults can refine their communication skills through practice and experience.

Online Tools and Resources: Many online tools and resources are designed to be user-friendly and accessible to individuals of all ages. From conducting surveys and utilising keyword research tools to exploring the latest trends on social media, these resources provide valuable insights that can inform decision-making.

Observing and Learning: The art of observing and learning from others, including your competitors, is a valuable skill that can be honed at any age. By studying successful individuals or businesses within your industry, you gain inspiration, absorb their strategies, and adapt them to suit your unique circumstances.

Creativity and Problem-Solving: Market research stimulates creative thinking and fosters problem-solving skills. It prompts individuals to think critically about their target audience's needs and discover innovative solutions to meet those needs. This nurtures creativity and empowers individuals to develop their problem-solving abilities, skills that hold value in various aspects of life.

Personal Growth and Development: Engaging in market research activities can lead to personal growth and development. By actively seeking feedback, embracing different perspectives, and continuously learning about your target audience, you expand your knowledge and understanding. This not only benefits your business or project but also contributes to personal growth and self-improvement.

Enhanced Decision-Making: Market research provides valuable insights that inform strategic decision-making. Whether you're a child contemplating a school project or an adult making critical business choices, understanding your target audience's needs and desires enables you to make informed decisions that are more likely to resonate and succeed.

Increased Success and Satisfaction: By investing time in market research, you heighten the prospects of creating products, services, or content that genuinely cater to your target audience's needs and desires. This, in turn, boosts your chances of achieving greater success, customer satisfaction, and overall fulfilment in your endeavours.

In a nutshell, these actions are open to individuals of all ages and yield a multitude of benefits, including improved communication skills, heightened problem-solving abilities, personal growth, and increased success. Devoting time to understanding your target audience is a valuable and worthwhile pursuit that sets you on a path towards greater achievements and satisfaction.

A lack of comprehensive research and understanding of the target market can lead to dire consequences, resulting in insolvency and the ultimate collapse of a company. Let us delve into the tale of Mark, an aspiring entrepreneur, and discover how his failure to conduct adequate market research contributed to his downfall:

Mark possessed a deep passion for crafting and selling handcrafted wooden furniture. He believed that his unique designs and exceptional craftsmanship would captivate customers and pave the way for a prosperous business. However, he committed a grave error by disregarding market research and failing to grasp the intricacies of his target market.

Without a thorough understanding of the preferences, needs, and purchasing patterns of his potential customers, Mark began producing furniture solely based on his own preferences and assumptions. He invested substantial amounts of time and money into creating elaborate and costly pieces without considering whether there was a genuine demand for such products.

As a result, Mark encountered significant challenges in selling his furniture. His pricing strategy did not align with the market, and his designs failed to resonate with his intended audience. Lacking a clear comprehension of what his customers truly desired, he was unable to effectively communicate the value of his products.

Meanwhile, Mark's competitors, who had dedicated time and resources to understand their target markets, thrived. They offered furniture that specifically appealed to distinct customer segments, addressing their unique requirements and preferences. These astute businesses had conducted meticulous market research, identified gaps in the market, and tailored their offerings accordingly.

Over time, Mark's sales dwindled, and he found himself burdened with unsold inventory. Despite his earnest efforts to promote his products through various marketing channels, his lack of insight into the target market resulted in minimal customer interest and disappointing sales performance.

Ultimately, Mark's business encountered severe financial difficulties, struggling to meet expenses and generate sufficient revenue. Plagued by mounting debts and a lack of viable market positioning, his company faced insolvency, leading to its eventual closure.

Mark's story serves as a cautionary tale, underscoring the significance of market research and a profound understanding of the target market. Had he devoted the time and effort to conduct thorough research, identify customer preferences, and align his products with market demand, the outcome could have been vastly different.

By gaining a comprehensive understanding of his target market, Mark could have adapted his designs, pricing strategies, and marketing approaches to better meet customer needs and stand out amidst fierce competition. Market research would have enabled him to identify emerging trends, anticipate customer preferences, and make informed decisions, steering his business towards success.

Mark's failure serves as a poignant reminder of the pivotal role that market research plays in the survival of a business. It is an indispensable step that should never be overlooked, as it provides the groundwork for developing products and services that genuinely resonate with the target market, enabling businesses to thrive and avoid the perils of insolvency.

Let's compare the experiences of Mark and Sarah, two individuals with contrasting approaches to market research, and explore the reasons behind their different outcomes:

Approach to Market Research:

Mark: Mark neglected market research, relying on his personal assumptions and preferences to guide his business decisions. He failed to understand his target market's needs and preferences, resulting in a mismatch between his products and customer demand.

Sarah: Sarah prioritised market research and actively engaged with her target audience. She sought feedback, conducted surveys, and observed trends in the fitness industry. Sarah's efforts allowed her to gain valuable insights into her audience's desires and tailor her offerings accordingly.

Understanding Customer Needs:

Mark: Due to his lack of market research, Mark had limited understanding of his customer's needs. He assumed that his unique designs and craftsmanship alone would attract customers, without validating whether there was genuine demand for his products.

Sarah: Sarah invested time and effort into understanding her target audience's fitness goals, preferences, and challenges. This enabled her to develop personalised coaching programmes and content that addressed her audience's specific needs, leading to a stronger connection and resonance with her customers.

Adaptability and Flexibility:

Mark: Without market research, Mark struggled to adapt his products and business strategies to meet customer expectations. He remained fixed on his initial assumptions, even when faced with low sales and minimal customer interest.

Sarah: Through ongoing market research, Sarah remained adaptable and open to making changes based on customer feedback. She fine-tuned her coaching programmes, workout plans, and content to better align with her audience's evolving needs, ensuring continuous relevance and customer satisfaction.

Competitive Analysis:

Mark: Mark failed to conduct a thorough analysis of his competitors, overlooking valuable insights that could have guided his product positioning and pricing strategies.

Sarah: Sarah carefully studied successful fitness coaches catering to a similar target market. She analysed their strategies, customer testimonials, and programme offerings, allowing her to identify effective approaches and differentiate her offerings in the market.

Customer Engagement and Communication:

Mark: Due to the lack of market research, Mark struggled to effectively communicate the value of his products to potential customers. His marketing efforts were less targeted, resulting in minimal customer engagement and low sales.

Sarah: Sarah actively engaged with her target audience through social media, surveys, and personal connections. She fostered genuine relationships, listened to her customers' feedback, and tailored her messaging to resonate with their aspirations and challenges. This led to higher customer engagement and increased sales.

Ultimately, Sarah's commitment to market research, understanding her target audience, adaptability, and effective communication contributed to her success. In contrast, Mark's lack of market research, limited understanding of customer needs, and reluctance to adapt hindered his progress.

The key takeaway is that market research is essential for businesses to thrive. It provides valuable insights into customer needs, preferences, and market dynamics. By investing time and effort in understanding their target audience, businesses like Sarah's can create offerings that truly resonate and meet customer expectations, while those like Mark's who overlook market research face an uphill battle in reaching their goals.

Fine-Tuning Your Pitch

The first step was to create your offer and pitch, the second step is to improve it. Crafting an irresistible offer and continually improving it is akin to embarking on an enthralling adventure. It's an ever-evolving journey that blends art, science, and customer-centricity, propelling your business to soaring heights of success. Let's delve into why this ongoing process is not only crucial but also incredibly captivating.

Envision yourself as an explorer, venturing into uncharted territories. Your initial offer is like a hidden treasure waiting to be discovered. By launching it and gathering customer feedback, you unlock the secrets of their desires and unmet needs. It's a thrill to unearth those hidden gems that can elevate your offer from good to extraordinary.

The marketplace is akin to a dynamic ocean, with waves of change constantly ebbing and flowing. Your offer, like a skilled surfer, needs to ride these waves with agility and finesse. By continually assessing market dynamics and staying attuned to customer preferences, you position yourself as a pioneer, ready to adapt, innovate, and catch the next big wave of opportunity.

Competition in the bustling marketplace is fierce. Your competitors are honing their strategies, refining their tools, and vying for the attention of your customers. But fear not! By continually improving your offer, you sharpen your competitive edge. It's akin to sharpening your sword, equipping yourself to slay the dragons of mediocrity and stand out from the crowd.

Fine-tuning your offer is not merely a process; it's an artistic endeavour. It's where imagination takes flight and creativity knows no bounds. As you delve deeper into the process, you unlock your creative potential, exploring innovative features, distinctive services, and captivating bundles. Picture yourself as an artist, brush in hand, adding vibrant strokes to your offer, crafting a masterpiece that captivates your audience.

Customers are the lifeblood of your business, and nurturing their affection and loyalty is paramount. By attentively listening to their feedback, understanding their evolving needs, and continually enhancing your offer, you cultivate a deep connection. It's a dance of reciprocity, where your customers feel seen, heard, and cherished, and in return, they become your fervent admirers and brand ambassadors.

Now, close your eyes and envision the exhilaration of witnessing your improved offer in action. The conversions it generates, the impact it has on your customers, and the triumph it brings is an adrenaline rush like no other. It's akin to standing atop a mountain, gazing upon the panoramic view of accomplishments and knowing that your relentless pursuit of improvement has borne fruit.

So, creating an offer is merely the genesis of a captivating journey. By continuously fine-tuning, adapting, and enhancing your offer, you embark on a mesmerising adventure of discovery, innovation, and customer-centricity. So, embrace the excitement, ignite your creativity, and let your offer radiate as a beacon of value, leaving an indelible impression on your customers and propelling your business to extraordinary heights.

To fine-tune our pitch and offer, we now delve into the paint points of your potential buyer.

Imagine you're a passionate home chef, dedicated to creating culinary masterpieces that impress your family and friends. But there's a problem: your kitchen knives are a nightmare to work with. They're blunt, unreliable, and constantly frustrate your efforts to create beautifully chopped ingredients. The joy of cooking has become a tedious and annoying chore.

Enter the world of two knife retailers: KnifeHaven and EpicCut. KnifeHaven believes in showcasing the technical aspects of their knives, highlighting the quality of the blade steel, ergonomic handles, and precision craftsmanship. On the other hand, EpicCut takes a different approach, understanding the pains and struggles of home chefs like yourself.

EpicCut knows that you've had enough of struggling with subpar knives. They understand the annoyance of uneven cuts, squashed tomatoes, and the time wasted trying to chop through tough ingredients. They empathise with your desire for a hassle-free cooking experience and offer a solution that goes beyond the product itself.

With EpicCut, you're not just buying a set of knives; you're investing in a transformative culinary journey. They offer a personalised consultation where a knife expert will understand your specific cooking style, preferences, and pain points. Based on this information, they'll recommend a set of knives that perfectly suits your needs, ensuring effortless slicing, dicing, and chopping. But that's not all!

EpicCut goes the extra mile by providing additional services to ensure your satisfaction. They offer free knife sharpening for a lifetime, guaranteeing that your knives will always be in top-notch condition. They even provide access to exclusive cooking tutorials and recipes, helping you enhance your skills and create culinary masterpieces like never before.

As a passionate home chef, the choice becomes clear. While KnifeHaven focuses on the technical features, EpicCut offers a complete solution that addresses your pain points and takes your cooking experience to new heights. Their approach resonates with you on a deeper level because they understand your frustrations and offer a comprehensive solution.

By positioning themselves as problem solvers, EpicCut sets themselves apart from competitors like KnifeHaven. They create an apples-to-oranges comparison, where the emphasis is on a personalised and pain-relieving experience rather than just the technical specifications of the knives.

This example illustrates the power of understanding your customers' pain points and crafting an irresistible offer that addresses their needs. By going beyond the product and offering a comprehensive solution, you can capture the hearts and loyalty of customers who are tired of the same old struggles. So, whether you're selling knives, cars, or consulting services, remember to tap into your customers' pains, provide relief, and turn their experience into an unforgettable journey.

To create a compelling and persuasive offer that resonates with your target audience, it's crucial to delve into their pains, concerns, and problems, too. By addressing these issues directly, you can position your offer as the ultimate solution. Here's a step-by-step guide to uncovering the pains and concerns of buyers and incorporating them into your messaging, along with examples:

Conduct Customer Surveys and Interviews: Engage with your existing customers or target audience and inquire about their greatest challenges and concerns in relation to your industry or niche. Use open-ended questions to encourage detailed responses. For instance, you could ask, "What are the main obstacles you face when striving to achieve [desired outcome]?"

Analyse Customer Feedback and Reviews: Pay close attention to customer feedback, reviews, and testimonials. Look for recurring themes or specific pain points mentioned by multiple customers. These insights can offer valuable guidance on the common concerns of your target audience. For example, if you operate an e-commerce business, you may notice customers frequently highlighting issues with product delivery or sising.

Engage in Social Listening: Monitor social media platforms, online forums, and review websites to listen in on conversations and discussions relevant to your industry. Identify the pain points, complaints, and challenges that people express within these online communities. This can provide real-time understanding of your target audience's concerns. For instance, if you're in the fitness industry, you may discover that many individuals struggle with finding time to exercise due to busy lifestyles.

Create Buyer Personas: Develop detailed buyer personas that represent different segments of your target audience. Include their pain points, concerns, and challenges within these personas. This helps you visualise and empathise with your customers on a deeper level. For example, one persona may represent a time-strapped professional who aspires to eat healthily but finds it difficult to access quick and nutritious meal options.

Align Pain Points with Offer Benefits: Once you've identified the pain points and concerns of your target audience, align them with the benefits and solutions that your offer provides. Craft your messaging to clearly demonstrate how your product or service addresses these pain points. For example, if you offer time-saving meal prep services, emphasise how it eliminates the stress and hassle of meal planning and cooking for busy individuals.

Use Emotive Language: Incorporate emotive language that resonates with your audience's pain points and concerns. Highlight the emotional impact of the problems they face and how your offer can bring relief and transformation. For instance, instead of simply stating that your product saves time, you could say, "Bid farewell to frantic mornings and savour quality time with your loved ones by utilising our time-saving solution."

Share Success Stories and Testimonials: Harness the power of social proof by sharing success stories and testimonials from satisfied customers who have experienced relief from their pain points through your product or service. Highlight how your offer has transformed their lives and addressed their specific concerns. For example, if you provide financial planning services, share a testimonial from a client who achieved financial security and peace of mind through your guidance.

Demonstrate Value and Results: Clearly communicate the value your offer provides and the results customers can expect by addressing their pain points. Use quantifiable data or statistics to illustrate the effectiveness of your solution. For example, if you offer a weight loss program, highlight the average weight loss achieved by your clients.

Offer a Risk-Free Guarantee: Address the concerns and apprehensions of potential buyers by providing a robust guarantee that eliminates any perceived risk. Assure them that if your solution doesn't deliver the promised results, they will receive a refund or an alternative solution. This instils confidence and reduces resistance to making a purchase.

Continuously Adapt and Improve: Regularly gather feedback from your customers to ensure you stay attuned to their evolving pains and concerns. Adapt your offer, messaging, and customer experience accordingly to maintain relevance and deliver ongoing value.

By thoroughly understanding the pains, concerns, and problems of your target audience, you can tailor your offer to provide the most compelling solution. Incorporate these insights into your messaging, and you'll be well-equipped to persuade potential buyers that your product or service is precisely what they need to overcome their challenges and achieve their desired outcomes.

Having immersed yourself in the depths of your target market's consciousness, the time has come to unveil the sorcery that lies in crafting an offer so irresistible, it will leave your customers spellbound. Prepare yourself to unlock the secret techniques that will bewitch and captivate your audience, leaving them eagerly awaiting what you have in store:

Unleash the Value: Get your thinking cap on and brainstorm the most awe-inspiring value you can deliver to your customers. Imagine the transformation that will leave them in awe, propelling them from their current state to a whole new level of success. It's the result they've been dreaming of, and you hold the key to making it happen.

Language that Speaks their Lingo: To truly connect with your target market, you need to speak their language, not the dull jargon of the industry. Dive into their world, tap into their passions, and use words that make their hearts skip a beat. If you're selling adventure gear, talk about conquering peaks, epic expeditions, and adrenaline-fuelled thrills that ignite their spirit of adventure.

Reasons that Wow: When you present your irresistible offer, you need to have a compelling reason why you're blowing their minds. People have become skeptical of empty promises, so you must provide a rock-solid justification for the incredible value you're offering. Whether it's clearing out stock, celebrating a milestone, or simply wanting to make their lives extraordinary, let your reason shine.

Stack the Value Tower: Prepare to blow their socks off by stacking your offer with mind-blowing bonuses. These goodies should be so irresistible that they can't help but think, "I'd be daft not to take this deal!" Think exclusive access to VIP events, personalised coaching sessions, or even a luxurious getaway to reward their decision. Make the bonuses so tempting that they can't resist diving headfirst into your offer.

Upsell like a Pro: Strike while the iron is hot and offer complementary products or services that take their experience to the next level. It's the moment when they're craving more, so why not satisfy their desires with an upsell? Think of it as the cherry on top of an already scrumptious dessert. From deluxe add-ons to premium upgrades, give them the opportunity to indulge and elevate their experience.

Payment Made Easy: Break down the financial barriers by providing flexible payment options that make your offer more attainable. Help them overcome the "big-ticket" hurdle by presenting a payment plan that eases the strain on their wallets. It's like offering a golden ticket to their dreams, allowing them to enjoy the benefits while keeping their finances in check.

Rock-Solid Guarantee: In a world of empty promises, be the shining knight in armour with an outrageous guarantee. Sweep away their doubts and fears by assuring them that you've got their back. It's a risk-free transaction where the burden lies on your shoulders. Make it clear that their satisfaction is not just a goal, but an absolute guarantee. It's time to build trust and instil confidence like never before.

Scarcity Sensation: Ignite the fire of urgency by introducing a dash of scarcity to your offer. Create a buzz, light the fuse, and watch as their fear of missing out drives them into action. Limited-time deals, exclusive editions, or limited stock availability will make their hearts race. It's a game where time is of the essence, and they won't want to miss out on the golden opportunity you're presenting.

Prepare yourself for the moment of truth, where your offer becomes a magnet, pulling customers towards you with irresistible force. With value that leaves them speechless, language that speaks to their souls, reasons that defy skepticism, stacked bonuses, upsells that take their breath away, flexible payment plans, rock-solid guarantees, and the thrill of scarcity, your offer will shine like a beacon, capturing hearts and transforming lives.

Let's explore the captivating story of Emma, a talented web developer, who applied the steps mentioned today to enhance her pitch and connect with her target audience in a compelling way. Here's a more detailed account of her journey:

Research and Understanding: Emma embarked on an extensive market research journey, diving deep into the needs and pain points of her target audience. She conducted surveys, interviews, and analysed industry trends to gain a comprehensive understanding of the challenges businesses faced with their websites. She discovered that many small businesses struggled with slow-loading websites, outdated designs, poor user experience, and difficulties in managing content updates.

Example: During her research, Emma interviewed a local bakery owner who shared their frustration about losing potential customers due to their outdated website, which didn't showcase their delicious creations effectively. This insight fuelled Emma's determination to help businesses overcome such challenges.

Aligning with Pain Points: Armed with her research findings, Emma tailored her pitch to address the specific pain points of her target audience. She crafted a compelling narrative around how a well-designed, user-friendly website could significantly impact a business's online presence, customer engagement, and ultimately, their revenue.

Example: In her pitch, Emma shared the story of a boutique clothing store that experienced a 50% increase in online sales after she revamped their website, making it visually appealing and mobile-responsive. The store owner expressed their delight at how the new website accurately reflected their brand image, attracted more visitors, and resulted in higher conversions.

Value Proposition: Emma crafted a strong value proposition that highlighted her expertise in creating bespoke websites tailored to each client's unique needs. She emphasised her ability to align design aesthetics with brand identity and create intuitive navigation for enhanced user engagement. She also stressed the importance of responsive design, SEO optimisation, and seamless integration of key functionalities such as e-commerce or booking systems.

Example: Emma described how she collaborated with a local yoga studio, creating a website that captured the serene ambiance of their space and integrated online class booking functionality. The studio saw a significant increase in class registrations and positive customer feedback, as the new website facilitated easy exploration of class schedules and seamless registration.

Emotive Language: To make her pitch resonate emotionally, Emma used evocative language that connected with her audience's aspirations and desires. She emphasised how her web development skills could transform businesses, helping them leave a lasting impression on their customers and stand out in the competitive online landscape.

Example: Emma painted a vivid picture of a coffee shop owner's dream to create an online platform that not only showcased their specialty brews but also evoked the aroma and cozy ambiance of their café, enticing customers to visit in person. By emphasising the emotional connection, Emma conveyed the potential of a well-crafted website to create a unique and immersive brand experience.

Demonstrating Results: Emma backed up her pitch with impressive case studies and success stories. She showcased the measurable results her clients achieved after working with her, such as increased website traffic, higher conversion rates, improved search engine rankings, and positive customer feedback.

Example: Emma shared how she helped a local tour agency optimise their website for search engines, resulting in a 30% increase in organic website traffic and a significant boost in bookings. The agency praised Emma's expertise in crafting compelling content, incorporating captivating visuals, and implementing effective SEO strategies that helped them attract more customers and grow their business.

Social Proof: To further strengthen her pitch, Emma incorporated testimonials from satisfied clients who praised her technical expertise, attention to detail, and ability to translate their vision into a stunning online presence. This social proof helped build trust and credibility, showcasing her track record of delivering exceptional results.

Example: Emma featured a testimonial from a client in the fitness industry who highlighted how her beautifully designed website played a vital role in attracting new members and showcasing their class offerings effectively. The client expressed their appreciation for Emma's professionalism, collaborative approach, and the positive impact her website had on their business growth.

Continuous Improvement: Emma had a growth mindset and actively sought feedback from her clients. She used their insights to refine her development process, stay updated with the latest design trends, and continually enhance her skills to deliver exceptional results. She embraced new technologies, explored innovative solutions, and attended industry conferences and workshops to stay at the forefront of web development trends.

Example: Emma implemented client feedback to create an intuitive user interface for a local restaurant's website, resulting in improved online reservations and positive customer reviews about the seamless booking experience. By actively seeking feedback and continuously improving her services, Emma showcased her commitment to client satisfaction and her dedication to staying ahead in the ever-evolving digital landscape.

By weaving compelling examples and captivating storylines into her pitch, Emma captivated her audience's attention and effectively communicated the value of her web development services. Her ability to address her target audience's pain points, share success stories, demonstrate her expertise, and showcase social proof contributed to her growing client base, a strong reputation, and long-term success in the competitive web development industry.

Honing your pitch is akin to being a seasoned surfer riding the waves of change. Just as the ocean swells and shifts, the needs, interests, and requirements of buyers are in a perpetual state of flux. Let us explore why continuously refining your pitch is not just important, but an invigorating necessity:

Dancing to the Rhythm of Changing Needs: Envision a skilled DJ who effortlessly gauges the beats that will get the crowd moving. By continuously fine-tuning your pitch, you can embody that DJ of the business world. As the needs of buyers change, your pitch must be in tune with the latest trends, challenges, and aspirations. By remaining updated and adapting your messaging, you become the irresistible melody that resonates with your target audience.

Example: A technology company offering cybersecurity services. As cyber threats evolve, the pitch must reflect the latest dangers and showcase innovative solutions that address those concerns. Fine-tuning the pitch allows the company to stay one step ahead, providing buyers with the peace of mind they yearn for.

Outshining the Competition: In a bustling marketplace, standing out is paramount. Continuously refining your pitch ensures that you shine brighter than the neon lights of your competitors. By understanding your unique selling points and incorporating them into your messaging, you become a captivating beacon that draws buyers in.

Example: Picture a fashion brand that possesses an innate understanding of its target audience. By refining its pitch, the brand not only showcases trendy designs but also underscores its commitment to sustainability. This distinctive approach sets it apart from competitors, captivating the hearts of eco-conscious buyers.

Riding the Wave of Industry Trends: Much like catching the perfect wave, staying atop industry trends can propel your business to new heights. By continuously fine-tuning your pitch, you can ride those trends and exhibit how your offerings align with the latest industry developments.

Example: An innovative food delivery service that recognises the surging demand for plant-based options. By refining its pitch to highlight an extensive range of delectable and sustainable plant-based meals, the company positions itself as a vanguard in catering to evolving dietary preferences and lifestyle choices.

Engaging with the Ever-Changing Customer: Customers are the lifeblood of any business, and their preferences can shift as swiftly as the wind. Fine-tuning your pitch enables you to adapt to their ever-evolving desires, connecting directly with their emotions and intellect. It is akin to an ongoing conversation that keeps getting better with time.

Example: A skincare brand that heeds customer feedback and adjusts its pitch accordingly. By comprehending shifting beauty trends and concerns, the brand refines its messaging to address specific skin issues, fostering a personal connection that cultivates trust and loyalty.

Unleashing the Power of Conversion: Imagine a magician honing their tricks, captivating the audience with each deft movement. Similarly, fine-tuning your pitch can work wonders on your conversion rates. By analysing data, gathering feedback, and making iterative improvements, you can unlock the power of persuasion, transforming prospects into devoted customers.

Example: An e-commerce platform that continually optimises its pitch based on customer behaviour data. By discerning what resonates with their audience, they refine their messaging, offers, and user experience, resulting in higher conversion rates and repeat purchases.

In the ever-shifting landscape of business, continuously refining your pitch is akin to being a skilled artist, shaping your masterpiece with each stroke. It allows you to adapt, captivate, and lead the way in a dynamic marketplace. So embrace the exhilarating journey of fine-tuning your pitch and witness your business soar to new heights, riding the waves of success.

Here are some before and after pitches that were continuously improved:

Before Fine-Tuning: Imagine a local bakery struggling to attract customers amidst fierce competition. Their initial offer was a generic "Buy One, Get One 10% Off" promotion, which failed to generate much interest or excitement.

After Fine-Tuning: After diligently fine-tuning their offer, the bakery transformed their messaging and created an irresistible offer that set them apart. Their new offer became: "Indulge in the Ultimate Sweet Escape- Buy One Decadent Cake, Get a Box of Gourmet Cupcakes FREE!"

The refined offer capitalised on customers' desire for indulgence and variety, creating a sense of anticipation and delight. By providing a free box of gourmet cupcakes alongside a purchase of a decadent cake, the bakery captured attention and enticed customers to experience a full range of their delectable treats.

Before Fine-Tuning: A software development company struggled to differentiate itself in a saturated market. Their initial offer simply highlighted technical features and benefits, failing to connect with potential clients.

After Fine-Tuning: Realising the need to appeal to customers' pain points and aspirations, the software company refined their offer to focus on the outcomes and transformative benefits. Their new offer became: "Unlock Your Business's Full Potential with Our Custom Software- Boost Efficiency, Streamline Operations, and Scale for Success!"

The refined offer spoke directly to the pain points faced by businesses, highlighting the tangible benefits of increased efficiency, streamlined operations, and scalable growth. By positioning their software as a solution that empowers businesses to thrive, the company crafted an irresistible offer that resonated with their target audience.

Before Fine-Tuning: An online fitness coach struggled to convert prospects into clients despite offering valuable training programs. Their initial offer relied on generic discounts, which failed to inspire action or create a sense of urgency.

After Fine-Tuning: Recognising the importance of addressing customers' specific fitness goals and challenges, the fitness coach refined their offer to target these pain points. Their new offer became: "Achieve Your Dream Body in 12 Weeks- Personalised Training Program + Nutritional Guidance + 24/7 Support. Limited Spots Available!"

The refined offer highlighted the personalised nature of the training program, the comprehensive support provided, and the scarcity of available spots. By speaking directly to customers' desires for individualised guidance and achieving their dream body, the fitness coach created an irresistible offer that motivated prospects to take immediate action.

Before Fine-Tuning: "Explore the Amazon rainforest with our exciting expedition package. See stunning landscapes, encounter wildlife, and enjoy a helicopter ride and gourmet dining experience."

After Fine-Tuning: "Embark on an unforgettable journey through the untamed wilderness of the Amazon rainforest. Immerse yourself in breathtaking landscapes, encounter exotic wildlife up close, and experience the thrill of exploring uncharted territories. As an added bonus, we'll include a private helicopter ride over the lush canopies and a gourmet dining experience under the stars. This is the ultimate adventure for those seeking the extraordinary."

The refined offer highlights the unique and thrilling aspects of the journey, such as exploring uncharted territories, private helicopter rides, and gourmet dining. This creates a sense of adventure and exclusivity, making it more appealing to adventure seekers.

Before Fine-Tuning: "Transform your fitness with our 90-day programme. Our trainers will guide you through workouts, nutrition plans, and provide support."

After Fine-Tuning: "Unleash your full potential and sculpt the body of your dreams with our 90-day transformation programme. Our team of expert trainers will guide you through personalised workouts, nutrition plans, and mindset coaching. As an added bonus, you'll receive exclusive access to our members-only online community for ongoing support and motivation. Get ready to unleash the fittest version of yourself and achieve the results you've always desired."

The improved offer emphasises the potential for personal transformation and achieving desired fitness goals. The addition of personalised workouts, nutrition plans, mindset coaching, and access to an online community adds value and creates a comprehensive solution, making it more compelling.

Before Fine-Tuning: "Attend our business bootcamp to learn strategies for growth and success."

Fine-Tuning: "Elevate your business to new heights with our intensive Business Mastery Bootcamp. Learn from industry leaders, gain insider strategies, and master the art of scaling your business for exponential growth. As an added bonus, you'll receive one-on-one coaching sessions, access to our exclusive network of successful entrepreneurs, and a VIP ticket to our annual business summit. Unlock your business's full potential and conquer the world of entrepreneurship."

The refined offer focuses on the exclusive benefits of the Business Mastery Bootcamp, such as learning from industry leaders, insider strategies, one-on-one coaching, and access to a network of successful entrepreneurs. This positions it as a high-value opportunity for business growth and success.

Before Fine-Tuning: "Plan your dream wedding with our all-inclusive package."

After Fine-Tuning: "Experience the wedding of your dreams with our all-inclusive wedding package. From a picturesque venue and exquisite décor to personalised menu selections and a dedicated wedding planner, we'll take care of every detail. As an added bonus, we'll arrange a romantic honeymoon getaway to a luxurious destination of your choice. Say 'I do' in style and create memories that will last a lifetime."

The improved offer highlights the all-inclusive nature of the package, including a picturesque venue, exquisite décor, personalised menu selections, a dedicated wedding planner, and a romantic honeymoon getaway. This creates a sense of luxury and convenience, making it more enticing for couples.

Before Fine-Tuning: "Indulge in a relaxing spa retreat."

After Fine-Tuning: "Indulge in pure bliss and rejuvenation with our exclusive spa retreat package. Relax with luxurious massages, refreshing facials, and soothing body treatments in a serene oasis. Experience the healing power of our expert therapists and unwind in lavish accommodations. As an added bonus, enjoy access to our state-of-the-art wellness facilities and a personalised wellness consultation. Treat yourself to a truly revitalising escape."

The refined offer focuses on the exclusive and indulgent aspects of the retreat, such as luxurious massages, refreshing facials, soothing body treatments, access to wellness facilities, and a personalised wellness consultation. This enhances the value proposition and creates a sense of pampering and rejuvenation.

Before Fine-Tuning: "Get the latest tech gadgets at our store."

After Fine-Tuning: "Step into the world of cutting-edge technology with our Tech Enthusiast's Paradise offer. Immerse yourself in the latest gadgets, from state-of-the-art smartphones to virtual reality headsets. Gain early access to new product releases, exclusive discounts, and special promotions. As an added bonus, receive complimentary tech support and access to our expert-led workshops and demonstrations. Embrace the future of technology and stay one step ahead."

The improved offer positions the package as a paradise for tech enthusiasts, offering early access to new releases, exclusive discounts, tech support, and expert-led workshops. This creates a sense of being at the forefront of technology and gaining valuable knowledge and experiences.

Before Fine-Tuning: "Explore gourmet cuisine with our food adventure."

After Fine-Tuning: "Embark on a culinary journey like no other with our Gourmet Food Adventure. Explore a diverse array of gourmet cuisines, tantalise your taste buds with exquisite flavours, and savour unforgettable dining experiences at renowned restaurants. Delight in behind-the-scenes access to top chefs, private cooking classes, and exclusive tasting events. As an added bonus, receive a curated collection of rare spices and artisanal ingredients to elevate your own culinary creations."

The refined offer emphasises the unique experiences of the food adventure, including diverse cuisines, behind-the-scenes access, private cooking classes, and a curated collection of rare spices. This creates a sense of culinary exploration and elevates the offer beyond a simple dining experience.

Before Fine-Tuning: "Revamp your home with our design services."

After Fine-Tuning: "Transform your living space into a sanctuary of style and comfort with our Ultimate Home Makeover package. Our team of interior design experts will curate a bespoke design plan tailored to your preferences and lifestyle. From furniture and décor selection to colour schemes and spatial layout, we'll bring your vision to life. As an added bonus, enjoy exclusive discounts on premium home furnishings and a complimentary consultation with a renowned architect. Create a home that truly reflects your unique style."

The improved offer highlights the comprehensive nature of the makeover package, including bespoke design plans, exclusive discounts on premium furnishings, and a complimentary consultation with a renowned architect. This offers a complete home transformation experience, making it more appealing and valuable to customers.

These examples demonstrate the power of fine-tuning offers to create compelling propositions that address customers' specific needs, desires, and pain points. By adding unique elements, bonuses, and personalisation, the revised offers become more attractive and appealing to potential customers, increasing the chances of conversion and customer satisfaction.

Through fine-tuning their offers, these businesses transformed lacklustre propositions into compelling, irresistible offers. By understanding their customers' desires, pain points, and aspirations, and aligning their messaging accordingly, they were able to captivate their audience, drive conversions, and achieve greater success.

The Art of Captivating Copywriting to Win Hearts and Sales

Imagine this: You're in a bustling marketplace, surrounded by competing businesses vying for attention. Your aim is to stand out, to capture the interest and imagination of your prospects. How can you achieve that? The answer lies in the power of compelling copywriting.

Writing captivating words that clearly articulate why a prospect should choose you over your competitors is the master skill of marketing. It's the ability to create an emotional connection and motivate action. This skill will reward you more than any other in the world of business.

Now, let's delve deeper into the world of direct response marketing, where we unleash the secret techniques of persuasive copywriting. Unlike traditional, dull, "professional" copy, direct response copy is like a magnetic force that irresistibly draws attention.

Emotional direct response copywriting utilises attention-grabbing headlines, persuasive sales copy, and compelling calls to action. It's the art of "salesmanship in print," where words come alive and emotions are ignited.

Some businesses believe this type of copy is not suitable for their market, especially those targeting professional or corporate clients. However, dismissing emotional direct response copywriting would be a grave mistake.

Here's the truth: from the CEO of a global corporation to the janitor sweeping the floors, we are all emotional beings. Our buying decisions are driven by emotions, and we use logic to justify them later. "Darling, I bought that sports car for its advanced safety features and impeccable German engineering." Yeah, right.

It's fascinating how many business owners possess vibrant personalities and engaging conversational skills in person. However, when it comes to their marketing materials and sales copy, they freeze up. Suddenly, they adopt a bland, "professional" tone and use jargon that has no place in genuine conversation. You know the type of language I'm talking about—phrases like "best-in-class solutions," "synergistic partnerships," and "strategic optimisation." These are words they would never utter in everyday dialogue.

But here's the thing: people buy from people, not faceless corporations. Building relationships and establishing rapport is well understood in one-on-one sales. Yet, when it comes to marketing, many business owners believe they must suppress their personality and adopt a corporate facade. That's where they go wrong.

Copywriting is the art of salesmanship in print. When you write your sales copy, envision yourself engaging in a personal conversation with a single individual. Inject personality, authenticity, and opinion into your words.

Using monotonous, uninspiring, "professional" sales copy is the fastest way to lose the interest of your customers and prospects. It's like serving them a tasteless meal in a world full of exciting culinary experiences. Don't be another "me-too" business. Stand out and be memorable.

People crave authenticity, personality, and a fresh perspective. Even if they disagree with you, they'll respect you for being real and unafraid to express your thoughts. Your marketing materials should be an extension of yourself, not a shield to hide behind.

Just think about the power of adding personality to your business. Consider creating a video for your website where you passionately describe your products and services. It could be as simple as recording yourself with a handheld camera or even a smartphone. Embrace social media as a two-way communication medium to engage with your customers and prospects. Show them the real you, and watch the deeper connections and stronger relationships blossom.

Copywriting plays a crucial role in various aspects of a business, including marketing, sales, and bidding. Here's a detailed explanation of how copywriting can be used effectively in each of these areas:

Marketing:

Branding: Copywriting helps establish and communicate a brand's identity and values. It enables businesses to craft a unique and compelling brand voice that resonates with their target audience.

Content Creation: Copywriting is essential for creating engaging content such as blog posts, social media posts, email newsletters, and website copy. Well-crafted content helps businesses attract and retain customers, build brand awareness, and drive engagement.

Advertising: Copywriting plays a pivotal role in creating persuasive advertising campaigns. It involves crafting compelling headlines, taglines, and ad copy that capture attention, generate interest, and motivate action.

SEO: Effective copywriting ensures that content is optimised for search engines, helping businesses improve their search rankings and attract organic traffic. By incorporating relevant keywords and providing valuable information, copywriters can enhance a company's online visibility and reach

Sales:

Product Descriptions: Copywriting is used to create compelling product descriptions that highlight the features, benefits, and unique selling points of a product or service. Well-crafted descriptions can effectively persuade potential customers to make a purchase.

Sales Collateral: Copywriters create persuasive sales collateral such as brochures, sales letters, and presentations. These materials are designed to convince prospects, address their pain points, and showcase how the product or service can meet their needs.

Landing Pages: Copywriting is critical for creating high-converting landing pages. Clear, concise, and persuasive copy guides visitors through the sales funnel, encourages them to take action, and increases conversion rates.

Sales Scripts: Copywriters develop sales scripts that provide sales teams with persuasive language and key talking points to effectively communicate the value of a product or service to potential customers.

Bidding:

Proposals: Copywriting is used to create compelling proposals that clearly outline the value and benefits of a company's offerings. Persuasive copy can help businesses stand out from competitors and increase their chances of winning bids.

Bid Responses: Copywriters craft bid responses that address the specific requirements and criteria outlined in a request for proposal (RFP). Well-written responses showcase a company's capabilities, expertise, and competitive advantage, increasing the likelihood of winning the bid.

Case Studies: Copywriters develop persuasive case studies that highlight successful projects or client testimonials. These case studies demonstrate a company's track record, credibility, and ability to deliver results, strengthening its bid proposals.

As you can see, copywriting is an integral part of a business's marketing, sales, and bidding strategies. It enables businesses to effectively communicate their brand identity, engage with their target audience, persuade potential customers, and differentiate themselves from competitors. By leveraging the power of words, businesses can create compelling copy that drives success in various areas of their operations.

The Alchemy of Language: Language, like magic, has the ability to transform ordinary thoughts into extraordinary visions. As a copywriter, you hold the key to this linguistic alchemy. Let us unlock the enchanted words and phrases that possess the power to weave spells of persuasion:

Ignite: Ignite their curiosity and set their hearts ablaze with desire.

Enchant: Cast a spell of enchantment with words that mesmerise and captivate.

Illuminate: Illuminate their path to success and guide them towards a brighter future.

Unveil: Unveil the secrets and mysteries that lie within your offering.

Spark: Spark their imagination and kindle the flames of possibility.

Empower: Empower them to unleash their true potential and achieve greatness.

Seduce: Seduce their senses with alluring promises and irresistible offers.

Conquer: Conquer their doubts and fears, leading them towards triumph and victory.

Spellbinding Headlines: In the realm of copywriting, headlines act as enchanting incantations, summoning the attention of your audience and drawing them deeper into your world. Let us delve into the realm of bewitching headlines, where mere words possess the power to cast a spell:

"Unlock the Forbidden Secrets of Success: Discover the Key to Prosperity"

"Journey to a World Beyond Imagination: Experience the Adventure of a Lifetime"

"Harness the Power of the Elements: Transform Your Life with Ancient Wisdom"

"Sorcery for Your Senses: Indulge in the Divine Delights of our Exquisite Cuisine"

"Unleash Your Inner Hero: Conquer Fear and Embrace Your True Potential"

Conjuring Emotional Enchantment: Emotions are the raw materials from which we weave spells of persuasion. By harnessing the right emotional triggers, you can forge a powerful connection with your audience. Allow us to unveil examples of emotional enchantment in copywriting:

Fear: "Banish the Shadows of Uncertainty: Embrace a Future of Confidence and Security"

Excitement: "Prepare for a Heart-Pounding Journey: Brace Yourself for Thrills Beyond Imagination"

Curiosity: "Unravel the Mysteries of Success: Enter a World of Infinite Possibilities"

Desire: "Indulge in Pure Opulence: Surrender to the Luxurious Charms of our Exquisite Retreat"

Belonging: "Join the Fellowship of Visionaries: Unite with Like-Minded Souls on a Quest for Greatness"

The Magic of Words: Words possess an undeniable power to evoke emotions, ignite desires, and inspire action. In the realm of copywriting, the right combination of words can paint vivid pictures, evoke laughter or tears, and ultimately compel your audience to take the desired action. Let's explore a few captivating examples:

Example 1: Airbnb's tagline, "Belong Anywhere," instantly sparks a sense of wanderlust, inviting you to explore the world, connect with new cultures, and create unforgettable memories.

Example 2: Coca-Cola's timeless slogan, "Open Happiness," taps into our deepest desires for joy, unity, and shared experiences. It paints a picture of a refreshing drink that goes beyond quenching thirst—it brings people together in moments of pure happiness.

Crafting Compelling Copy: The art of copywriting involves a delicate balance of creativity, psychology, and strategic thinking. Here are key techniques and elements to consider when crafting your own mesmerising copy:

Understanding the Heartbeat of Your Audience: Take the time to truly understand your target audience—their dreams, fears, aspirations, and pain points. This knowledge forms the foundation of your copy and allows you to speak directly to their hearts and minds.

Hypnotic Headlines: Your headline is the first impression, the captivating invitation that draws readers into your world. Craft headlines that pique curiosity, evoke emotion, and promise a transformative experience. For example, "Unleash Your Inner Creative Genius: Discover the Art of Limitless Imagination."

Storytelling Magic: Weaving stories into your copy captivates your audience, immerses them in a narrative, and creates a powerful connection. Paint vivid scenes, introduce relatable characters, and take readers on a journey that showcases the benefits of your product or service.

Persuasive Language: Embrace the power of words that trigger emotions, create urgency, and inspire action. Choose words like "unforgettable," "exclusive," "limited-time offer," or "transform your life" to make your copy irresistible.

Real-World Transformations: Copywriting has the remarkable ability to transform businesses and reshape their fortunes. Here are a few captivating case studies:

Case Study 1: Mailchimp's playful and engaging copy turned a mundane task—email marketing— into a delightful experience. By injecting personality and wit into their brand voice, they transformed an industry and built a loyal following of users who fell in love with their product.

Case Study 2: The Dollar Shave Club disrupted the razor industry with their viral video ad that mixed humour, relatability, and a bold brand message. This witty copy and charismatic storytelling propelled them from obscurity to a multi-million-pound business.

Copywriting is the secret weapon that sets exceptional businesses apart from the rest. It allows you to connect with your audience on a deeper level, spark desire, and drive action. By mastering the art of copywriting, you can create a powerful brand presence, inspire loyalty, and propel your business to new heights. So, unleash your creativity, embrace the magic of words, and let your captivating copy cast a spell on the hearts and minds of your audience. The possibilities are endless, and the rewards are extraordinary.

Once upon a time in a quaint village, there lived a passionate baker named John. He dreamt of creating a bakery that would delight the senses and leave a lasting impression on anyone who walked through its doors. With a heart full of ambition and hands skilled in the art of baking, John set out on his entrepreneurial journey.

As the aroma of freshly baked bread and pastries wafted through the air, John opened the doors to his small boutique bakery. His creations were divine, meticulously crafted with love and attention to detail. Each pastry was a work of art, a symphony of flavours waiting to be savoured. However, there was one issue that John encountered—the sweet symphony of his bakery was lost amidst the hustle and bustle of the town.

Determined to share his culinary wonders with the world, John sought the guidance of a talented copywriter. This master of words possessed a gift for turning mere sentences into captivating tales that danced in the minds of readers. They understood the power of storytelling and knew how to wield it to ignite desire and create a sense of longing.

The copywriter stepped into John's bakery, observing the gleaming display of pastries and the passion that radiated from John's eyes. With a mischievous grin, they began crafting tales that would breathe life into John's creations.

With every pastry, the copywriter spun a tale of its origin. They shared stories of secret family recipes passed down through generations, whispered in hushed tones and treasured like precious gems. The tales painted vivid pictures of the bakery's inner workings, where time-honoured techniques merged with John's artistic touch to create magic on a plate.

But the magic didn't stop there. The copywriter took to social media, conjuring captivating images and pairing them with words that stirred desire. They transported the audience to a world where the delicate flakiness of a croissant could transport them to the streets of Paris, where the first bite of a velvety chocolate cake could unleash a flood of childhood memories.

Customers couldn't resist the allure of John's bakery as they scrolled through their social media feeds. The enchanting visuals and clever captions acted as a siren's call, drawing them closer to the sweet wonders that awaited them.

Emboldened by the success of their online presence, the copywriter turned their attention to John's website. They wove a symphony of words that not only described the pastries but also showcased the bakery's commitment to quality, the locally sourced ingredients, and the meticulous craftsmanship that went into each creation. The website became a portal to pastry paradise, enticing visitors to step into John's world and indulge in a symphony of flavours.

Word spread throughout the village. The tantalising tales, the mesmerising social media posts, and the captivating website copy wove a spell that no one could resist. Customers flocked to John's bakery, their senses heightened by anticipation. They walked through the doors, their mouths watering and their hearts full of excitement.

With each bite, customers discovered that John's creations were not simply baked goods—they were portals to moments of pure bliss. The power of well-crafted words had transformed John's bakery from a hidden gem to the talk of the town.

As the story of John's bakery spread far and wide, people from neighbouring villages made the journey to experience the magic for themselves. John's dream had come true, thanks to the skilful storytelling of the copywriter who had sprinkled their words like fairy dust, turning dough into doughnuts and dreams into reality.

And so, John's bakery stood as a testament to the power of captivating copywriting. It was a place where the love for baking, combined with the art of storytelling, created an enchanting experience that would forever linger in the hearts and taste buds of those who had the pleasure of stepping into its world.

John employed the power of storytelling as a copywriting technique to captivate his audience and create an emotional connection with his bakery. By infusing his pastries with narratives, he transported his customers to a world where each treat held a story, a tradition, and a moment of delight waiting to be savoured.

The use of storytelling worked wonders for John in several ways. First, it engaged his customers on an emotional level. As they read or heard about the secret family recipes and the passion behind each creation, they became emotionally invested in the bakery. They felt connected to the history, the heritage, and the love that went into every pastry.

Secondly, storytelling made John's bakery memorable. By associating unique narratives with his pastries, he differentiated his offerings from those of his competitors. Customers didn't just see pastries; they saw edible stories that they couldn't find anywhere else. This distinctiveness created a sense of exclusivity and increased the perceived value of his products.

Moreover, storytelling sparked curiosity and desire. The tales woven around the pastries ignited the customers' imagination, transporting them to different times and places. They yearned to experience the emotions and flavours described in the stories, making a visit to John's bakery irresistible.

Additionally, storytelling allowed John to showcase the craftsmanship and attention to detail that went into his creations. The stories emphasised the bakery's commitment to quality, authenticity, and the use of locally sourced ingredients. This elevated the perception of his pastries and positioned them as premium products worth experiencing.

Overall, John's use of storytelling as a copywriting technique helped him create an emotional connection with his audience, differentiate his bakery from competitors, increase the perceived value of his pastries, and spark curiosity and desire. It transformed his bakery into a place where customers didn't just buy pastries but became part of a captivating narrative, enriching their experience and fostering customer loyalty.

Here are 50 copywriting techniques that you can use:

Emotional Appeal: Evoke emotions that resonate with your audience. By tapping into their desires, fears, or aspirations, you can create a powerful connection. Example: "Experience the joy and freedom of our luxury holiday packages, where you can escape the daily grind and create lifelong memories with your loved ones."

Storytelling: Create engaging narratives to captivate readers. Stories have the power to evoke emotions and make your message more memorable. Example: "Imagine stepping into a room filled with the enticing aroma of freshly baked biscuits, as the warm, gooey centers melt in your mouth, taking you back to cherished childhood moments."

Persuasive Language: Use words and phrases that compel action. Employ strong verbs, adjectives, and power words to convey a sense of urgency and persuade your audience. Example: "Don't miss out on this exclusive opportunity to transform your life and unlock your full potential. Take charge and grasp the reins of your success today."

Benefit-focused Approach: Highlight the benefits of your product or service. Clearly communicate how your offering can solve a problem or improve the lives of your customers. Example: "Our revolutionary fitness programme will help you shed unwanted weight, boost your energy levels, and regain your confidence, so you can embrace a healthier and happier lifestyle."

Audience Segmentation: Tailor your message to specific target segments. Understand your audience's unique needs, preferences, and pain points, and address them directly in your copy. Example: "Calling all adventure enthusiasts! Discover awe-inspiring landscapes, adrenaline-pumping activities, and unforgettable experiences tailored exclusively for you."

Power Words: Incorporate impactful and attention-grabbing words. These words have a strong emotional or sensory impact and can leave a lasting impression. Example: "Unleash your untapped potential with our groundbreaking strategies that will catapult you to unprecedented success."

Social Proof: Include testimonials and evidence of your product's success. Showcasing positive reviews and great experiences helps build trust and credibility. Example: "Join the thousands of satisfied customers who have transformed their finances with our proven wealth management system."

Call-to-Action (CTA): Craft clear and compelling CTAs to prompt action. Use persuasive language and create a sense of urgency to encourage an immediate response. Example: "Don't hesitate! Grab your limited-time offer now and take the first step towards a brighter future."

Urgency: Create a sense of urgency to encourage immediate action. Highlight time-limited offers, limited availability, or impending deadlines to prompt a response. Example: "Limited stock available! Secure your place for this exclusive collector's edition before it's gone forever."

Scarcity: Highlight limited availability or exclusive offers to increase desirability. Convey that the opportunity is rare or exclusive, creating a sense of urgency to act quickly. Example: "Be one of the privileged few to own this meticulously handcrafted masterpiece. Limited to only 100 pieces worldwide."

Repetition: Repeat key phrases or messages to reinforce their importance and create a lasting impact. Example: "Discover a world of possibilities. Discover a world of adventure. Discover our exclusive travel experiences."

Rhetorical Questions: Pose thought-provoking questions to engage readers and encourage them to reflect on their needs or desires. Example: "Are you tired of feeling exhausted all the time? Ready to take control of your energy levels and live life to the fullest?"

Contrast: Highlight the differences between two options or scenarios to emphasise the benefits of choosing your product or service. Example: "Don't settle for mediocrity when you can experience excellence. Upgrade to our premium package and elevate your lifestyle."

Power of Three: Use groups of three to make your message more memorable and impactful. Example: "Discover, Explore, Transform. Unleash the power within and embark on a journey of personal growth."

FOMO (Fear of Missing Out): Create a sense of urgency and exclusivity by emphasising the unique opportunities or benefits that customers may miss out on if they don't act quickly. Example: "Limited spots available! Join our elite community of entrepreneurs and gain exclusive access to game-changing strategies."

Anticipation: Build anticipation and excitement for an upcoming product launch or event by gradually revealing enticing details over time. Example: "Coming soon: The revolutionary gadget that will redefine the way you experience technology. Stay tuned for the big reveal!"

AIDA (Attention, Interest, Desire, Action): Structure your copy to capture attention, generate interest, create desire, and prompt action. Example: "Attention! Are you tired of mundane workouts? Discover our fitness program that will ignite your interest, fuel your desire, and propel you towards a healthier, fitter you. Take action now!"

Curiosity: Spark curiosity by teasing information or solutions that readers can only uncover by engaging with your product or service. Example: "Unlock the secret to radiant skin. Discover the age-defying ingredient that dermatologists don't want you to know about."

Metaphors and Similes: Use figurative language to create vivid imagery and make complex concepts more relatable. Example: "Our software is like a Swiss Army knife for productivity, empowering you with versatile tools that tackle any task."

Personalisation: Tailor your copy to resonate with individual readers, addressing their specific needs and preferences. Example: "Looking to revamp your style? Our personalised fashion consultations will ensure you always look and feel your best, no matter the occasion."

Storytelling: Use the power of storytelling to engage your audience emotionally and create a connection with your brand. Example: "Imagine standing at the edge of a majestic waterfall, feeling the mist on your face and the rush of exhilaration. Our adventure tours will take you to breathtaking places that will leave you with unforgettable stories to share."

Social Proof: Highlight testimonials, reviews, or endorsements from satisfied customers to build trust and credibility. Example: "Join thousands of happy customers who have achieved their fitness goals with our revolutionary workout program. Hear what they have to say about their incredible transformations."

Call to Action (CTA): Clearly instruct readers on the desired action you want them to take, whether it's making a purchase, signing up for a newsletter, or contacting you for more information. Example: "Don't miss out on this limited-time offer! Click here to claim your exclusive discount and start your journey to a healthier lifestyle today."

Emotional Appeal: Tap into the emotions of your audience by addressing their desires, fears, or aspirations. Example: "Experience the joy of financial freedom. Say goodbye to financial stress and embrace a life of abundance with our proven wealth-building strategies."

Exclusivity: Create a sense of exclusivity or prestige by offering limited editions, VIP access, or membership benefits. Example: "Be part of an elite circle of innovators. Join our exclusive membership programme and gain access to insider events, industry insights, and networking opportunities."

Urgency: Encourage immediate action by emphasising time-limited offers, countdowns, or limited stock availability. Example: "Only 24 hours left to secure your spot in our intensive workshop. Don't miss out on this opportunity to learn from industry experts and take your skills to the next level."

Benefit-Oriented Language: Clearly communicate the benefits and value of your product or service rather than focusing solely on features. Example: "Unlock the secrets of efficient time management and reclaim your productivity. Our time-saving tools will help you achieve more in less time."

Authority: Position yourself as an expert or industry leader to instil confidence and credibility in your audience. Example: "With years of research and endorsements from top professionals in the field, our skincare products are trusted by beauty experts worldwide."

Sensory Language: Engage multiple senses by using descriptive and vivid language that allows readers to imagine how your product or service feels, smells, tastes, or sounds. Example: "Indulge in the rich aroma and velvety smoothness of our artisanal coffee, sourced from the finest coffee beans around the world."

Benefit Stacking: Highlight multiple benefits or features in a compelling way to demonstrate the value your product or service offers. Example: "Our all-in-one software streamlines your workflow, saves you time, and boosts your productivity, enabling you to focus on what truly matters—growing your business."

Scarcity: Create a sense of scarcity or limited availability to motivate action and prevent potential customers from procrastinating. Example: "Hurry, only 5 spots left for our exclusive workshop. Reserve your seat now before they're gone!"

Comparison: Highlight the advantages of your product or service by comparing it to competitors or alternative options. Example: "Unlike traditional cleaning products that leave residue and contain harmful chemicals, our eco-friendly solution provides a safer and more effective way to keep your home spotless."

Testimonials: Feature testimonials from satisfied customers to provide social proof and build trust. Example: "Don't just take our word for it. Hear what our customers have to say about their incredible experiences with our travel agency."

Curiosity: Create intrigue and captivate your audience by posing thought-provoking questions or teasing intriguing information. Example: "Discover the secret to unlocking unlimited creativity. Can you imagine what you could achieve if you had the key?"

Personalisation: Tailor your message to resonate with the individual needs and desires of your target audience. Example: "Looking for a skincare routine that's as unique as you are? Our personalised skincare solutions are specially formulated to address your specific concerns."

Social Responsibility: Emphasise your brand's commitment to social causes or environmental sustainability to appeal to socially conscious consumers. Example: "By choosing our eco-friendly products, you're not just caring for your skin, but also supporting sustainable practices that protect our planet."

Anticipation: Build anticipation and excitement by teasing upcoming product launches, events, or exclusive content. Example: "Get ready for the biggest sale of the year! Mark your calendars for our upcoming Black Friday extravaganza."

Repetition: Reinforce key messages or benefits by repeating them throughout your copy to enhance memorability. Example: "Achieve your fitness goals faster, feel stronger, and look better than ever. Our program is designed to help you transform your body and boost your confidence."

Hypotheticals: Use hypothetical scenarios or "what-if" questions to help readers visualise the potential outcomes of using your product or service. Example: "Imagine waking up each morning feeling refreshed and energised. With our revolutionary sleep aid, a good night's sleep is no longer a dream."

Storytelling: Engage your audience by weaving a compelling narrative that showcases how your product or service has positively impacted the lives of others. Example: "Meet Sarah, a working mum who used our meal planning service to save time and stress, allowing her to enjoy more quality moments with her family."

Urgency: Create a sense of urgency to prompt immediate action from your audience. Example: "Limited time offer! Grab your exclusive discount before it expires at midnight tonight."

Exclusivity: Highlight the exclusivity or uniqueness of your product or offer to make it more desirable. Example: "Introducing our exclusive VIP membership programme, granting you access to premium content, special discounts, and priority customer support."

FOMO (Fear of Missing Out): Tap into the fear of missing out by showcasing the benefits or experiences that your audience could miss if they don't take action. Example: "Join thousands of satisfied customers who have already transformed their lives. Don't miss out on the opportunity to achieve your goals."

Vivid Imagery: Paint a vivid picture in the minds of your audience by using descriptive language and imagery to make your message more engaging. Example: "Immerse yourself in a tropical paradise with pristine white-sand beaches, turquoise waters, and breathtaking sunsets."

Social Proof: Use social proof in the form of reviews, ratings, or endorsements to build credibility and trust. Example: "Rated 5 stars by over 1,000 satisfied customers. Join the ranks of those who have experienced the quality and excellence of our products."

Call-to-Action (CTA): Clearly and compellingly direct your audience to take the desired action, such as making a purchase or signing up for a newsletter. Example: "Don't wait any longer! Click the 'Buy Now' button to claim your exclusive offer and start your journey to success."

Emphasise Benefits: Focus on the benefits that your product or service provides, rather than just listing features, to show how it can improve the lives of your audience. Example: "Experience the freedom of wireless headphones, allowing you to enjoy your favourite music anytime, anywhere, without the hassle of tangled wires."

Authority: Position yourself or your brand as an expert or authority in your industry to gain credibility and trust. Example: "Recommended by top fitness trainers and trusted by athletes worldwide, our supplements are backed by science and proven results."

Problem-Solution: Clearly identify the problem or pain point that your audience is facing, and then present your product or service as the ideal solution. Example: "Tired of spending hours cleaning? Our innovative robotic vacuum takes care of the dirty work, giving you more time to relax and enjoy life."

Emotional Appeal: Tap into the emotions of your audience by appealing to their desires, aspirations, or fears to create a strong connection and engagement. Example: "Imagine the joy and pride you'll feel when you step into your dream home, meticulously designed to reflect your unique style and personality."

<u>Mindful Copywriting</u>

As a business owner, imagine you're trying to attract new customers to your product or service. To effectively communicate and persuade them, you need to understand their needs, motivations, and concerns. By entering the conversation already happening in their minds, you can tailor your message to resonate with them on a deeper level.

First, you need to conduct market research and gain insights into your target audience. Understand their pain points, challenges, and aspirations. This will help you speak their language and craft a message that captures their attention and addresses their specific needs.

Next, address any objections or hesitations they may have. Anticipate their concerns and provide clear and compelling solutions. For example, if potential customers are worried about the quality or reliability of your product, highlight customer testimonials and case studies that demonstrate its effectiveness.

To make your message more impactful, you can share stories of existing customers who have benefited from your product or service. Highlight the positive outcomes, success stories, and tangible results they've experienced. By showcasing great examples, you build credibility and trust, making it easier for prospective customers to connect with your business.

Now, let's explore some case studies that demonstrate the power of entering the conversation already going on in your prospect's mind:

Case Study 1: A Software Company A software company develops a productivity tool for small businesses. Through market research and customer feedback, they discover that many business owners struggle with time management and team collaboration. In their marketing campaigns, they focus on addressing these pain points, highlighting how their software streamlines workflows and enhances collaboration. By entering the conversation already happening in the minds of business owners, the company attracts a large customer base and experiences significant growth.

Case Study 2: A Fitness Studio A fitness studio wants to attract new clients to their classes. They conduct surveys and interviews to understand the motivations and goals of their target audience. Through their research, they discover that many people are seeking a fun and supportive environment to achieve their fitness goals. In their marketing messaging, they emphasise the community and camaraderie that their studio offers, showcasing success stories of individuals who have transformed their health and fitness. By entering the conversation already happening in the minds of fitness enthusiasts, the studio attracts a loyal clientele and establishes itself as a go-to fitness destination.

Case Study 3: A Restaurant A restaurant wants to increase foot traffic during weekdays. They conduct customer surveys and observe dining patterns to understand the challenges and preferences of their target audience. Through their research, they discover that many people are looking for convenient and affordable dining options during lunchtime. In their marketing efforts, they promote lunchtime specials and highlight the quick service and affordable pricing of their menu. By entering the conversation already happening in the minds of busy professionals, the restaurant sees a significant increase in weekday lunchtime customers.

Case Study 4: An E-commerce Store An e-commerce store specialises in sustainable fashion. Through market research and customer feedback, they discover that their target audience is increasingly concerned about the environmental impact of fast fashion. In their marketing campaigns, they enter the conversation by highlighting their eco-friendly practices, such as using organic materials and promoting fair trade. By aligning their message with the values and concerns of their target audience, the e-commerce store attracts environmentally conscious shoppers and builds a loyal customer base.

Case Study 5: A Marketing Agency A marketing agency wants to attract small businesses looking to improve their online presence. They conduct surveys and interviews to understand the pain points of their target audience. Through their research, they find that many small business owners struggle with digital marketing and are overwhelmed by the complexity of online advertising. In their marketing messaging, the agency addresses these concerns by offering simplified solutions, such as affordable social media management packages or step-by-step guides for improving online visibility. By entering the conversation already happening in the minds of small business owners, the agency establishes itself as a trusted partner and experiences a surge in client inquiries.

Case Study 6: A Home Cleaning Service A home cleaning service wants to expand its customer base. They conduct market research and customer interviews to understand the needs and preferences of their target audience. Through their research, they discover that busy professionals value convenience and reliability when it comes to hiring a cleaning service. In their marketing efforts, the cleaning service enters the conversation by emphasising their flexible scheduling options, online booking system, and thorough background checks for their cleaning staff. By addressing the specific concerns of their target audience and positioning themselves as a trustworthy and hassle-free option, the cleaning service attracts new customers and increases its market share.

These examples demonstrate how businesses can successfully enter the conversation already happening in the minds of their target audience by understanding their needs, concerns, and aspirations. By tailoring their messaging and offering solutions that align with those thoughts and desires, businesses can effectively connect with their prospects and drive meaningful engagement and growth.

<u>How to learn copywriting</u>

Learning new copywriting skills is an exciting journey that requires dedication and practice. Here's a step-by-step guide to effectively learn and develop your copywriting skills:

Set Clear Goals: Start by defining your goals and the specific copywriting skills you want to learn or improve. For example, you may want to enhance your storytelling abilities, refine your persuasive writing techniques, or strengthen your headline writing skills. Clear goals will help you focus your efforts and measure your progress.

Study the Fundamentals: Begin by understanding the foundational principles of copywriting. Learn about persuasive writing techniques, target audience analysis, marketing psychology, and the different components of copy such as headlines, subheadings, body text, and calls to action. Familiarise yourself with the techniques used in effective copywriting.

Read Widely: Immerse yourself in the world of copywriting by reading books, articles, and blogs on the subject. Study successful copywriting examples and dissect what makes them effective. Pay attention to the style, tone, structure, and language used in different types of copy. By exposing yourself to various styles and voices, you can expand your creative repertoire.

Practice Regularly: The key to learning copywriting is practice. Set aside dedicated time to write and experiment with different copywriting techniques. Start with small projects like writing social media posts, product descriptions, or blog articles. Gradually challenge yourself with more complex assignments such as crafting sales letters or creating advertising campaigns. The more you practice, the better you'll become at applying different copywriting techniques.

Seek Feedback: Share your work with peers, mentors, or online communities and ask for constructive feedback. Feedback helps you identify areas for improvement and provides valuable insights from experienced copywriters. Take their suggestions to heart and refine your copywriting skills accordingly.

Emulate Successful Copywriters: Study the work of renowned copywriters and try to emulate their style and techniques. Practice rewriting successful copy to understand the nuances and strategies they employ. While you should develop your unique voice, learning from established experts can provide valuable guidance and inspiration.

Take Copywriting Courses or Workshops: Consider enrolling in copywriting courses or attending workshops led by industry professionals. These structured learning experiences can accelerate your understanding of copywriting principles and provide hands-on practice opportunities. Look for courses that offer practical exercises, real-world examples, and feedback from instructors.

Build a Portfolio: As you gain experience, create a portfolio of your best copywriting samples. This serves as evidence of your skills and can be showcased to potential clients or employers. Include a variety of copywriting projects to demonstrate your versatility and ability to adapt to different industries and target audiences.

Stay Curious and Updated: Copywriting is a dynamic field, so it's important to stay curious and updated with industry trends and changes. Continuously seek opportunities to learn, whether through reading industry blogs, attending webinars, or joining copywriting communities. Stay abreast of new techniques, tools, and strategies to enhance your copywriting skills.

Practice Continuous Improvement: Copywriting is a skill that can always be improved. Regularly reflect on your work, analyse what worked and what didn't, and strive to refine your techniques. Learn from both successes and failures, and embrace a growth mindset that values continuous improvement.

Join Writing Communities: Engage with writing communities, both online and offline, to connect with fellow copywriters and exchange ideas. Participate in forums, social media groups, or local writing meet-ups. Collaborating with like-minded individuals can provide valuable insights, support, and opportunities for growth. You can receive feedback, share resources, and learn from the experiences of others in the field.

Analyse Competitors: Study the copywriting strategies employed by your competitors in the industry or niche you're interested in. Examine their website copy, adverts, social media content, and sales materials. Identify their strengths and weaknesses. By understanding what your competitors are doing, you can identify opportunities to differentiate yourself and develop unique selling propositions that resonate with your target audience.

Conduct A/B Testing: Experiment with different versions of your copy by conducting A/B tests. Create multiple variations of headlines, calls to action, or email subject lines, and measure the response rates and conversion rates of each version. A/B testing allows you to gather data-driven insights into what copy elements resonate better with your audience and drive better results. This experimentation helps you refine your copywriting skills based on real-world feedback.

Seek Mentors: Find experienced copywriters who can mentor and guide you in your learning journey. Look for industry professionals, attend conferences, or reach out to established copywriters for mentorship or advice. Having a mentor can provide valuable insights, personalised guidance, and feedback specific to your goals and challenges. They can offer practical tips, share their experiences, and help you navigate the copywriting landscape.

Continuous Learning: Cultivate a mindset of continuous learning by staying curious and exploring new areas of copywriting. Expand your knowledge by delving into related disciplines such as psychology, marketing, storytelling, or design. Attend webinars, listen to podcasts, or enrol in courses that focus on specific aspects of copywriting or complementary skills. Embracing lifelong learning ensures you stay adaptable and equipped with the latest tools and techniques in the ever-evolving field of copywriting.

How to get better at copywriting

To improve your copywriting skills and become a more effective copywriter, consider the following tips:

Study Successful Copy: Analyse and dissect successful copy from various mediums such as advertisements, sales letters, websites, and social media campaigns. Pay attention to the structure, tone, language, and persuasive techniques used. Understand how the copy engages the target audience, builds desire, and prompts action. Learn from the best and apply their strategies to your own writing.

Practice Regularly: Copywriting is a skill that improves with practice. Set aside dedicated time to write and experiment with different copywriting techniques. Start with small exercises to focus on specific skills, such as crafting compelling headlines or writing persuasive calls to action. As you gain confidence, take on more complex assignments and challenge yourself to write in different styles and tones.

Embrace the Power of Editing: Great copy is often the result of careful editing. Review your work critically and make revisions to improve clarity, flow, and impact. Remove unnecessary words, tighten sentences, and ensure your message is concise and compelling. Editing allows you to refine your ideas and polish your copy to make it more effective.

Read Widely: Expand your knowledge and exposure to different writing styles by reading extensively. Explore various genres, including fiction, non-fiction, articles, and blogs. Pay attention to the way authors use language, structure their sentences, and engage readers. Reading widely helps you develop a versatile writing style and enhances your understanding of effective communication.

Seek Feedback: Share your copywriting work with trusted peers, mentors, or professionals in the field and ask for constructive feedback. Listen to their suggestions and use their insights to improve your writing. Consider joining writing groups or online communities where you can exchange ideas, receive feedback, and learn from others.

Continuously Learn and Stay Updated: Copywriting is a dynamic field that evolves with changing trends and consumer preferences. Stay updated with industry news, attend webinars or workshops, and participate in relevant courses. Continuously learning and staying informed about new techniques, technologies, and best practices will keep your copywriting skills sharp and relevant.

Test and Measure Results: When possible, test different versions of your copy to see what resonates best with your audience. A/B testing can help you identify the most effective headlines, calls to action, or messaging approaches. By measuring the results of your copy, you can make data-driven decisions and further refine your writing strategies.

Embrace Creativity and Innovation: Copywriting is a creative discipline. Allow yourself to think outside the box, experiment with new ideas, and take risks. Don't be afraid to challenge conventions and explore unconventional approaches. Innovative and creative copy often stands out and captures the attention of readers.

Develop Empathy for Your Audience: Understand your target audience deeply and empathise with their needs, desires, and pain points. Tailor your copy to address their specific challenges and aspirations. By connecting emotionally with your audience, your copy will resonate more strongly and drive desired actions.

Never Stop Learning: Copywriting is a lifelong learning process. Stay curious, seek inspiration from various sources, and continuously seek opportunities to improve your skills. Attend conferences, join professional associations, and engage in networking to stay connected with industry trends and connect with fellow copywriters.

Master the Art of Storytelling: Develop your storytelling abilities to create engaging narratives that captivate your audience. Use storytelling techniques to evoke emotions, convey your message, and make your copy more memorable.

Hone Your Research Skills: Conduct thorough research to gather relevant information and insights about your target audience, industry trends, and competitive landscape. The more you know, the better you can tailor your copy to resonate with your audience and differentiate yourself from competitors.

Develop a Strong Unique Selling Proposition (USP): Clearly identify and articulate what sets your product or service apart from others in the market. Craft a compelling USP that communicates the value and benefits customers will receive by choosing your offering.

Understand Conversion Psychology: Familiarise yourself with the principles of conversion psychology, such as social proof, scarcity, urgency, and the psychology of persuasion. Apply these principles strategically in your copy to influence customer behaviour and increase conversions.

Enhance Your Editing Skills: Sharpen your editing skills to ensure your copy is error-free, concise, and impactful. Pay attention to grammar, punctuation, spelling, and sentence structure. Edit for clarity, coherence, and consistency to deliver a polished final piece of copy.

Develop a Strong Headline Writing Technique: Master the art of writing compelling headlines that grab attention and entice readers to continue reading. Experiment with different headline formulas, such as curiosity, numbers, and emotional triggers, to discover what resonates best with your target audience.

Study Consumer Psychology: Gain insights into consumer behaviour, motivations, and decision-making processes. Understand what drives customers to make purchasing decisions and incorporate psychological triggers into your copy to influence their actions.

Cultivate a Unique Writing Voice: Find your own unique writing voice that reflects your personality and resonates with your target audience. Develop a consistent tone and style that sets you apart and makes your copy instantly recognisable.

Practice Writing Different Copy Formats: Expand your repertoire by practising writing copy for various formats, such as emails, landing pages, social media ads, video scripts, and sales funnels. Each format requires a different approach and style, so diversify your skills by tackling different copywriting challenges.

Stay Updated with Digital Marketing Trends: Keep up with the latest trends and advancements in digital marketing. Stay informed about new platforms, technologies, and strategies that can impact the effectiveness of your copy. Embrace digital channels and adapt your writing style to suit online platforms and mobile devices.

Develop Empathy for Your Client's Brand: When writing for clients, take the time to understand their brand identity, values, and target audience. Align your copy with their brand voice and capture the essence of their business. Show a genuine interest in their success and create copy that truly represents their brand.

Practice Concise Writing: Learn to communicate your message concisely without sacrificing clarity. Avoid unnecessary jargon, filler words, and overly complex sentences. Embrace simplicity and brevity to make your copy more accessible and impactful.

Study Copywriting Legends: Learn from the copywriting greats who have shaped the industry. Study the works of legends such as David Ogilvy, Eugene Schwartz, and Gary Halbert to gain insights into their techniques and strategies. Apply their timeless principles to your own writing.

Develop Strong Calls to Action (CTAs): Craft compelling and persuasive calls to action that encourage readers to take the desired action. Use action verbs, create a sense of urgency, and clearly communicate the benefits of acting now.

Embrace Continuous Improvement: Copywriting is a skill that can always be refined. Embrace a growth mindset and continually seek opportunities for self-improvement. Attend workshops, conferences, and seminars, and invest in your professional development to stay ahead in the ever-evolving field of copywriting.

Remember, improving your copywriting skills takes time and practice. Be patient with yourself and embrace the learning process. By consistently honing your craft and incorporating these strategies, you'll become a more skilled and effective copywriter.

<u>How to add new copywriting skills for tenders:</u>

Tenders refer to formal invitations by clients or organisations for businesses to submit proposals or bids to provide goods, services, or projects. They are typically used in the public sector or larger private sector contracts. Winning tenders can provide significant business opportunities and revenue for companies.

To find tenders, businesses can explore various sources such as government procurement portals, online tender platforms, trade publications, and industry-specific websites. Additionally, networking, attending industry events, and building relationships with potential clients can lead to tender opportunities.

Bid writing is the process of preparing and submitting a compelling proposal or bid in response to a tender. It involves crafting a persuasive document that highlights the company's capabilities, relevant experience, competitive advantages, and a clear understanding of the client's requirements. Effective bid writing increases the chances of winning tenders by presenting a compelling case to the client and demonstrating that the company is the best fit for the project.

Learning bid writing is crucial as it equips businesses with the skills and knowledge to create well-structured and persuasive bids. It allows businesses to showcase their strengths, differentiate themselves from competitors, and effectively communicate their value proposition to potential clients. By learning bid writing, businesses can significantly increase their success rate in winning tenders, leading to growth, increased revenue, and expanded opportunities.

A few steps that help:

Understand the Tendering Process:

Research the different stages involved in the tendering process, such as pre-qualification, expression of interest, and submission of formal bids.

Understand the specific requirements of public sector tenders, such as complying with procurement regulations or using designated tender platforms.

Research Tendering Guidelines:

Carefully review the tender documents provided by the client, including the Request for Proposal (RFP) or Invitation to Tender (ITT).

Pay attention to evaluation criteria, submission deadlines, required documents, and any specific formatting or content guidelines.

Analyse Successful Bids:

Study successful bids in your industry or sector. For example, analyse a winning bid for a construction project or a service contract.

Look for common elements such as clear value propositions, well-structured responses, strong evidence of capabilities, and persuasive language.

Develop Strong Proposal Writing Skills:

Focus on writing clear, concise, and persuasive proposals that address the client's requirements.

Use compelling language to demonstrate your unique expertise and differentiate your bid from competitors. For example, highlight past achievements, relevant experience, and key differentiators.

Conduct Thorough Research:

Research the client's organisation, including their mission, values, and strategic priorities.

Understand the client's industry, competitors, and current challenges to tailor your bid accordingly. For instance, if the client is in the healthcare sector, highlight your experience in delivering healthcare-specific solutions.

Seek Training and Guidance:

Attend bid writing workshops or webinars conducted by professional organisations or industry experts.

Engage with bid writing consultants who can provide personalised guidance and tips based on their experience with successful tenders.

Practise Writing Bids:

Practise writing bids for different scenarios. For instance, create a hypothetical bid for a software development project or a consultancy service.

Refine your writing skills by receiving feedback from experienced bid writers or mentors, and make necessary revisions to improve your bid quality.

Collaborate with Industry Peers:

Engage with other bid writers or professionals in your industry through online forums or networking events.

Exchange best practices, share insights, and learn from their experiences in tendering for various projects.

Gain Experience through Subcontracting:

Collaborate with established companies by subcontracting on their bids.

This allows you to gain practical experience in the tendering process and understand the dynamics of successful bid preparation.

Learn from Unsuccessful Bids:

Review unsuccessful bids to identify areas for improvement.

Assess the weaknesses in your bid and learn from the feedback provided by the client or evaluators to enhance your future bids.

Keep Up with Industry Trends:

Subscribe to industry publications, newsletters, or online forums to stay updated on the latest trends and developments in bid writing.

Follow blogs or websites that provide insights into successful bidding strategies or changes in procurement regulations.

Seek Feedback and Continuous Improvement:

Request feedback from clients or evaluators on your bids, even if you are not successful.

Use their feedback to identify areas for improvement, refine your bid writing approach, and increase your chances of success in future tenders.

By incorporating these examples, you can apply each step effectively in your bid writing journey. Remember that practice, continuous improvement, and staying up-to-date with industry trends are essential for mastering the art of winning tenders.

<u>How to improve copywriting for tenders</u>

Understand the Bid Requirements: Begin by thoroughly understanding the bid requirements and the client's needs. Study the request for proposal (RFP) or tender documents to grasp the specific objectives, evaluation criteria, and submission guidelines.

Research the Client and Their Industry: Conduct extensive research on the client, their industry, and their competitors. Gain an in-depth understanding of their unique challenges, goals, and values. This research will help you tailor your bid to resonate with the client and demonstrate your comprehension of their specific requirements.

Develop a Compelling Executive Summary: Craft a captivating executive summary that provides a concise overview of your bid. Highlight the key benefits and outcomes the client can expect from your proposal. Make it compelling and persuasive to capture the client's attention right from the start.

Focus on Value Proposition: Clearly articulate the unique value proposition of your bid. Showcase how your solution addresses the client's pain points and offers tangible benefits. Emphasise the value they will receive by choosing your bid over competitors.

Use Clear and Persuasive Language: Write in a clear and persuasive manner. Use concise sentences and avoid jargon or complex terminology. Communicate your ideas effectively, ensuring that the client understands the value and benefits of selecting your bid.

Structure Your Bid Effectively: Organise your bid in a logical and coherent manner. Use headings, subheadings, and bullet points to improve readability and help the client navigate through the document. Clearly label each section to make it easy for evaluators to find the information they need.

Provide Supporting Evidence: Substantiate your claims with evidence and data. Include case studies, testimonials, or relevant statistics to validate your capabilities and track record. Provide tangible proof of your expertise and success in similar projects.

Address the Client's Concerns: Anticipate and address the client's potential concerns or objections within your bid. Show empathy and provide solutions or explanations that alleviate any doubts they may have. This demonstrates your commitment to understanding their needs and building trust.

Use Visuals and Graphics: Incorporate visuals and graphics strategically to enhance the visual appeal of your bid. Use charts, graphs, infographics, or images to present data, project timelines, or other relevant information. Visual elements can help convey complex information in a more digestible format.

Edit and Proofread Carefully: Take the time to carefully edit and proofread your bid. Check for grammar, punctuation, and spelling errors. Ensure that your writing is clear, concise, and error-free. A well-edited bid reflects professionalism and attention to detail.

Seek Feedback and Continuous Improvement: Share your bid with colleagues or industry professionals for feedback. Actively seek constructive criticism and identify areas for improvement. Use feedback to refine your copywriting skills and enhance future bids.

Learn from Successful Bids: Study successful bids in your industry to understand what makes them stand out. Analyse their structure, language, and presentation. Learn from their strengths and incorporate effective techniques into your own bid writing.

Attend Bid Writing Workshops or Courses: Consider attending bid writing workshops or enrolling in courses focused on bid writing. These learning opportunities can provide valuable insights, best practices, and hands-on exercises to enhance your bid writing skills.

Practice Regularly: Regularly practice writing bids to improve your skills. Challenge yourself with different scenarios, industries, and types of bids. The more you practice, the more comfortable and proficient you will become in crafting persuasive bid copy.

Stay Updated with Bid Writing Trends: Stay informed about the latest trends and innovations in bid writing. Follow industry publications, attend webinars, and participate in industry forums or associations to stay up-to-date with the evolving landscape of bid writing.

By following this guide and continually refining your bid writing skills, you can increase your chances of success and win more bids. Remember to tailor your approach to each bid opportunity, showcase your unique value proposition, and communicate effectively with the client. With dedication and practice, you can become a skilled bid writer and secure lucrative opportunities for your business.

Cultivating the Art of Naming

Where competition is fierce and attention spans are fleeting, a solitary word holds immense power - your brand name. It acts as the gateway to your business, leaving a lasting impression that can either propel you to success or hinder your progress. A well-chosen name possesses the ability to captivate, engage, and etch itself in the minds of your customers. Let's delve into why names are crucial and how they can shape the destiny of your brand.

The Art of Recognition: A name that resonates Consider iconic brands like Nike, Apple, or Coca-Cola. These names effortlessly evoke images, emotions, and associations. They are ingrained in our collective consciousness. A strong brand name generates recognition and recall, ensuring that when customers require a product or service within your niche, your name springs to mind effortlessly.

The Power of Differentiation: Standing out from the crowd In an overcrowded marketplace, a distinctive and memorable name becomes your competitive edge. It's your opportunity to establish a unique identity that sets you apart from the sea of uniformity. Think about brands like Tesla or Uber- their names instantly signal a departure from convention and symbolise innovation and disruption.

A Window to Your Brand's Soul: Personality and Values Your brand name has the potential to convey a wealth of information about your values, personality, and ethos. It becomes the conduit for shaping perceptions and forging connections with your target audience. Innocent Drinks, with its playful and whimsical name, conveys a commitment to naturalness and purity that resonates with health-conscious consumers.

Crafting the Promise: Communicating your value proposition A well-chosen name can encapsulate your unique selling proposition and communicate the benefits of your product or service. Consider Airbnb, where the name suggests the idea of finding a temporary home away from home, igniting feelings of comfort, adventure, and exploration.

The Power of Word-of-Mouth: Spreading the buzz A name that is simple, memorable, and easy to share can become a catalyst for word-of-mouth referrals. When people can effortlessly recall and pass along your name, it amplifies your brand's visibility and expands your reach. Just think of how Google became a household name synonymous with online search.

The Cultural Code: Bridging boundaries and embracing diversity In a globally interconnected world, names should transcend borders and resonate across cultures. A culturally sensitive and linguistically adaptable name ensures that your brand is embraced worldwide. Chevrolet learned this the hard way when the Nova model faced challenges in Spanish-speaking countries, as "no va" translates to "doesn't go."

Evolving with Vision: Adaptability and scalability Your brand name should possess the flexibility to grow and evolve alongside your business. It should adapt to encompass new product lines, ventures, or even unforeseen opportunities. Amazon, initially an online bookstore, seamlessly transitioned into a global e-commerce giant, leveraging its name to symbolise limitless exploration and an extensive range of offerings.

The Legal Fortress: Safeguarding your brand identity Selecting a name that is legally available and distinctive safeguards the integrity of your brand. Registering trademarks and securing domain names protect your business from potential conflicts and imitations, providing a solid foundation for growth and protection.

The power of a name cannot be underestimated. It's a strategic decision that demands thoughtful consideration, creativity, and a deep understanding of your target audience. So, take a moment to reflect on the immense potential held within a single word- your brand name. Utilise its power wisely, and witness its role as the catalyst for your brand's journey towards greatness.

Imagine a successful entrepreneur named Alex, who had a game-changing idea for a revolutionary fitness app. This app seamlessly combined personalised workout plans, nutrition tracking, and virtual coaching to help users achieve their fitness goals. Alex understood that the name of the app would play a vital role in its success, and he was determined to find the perfect name that would captivate his target audience and propel his product to viral fame.

After extensive brainstorming sessions and market research, Alex arrived at the name "FitGenius." This name perfectly encapsulated the app's core concept of delivering personalised fitness solutions through cutting-edge technology. It evoked a sense of intelligence, innovation, and expertise, aligning perfectly with the app's value proposition.

To ensure that FitGenius would stand out in the highly competitive fitness app market, Alex enlisted the expertise of a renowned branding agency. Together, they crafted a visually striking logo that combined elements of fitness, technology, and inspiration. The logo, along with the carefully chosen name, created a cohesive and memorable brand identity that resonated with fitness enthusiasts.

When FitGenius made its official debut, Alex launched a comprehensive marketing campaign to generate buzz and drive user adoption. He leveraged social media platforms, collaborated with fitness influencers, and even sponsored local fitness events. The name "FitGenius" caught the attention of fitness enthusiasts who were looking for an innovative and intelligent solution to their fitness challenges.

The impact of FitGenius was remarkable. Within weeks of its launch, the app gained viral traction, accumulating thousands of downloads and positive reviews. Fitness enthusiasts praised the app's intuitive interface, personalised workout plans, and the seamless integration of nutrition tracking. FitGenius became the go-to fitness app for individuals seeking a smart and effective way to achieve their fitness goals.

Real data and customer testimonials affirmed the success of FitGenius. It achieved an impressive 4.8-star rating on app stores, with over 90% of users expressing high satisfaction with the app's features and performance. The name "FitGenius" became synonymous with cutting-edge fitness technology, and the brand recognition soared within the fitness community.

Alex's well-executed strategy, combined with the powerful name "FitGenius," propelled the app to new heights. Within the first year, FitGenius surpassed the 1 million user mark and generated significant revenue through premium subscriptions and in-app purchases. The app's success not only transformed Alex's business but also empowered countless individuals to lead healthier and more fulfilling lives.

By selecting a name that resonates with the target audience and effectively communicates the product's value proposition, entrepreneurs can create a strong brand identity, fuel growth, and establish themselves as industry leaders.

In the early days of Amazon, its founder, Jeff Bezos, recognised the critical importance of selecting the right name for his ambitious online marketplace. He understood that the name needed to capture the essence of his vision and resonate with customers on a global scale. The story behind the name "Amazon" reflects the meticulous planning and strategic thinking that went into its selection.

Jeff Bezos wanted a name that conveyed the vastness and diversity of the products available on his platform. He wanted to create an online marketplace that could offer everything from A to Z, catering to customers' diverse needs. With this vision in mind, he began exploring different naming options.

During his research, Bezos stumbled upon the name "Amazon" while flipping through a dictionary. He was immediately drawn to the word's powerful imagery and the association with the Amazon River, the largest river in the world, known for its immense sise and abundance. The name perfectly embodied his vision of a limitless marketplace that offered an extensive selection of products.

Beyond the strong imagery, Bezos also recognised the strategic advantages of the name "Amazon." It would position his company at the top of alphabetical lists, giving it a prominent position in directories and search results. This simple yet effective strategy would help increase visibility and attract more customers to the platform.

The careful selection of the name "Amazon" proved to be a masterstroke. It captured the attention of customers, piquing their curiosity and encouraging them to explore the wide range of products available on the platform. The name became synonymous with convenience, variety, and limitless possibilities.

As Amazon's success soared, the name became deeply embedded in the global consciousness. Today, Amazon is not only the world's largest online marketplace but also a multinational conglomerate encompassing various industries. The name has become a household brand, representing not just e-commerce but also innovation, customer-centricity, and disruption.

The well-planned selection of the name "Amazon" played a significant role in the company's success. It reflected Jeff Bezos' strategic thinking, his vision for a vast marketplace, and his understanding of the importance of brand positioning. The name became a catalyst for Amazon's growth and dominance in the e-commerce industry, showcasing the power of a well-chosen and meticulously planned brand name.

I've had numerous discussions with entrepreneurs regarding the naming of their new products, services, or business ventures. It often goes like this: they seek my opinion on various name options and then proceed to explain the reasoning behind each name. But here's the crux of the matter – if you have to explain the name, it's already a missed opportunity. The name should speak for itself and instantly convey the nature of your offering. This principle applies to both prominent brands and small businesses alike.

Choosing the right name for your products, services, or businesses is a crucial step in establishing a strong brand identity and effectively communicating what you offer to your target audience. Here is a step-by-step guide on how to name your offerings and why each step is important, along with examples and case studies to illustrate their significance.

Understand Your Offering: Start by gaining a deep understanding of your products, services, or business. Consider their unique features, benefits, and the problems they solve. This step helps you identify the key elements that should be reflected in the name.

Example: Let's say you're launching a new range of eco-friendly cleaning products that are safe for the environment. Understanding the environmentally friendly aspect and the effectiveness of your products will guide your name selection process.

Define Your Target Audience: Clearly define your target audience, their demographics, preferences, and values. Understanding your audience helps you choose a name that resonates with them and creates a connection.

Example: If your target audience consists of health-conscious individuals who prioritise sustainable living, a name that highlights the eco-friendly nature of your products, such as "GreenEarth Clean," would be relevant and appealing.

Brainstorm Keywords and Concepts: Brainstorm a list of keywords, phrases, and concepts associated with your offerings. Consider the emotions and associations you want your name to evoke. This step helps you generate ideas and explore different naming possibilities.

Example: For a new online fashion boutique targeting young, trendy individuals, keywords like "style," "fashion," "chic," and "trend" could be considered as you brainstorm potential names.

Evaluate Naming Options: Narrow down your list of potential names and evaluate them based on several criteria, including memorability, uniqueness, ease of pronunciation, and relevance to your brand and offerings. Consider how the name aligns with your brand values and positioning.

Example: If you're starting a coffee shop with a cosy, vintage ambiance, names like "Brew & Co." or "Retro Beans" might evoke the desired atmosphere and resonate with your target audience.

Conduct Market Research: Before finalising a name, conduct market research to ensure it is not already in use by a competitor. This step helps you avoid legal issues and ensures your chosen name stands out in the market.

Example: If you plan to launch a digital marketing agency and have selected the name "Digital Boost," conducting a thorough search will help you confirm that no other agency is operating under a similar name in your industry.

Case Study: The company "Jaguar" named after the sleek and powerful big cat. The name effectively reflects the brand's focus on luxury, elegance, and high-performance vehicles.

Seek Feedback: Once you have a shortlist of potential names, seek feedback from impartial individuals, preferably from your target audience. Their input will provide valuable insights into how the names are perceived and help you identify any unintended associations or confusion.

Example: If you're considering two potential names for a fitness studio, "FitLife" and "ActiveZone," seeking feedback from fitness enthusiasts will help you understand which name resonates better and conveys the desired brand image.

Test with Focus Groups: If feasible, conduct focus groups to gather more detailed feedback on your shortlisted names. This step allows for deeper insights into consumer preferences and perceptions, helping you make an informed decision.

Example: A software company organising focus groups to test potential names for their project management tool. The feedback received can highlight any potential concerns or associations that may influence the final name choice.

Choosing the right name for your products, services, or businesses is essential as it plays a significant role in shaping your brand's identity and perception in the market. A well-chosen name can attract attention, resonate with your target audience, differentiate you from competitors

Imagine you're starting a plumbing repair business. Instead of a vague name like Aqua Solutions, which demands explanation, opt for a clear and straightforward name like Swift Plumbing Services. This immediately communicates your core service and what you stand for, leaving no room for ambiguity.

Here are some practical tips to guide you in selecting an effective name:

Embrace Simplicity: Aim for a name that is easy to pronounce, spell, and remember. Complexity can lead to confusion and hinder brand recognition.

Reflect Your Offering: Align your name with the essence of your product, service, or business. Consider the benefits, unique features, or the problem you solve. For instance, if you're launching a natural skincare brand, a name like PureGlow or OrganicRevive would clearly communicate your focus.

Understand Your Target Market: Conduct research and analyse your target audience's preferences, language, and cultural context. Ensure the name resonates with them and avoids any unintended negative connotations.

Test for Clarity: Seek feedback from impartial individuals within your target market. Present potential names and ask for their immediate associations and understanding. Their input will help you assess clarity and identify any confusing elements.

Ensure Availability: Undertake a comprehensive search to ensure the name is not trademarked or already in use by a similar business. Securing a unique and legally available name will safeguard your brand identity.

Descriptive Names: Opt for a name that clearly describes the nature of your offering. This approach helps potential customers immediately understand what your business is all about. Examples: QuickBooks, PayPal.

Evocative Names: Select names that evoke specific emotions or feelings related to your brand or offering. These names create a strong association with your product or service. Examples: Dove, Apple.

Brandable Names: Create a unique and memorable name that can become synonymous with your brand. These names may not have a direct connection to your offering but are catchy and distinguishable. Examples: Google, Nike.

Keyword-based Names: Incorporate relevant keywords or industry-specific terms in your name to improve search engine visibility and clearly indicate your area of expertise. Examples: TechCrunch, MarketingProfs.

Acronym Names: Use initials or abbreviations to create a short and snappy name. This strategy works well when the acronym is easily recognisable or represents a well-known phrase or concept. Examples: IBM (International Business Machines), UPS (United Parcel Service).

Compound Names: Combine two or more words to form a new name that captures the essence of your business. This approach allows for creativity and can result in unique and memorable names. Examples: Microsoft (Microcomputer + Software), LinkedIn (Link + Network).

Inventive Names: Create a completely new and original name that is not derived from any existing words. These names can be coined or invented and give your brand a distinct identity. Examples: Xerox, Kodak.

Location-based Names: Incorporate a specific geographic location in your name to highlight your local presence or target a specific regional audience. Examples: London Eye, New York Times.

Metaphorical Names: Use metaphors or symbolic names that represent the qualities or values associated with your offering. These names can evoke a sense of meaning or story. Examples: Adobe, Amazon.

Personal Names: Consider using your own name or the name of a founder or key figure associated with your business. This strategy adds a personal touch and can help build trust and credibility. Examples: Ford, Chanel.

By selecting a clear and meaningful name, you not only facilitate understanding for your target audience but also establish a strong foundation for your brand. Remember, your name is a vital component of your brand's identity and communication strategy. With careful consideration and a focus on clarity, you can make a lasting impression and stand out in a competitive market.

Here are a few ideas for how you can approach this now:

Define Your Brand Identity: For example, if you're starting a sustainable clothing brand targeting eco-conscious millennials, your brand identity might be focused on sustainability, modernity, and ethical fashion.

Brainstorm Keywords and Concepts: In this case, you could brainstorm keywords like "green," "eco," "conscious," "modern," "style," "fashion," "sustainability," "ethical," and "millennials."

Wordplay and Combination: Combine relevant keywords and experiment with wordplay. For instance, you could explore combinations like "EcoStyle," "GreenChic," or "ConsciousCouture." These names capture the essence of sustainability and fashion while being memorable and engaging.

Check Availability: Research the availability of these names by conducting trademark searches, checking domain availability (e.g., ecostyle.co.uk), and ensuring the names are not already used by similar businesses.

Test with Your Target Audience: Share the top name choices with your target audience or a focus group. Get their feedback and reactions to understand if the names resonate with them and align with their perception of your brand.

Consider Branding and Long-Term Viability: Evaluate how well each name aligns with your brand's visual identity. For example, imagine how each name would look in a logo and other marketing materials. Consider if the name allows room for future expansion or diversification of your product offerings.

Narrow Down and Refine: Based on the feedback and insights gathered, narrow down your list to the strongest contenders. For instance, after testing the names, you may find that "EcoStyle" resonates the most with your target audience and aligns well with your brand identity.

Check Linguistic and Cultural Considerations: Ensure the chosen name does not have negative connotations or unintended meanings in relevant languages or cultural contexts. For example, you would want to ensure that "EcoStyle" doesn't mean something negative or offensive in another language.

Seek Legal Advice: Consult with a legal professional or trademark specialist to ensure that "EcoStyle" or any other chosen name can be legally protected and registered as a trademark.

Test for Availability Again: Before finalising your decision, recheck the availability of trademarks, domain names (e.g., ecostyle.co.uk), and social media handles to secure your online presence and brand consistency.

By following these steps and using the examples provided, you can see how the exercise helps you generate creative name ideas, evaluate their viability, and refine them to find the perfect fit for your business or product. Remember to adapt the process to your specific industry and target audience to achieve the best results.

How to Reach Your Target Group with Precision

In the bustling world of entrepreneurship, there lived a determined businessperson named Alex. Armed with a brilliant business idea, Alex embarked on a mission to conquer the market and reach their target customers. However, they faced numerous challenges along the way, grappling with connecting to their audience and converting leads into sales. But as the saying goes, every great story has a turning point.

One fine day, Alex realised the importance of dedicating ample time and effort to truly understand their target customers. They set out on a journey to unravel the secrets of reaching and engaging their audience in a manner that would lead to sales and growth.

Step by step, Alex began their quest. They dived deep into researching their target audience, seeking to unveil their demographics, interests, and pain points. It was an arduous endeavour, filled with extensive market research, surveys, and interviews. But Alex persevered, determined to gain the insights needed to craft a bespoke approach.

Armed with a newfound understanding of their target customers, Alex focused on selecting the right communication channels. They knew that a scattergun approach wouldn't suffice. Instead, they analysed different platforms and channels, considering the preferences and behaviours of their audience. Social media platforms such as Facebook, Twitter, and LinkedIn became their trusted allies, alongside industry-specific forums and networking events.

With the channels in place, Alex turned their attention to crafting compelling messages that would captivate their audience. They realised the power of personalised communication, addressing the unique pain points and desires of their customers. Through careful language crafting, storytelling, and a touch of creativity, Alex forged a strong connection with their target audience.

But the journey didn't end there. Alex understood the importance of building relationships and trust. They actively engaged with their audience, offering valuable content, promptly responding to queries, and seeking feedback. This approach helped establish credibility and fostered a sense of trust and loyalty. Customers transformed from mere buyers to ardent advocates for Alex's business.

As the story unfolded, Alex's business experienced a remarkable transformation. Conversion rates skyrocketed, customer satisfaction reached unprecedented levels, and word of mouth spread like wildfire. Through their unwavering dedication to understanding their target customers and leveraging effective communication channels, Alex achieved the success they had dreamed of.

Today, Alex's business stands as a shining testament to the power of strategic communication. Their journey from struggle to triumph serves as an inspiration to fellow businesspeople, reminding them of the significance of truly understanding their customers and mastering the art of effective communication. So, let this tale be a reminder to all: with the right understanding and strategy, reaching new customers and achieving business growth is well within reach.

Understanding communication channels and knowing how to use them effectively can have a significant impact on generating sales and growing your business.

Here's why it's important:

Reach the Right People: Different channels attract different audiences. By understanding your target customers, you can select the best channels to reach them. This ensures your messages are seen by the right people, increasing the likelihood of converting them into customers.

Get Noticed: Utilising multiple channels enhances your brand's visibility. By establishing a presence on various platforms such as social media, email, content marketing, and advertising, you can reach a wider audience and connect with potential customers who may be active on different channels.

Engage and Connect: Communication channels provide opportunities to interact with your audience. Engaging with comments, participating in discussions, and responding to inquiries helps build trust, relationships, and a positive brand image.

Establish Authority: By sharing valuable insights and expertise, you can position your brand as an authority in your industry. This attracts customers who recognise your knowledge and rely on your products or services.

Build Customer Relationships: Communication channels enable ongoing relationships with customers. Through email, personalised messaging, and social media, you can nurture loyalty, encourage repeat purchases, and develop long-term relationships.

Make Informed Decisions: Channels that provide data and analytics offer insights into customer behaviour. This helps refine your marketing strategies, target specific segments, and optimise your communication efforts for better results.

Create Sales Opportunities: Effective communication channels guide potential customers towards making a purchase. By addressing their needs, pain points, and providing compelling offers, you can increase sales opportunities.

Drive Business Growth: A well-executed communication strategy contributes to business growth. By reaching new customers, nurturing relationships, and driving sales, you can expand your customer base, increase revenue, and create opportunities for further growth.

Knowledge about your communication channels enable you to identify and use them effectively to target the right audience, enhance brand visibility, engage with customers, establish authority, build relationships, make informed decisions, grasp sales opportunities, and drive business growth. It helps you connect with the right people, at the right time, with the right message, giving you a competitive advantage.

In the ever-evolving world of business, let me introduce you to my dear friend Chris, a budding entrepreneur with an ardent desire to connect with potential customers and propel their business to new heights. Recognising the paramount importance of leveraging diverse communication channels, Chris embarked on an exciting journey to identify the most effective ways to reach their target audience.

Let's delve into their exploration together:

Online Advertising Platforms: Chris swiftly realised the immense potential of platforms such as Google Ads, Facebook Ads, and LinkedIn Ads. They delved into understanding the intricacies of crafting captivating ad campaigns that resonated with their audience's interests and demographics.

For instance, Chris created a compelling Facebook ad campaign that showcased their unique product offerings, driving users to their website for more information.

Social Media Platforms: Chris was acutely aware of the power of social media in engaging potential customers. They strategically established a strong presence on platforms like Instagram, Twitter, and LinkedIn, tailoring their content to captivate each platform's unique user base.

Chris shared visually stunning images of their products on Instagram, accompanied by captivating captions and industry-relevant hashtags, successfully attracting the attention of their target audience.

Email Marketing: Understanding the value of building direct and personalised connections, Chris invested time and effort into email marketing. They implemented effective lead generation strategies and crafted engaging newsletters to nurture relationships with their subscribers.

To build a quality email list, Chris offered a free e-book that resonated with their audience's interests, incentivising visitors to share their email addresses.

Content Marketing: Chris recognised that providing valuable and informative content was key to establishing themselves as an industry expert and gaining the trust of potential customers. They devoted time to creating captivating blog articles, videos, and podcasts that addressed their audience's pain points and provided actionable solutions.

Through a series of insightful blog articles, Chris positioned themselves as a go-to resource for their target audience, establishing credibility and attracting a loyal following.

Influencer Marketing: Chris was keen to tap into the power of influential voices within their industry. They identified key influencers whose audience aligned with their target market and strategically collaborated with them to promote their products or services.

By partnering with a popular fitness influencer, Chris gained exposure to a wider audience. The influencer featured Chris's products in their workout videos and shared positive reviews with their dedicated followers.

Networking and Partnerships: Chris understood the immense value of building relationships with other businesses and professionals in their industry. They actively sought out opportunities for collaborations, joint ventures, and networking events to expand their reach and tap into new customer bases.

By forging a strategic collaboration with a complementary business, Chris created a win-win situation that allowed both parties to benefit from the shared customer base.

A careful and strategic approach will utilise various communication channels. Chris established a comprehensive framework to connect with their potential customers. They understood the significance of targeting the right audience, crafting compelling messages, and harnessing the unique strengths of each platform to maximise their business's growth potential. With unwavering determination, Chris set the stage for success on their entrepreneurial journey.

Email marketing campaigns tailored to the target audience. Example: A software company sends personalised email newsletters highlighting new features and updates to their existing customer base. Case Study: Increased customer engagement and product adoption by 20% through targeted email campaigns. How-to Tip: Segment your email lists based on customer preferences and behaviour for more personalised and relevant messaging.

Hosting webinars or virtual events to engage with prospects. Example: A marketing agency conducts a webinar on effective social media strategies, inviting industry professionals to participate. Case Study: Generated 50% more leads and converted 30% into clients through a series of educational webinars. How-to Tip: Promote your webinar across various channels and provide valuable content that addresses specific pain points of your target audience.

Utilising social media platforms to share valuable content and engage with the target audience. Example: A fashion brand regularly posts visually appealing content on Instagram and engages with followers through comments and direct messages. Case Study: Increased brand awareness and customer engagement by 40% through strategic social media marketing. How-to Tip: Create a content calendar and use social media scheduling tools to maintain a consistent presence and engage with your audience consistently.

Direct mail campaigns targeting specific demographics or industries. Example: A luxury real estate agency sends personalised direct mail packages to high-net-worth individuals in desirable neighbourhoods. Case Study: Achieved a 15% response rate and closed five high-value property sales as a result of targeted direct mail campaigns. How-to Tip: Use data analytics to identify your ideal target audience, and create compelling and personalised direct mail pieces that stand out.

Networking at industry events, conferences, or trade shows. Example: A software startup attends a technology conference to network with potential investors, partners, and clients. Case Study: Secured £500,000 in funding and formed strategic partnerships by networking at industry events. How-to Tip: Prepare an elevator pitch, research attendees beforehand, and actively engage in conversations to build meaningful connections.

Cold calling and following up with personalised phone conversations. Example: A business consulting firm cold calls targeted companies and follows up with personalised proposals and solutions. Case Study: Increased client acquisition by 25% through strategic cold calling and personalised follow-ups. How-to Tip: Research your prospects beforehand, prepare a script or talking points, and focus on building rapport and addressing their pain points.

Content marketing through blog posts, articles, and informative guides. Example: A digital marketing agency consistently publishes blog posts and articles offering valuable tips and insights on SEO. Case Study: Generated 100% more organic traffic and doubled leads through content marketing efforts. How-to Tip: Identify trending topics and frequently asked questions in your industry, and create high-quality, informative content that addresses those topics.

Leveraging search engine optimisation (SEO) techniques to increase online visibility. Example: An e-commerce store optimises its product pages and blog content to rank higher on search engine results pages. Case Study: Increased organic search traffic by 40% and achieved top rankings for targeted keywords. How-to Tip: Conduct keyword research, optimise on-page elements, create high-quality backlinks, and regularly monitor and update your SEO strategy.

Collaborating with influencers or industry experts to reach a wider audience. Example: A fitness brand partners with a popular fitness influencer to promote their products on social media. Case Study: Reached a new audience of over 500,000 potential customers and experienced a 30% increase in sales. How-to Tip: Identify influencers or experts relevant to your industry, build relationships with them, and collaborate on content or promotions that align with your brand.

Participating in online forums or industry-specific communities to engage with prospects. Example: A software developer actively participates in a programming forum, providing helpful insights and solutions to fellow developers. Case Study: Established credibility and gained new clients by engaging in discussions and sharing expertise in online communities. How-to Tip: Find industry-specific forums or communities where your target audience hangs out, and contribute valuable insights without overtly promoting your business.

Offering free trials or demos to showcase the value of products or services. Example: A software-as-a-service (SaaS) company offers a free 14-day trial of their project management software. Case Study: Increased conversion rates by 50% and converted trial users into paying customers through a free trial offering. How-to Tip: Clearly communicate the benefits and value of your product or service, provide an easy sign-up process, and nurture trial users with educational resources and personalised support.

Utilising targeted advertising on platforms like Google Ads or social media ads. Example: An online fashion retailer runs targeted Facebook ads to reach women aged 25-35 interested in sustainable fashion. Case Study: Achieved a 3x return on ad spend and increased website traffic by 50% through targeted advertising campaigns. How-to Tip: Define your target audience, research the platforms they frequent, create compelling ad copy and visuals, and continually optimise and test your ad campaigns.

Engaging in strategic partnerships or joint ventures with complementary businesses. Example: A web design agency partners with a marketing agency to offer comprehensive digital solutions to clients. Case Study: Expanded service offerings and increased client base by leveraging strategic partnerships. How-to Tip: Identify complementary businesses that share your target audience and values, build mutually beneficial partnerships, and collaborate on joint marketing efforts.

Providing educational resources, such as whitepapers or ebooks, to establish thought leadership. Example: A cybersecurity firm publishes a comprehensive whitepaper on data protection best practices for businesses. Case Study: Established credibility as an industry thought leader, generated quality leads, and increased conversions through educational resources. How-to Tip: Identify valuable topics within your industry, conduct in-depth research, and create well-designed, informative resources that provide actionable insights and solutions.

Utilising remarketing techniques to re-engage prospects who have shown interest in the past. Example: An e-commerce store retargets website visitors who abandoned their shopping carts with personalised ads showcasing the abandoned products. Case Study: Increased conversion rates by 30% and recovered lost sales through effective remarketing campaigns. How-to Tip: Install remarketing tags on your website, segment your audience based on their interactions, create personalised ads, and set up remarketing campaigns on platforms like Google Ads or social media.

Creating and distributing press releases to gain media coverage and exposure. Example: A tech startup issues a press release announcing the launch of their innovative mobile app. Case Study: Garnered media attention and increased brand visibility through press release distribution, leading to a significant spike in app downloads. How-to Tip: Craft a compelling press release, research relevant media outlets, distribute it through press release distribution services, and follow up with media contacts for potential coverage.

Implementing referral programmes to encourage satisfied customers to refer others. Example: An online subscription service offers discounts or rewards to customers who refer their friends or colleagues. Case Study: Increased customer acquisition and retention by 25% through a referral programme that incentivised existing customers to refer others. How-to Tip: Design an easy-to-use referral programme, provide incentives that are appealing to your customers, and actively promote it through various channels.

Leveraging video marketing through platforms like YouTube or Vimeo. Example: A cooking instructor creates and shares instructional recipe videos on YouTube to reach a wider audience. Case Study: Gained a substantial following, increased brand awareness, and expanded revenue streams through video marketing efforts. How-to Tip: Identify video content ideas that resonate with your target audience, create high-quality videos with engaging visuals and valuable information, optimise video titles and descriptions for search, and actively promote your videos on relevant platforms.

Engaging in affiliate marketing by partnering with affiliates who promote products or services. Example: An e-commerce store collaborates with influential bloggers or content creators who recommend and promote their products. Case Study: Expanded customer reach, increased website traffic, and boosted sales through affiliate partnerships. How-to Tip: Identify reputable affiliates in your industry, establish mutually beneficial partnerships, provide affiliates with promotional materials and tracking links, and offer competitive commission rates.

Utilising offline advertising channels such as radio, television, or print media. Example: A local car dealership runs radio advertisements targeting their specific geographic area. Case Study: Increased brand visibility and generated qualified leads through targeted offline advertising campaigns. How-to Tip: Identify offline advertising channels that align with your target audience and budget, create compelling ad content, and track and analyse the results to optimise your campaigns.

For a new business, here are some of the easiest communication channels to start with, along with a brief guide on how to utilise them effectively:

Website: Build a professional website to establish an online presence. For example, a bakery could create a website showcasing their products, location, and contact details, allowing customers to place orders online.

Email: Set up a business email address (e.g. info@yourbusiness.com) to communicate professionally. For instance, a marketing agency could send personalised email newsletters to clients, sharing industry insights, tips, and updates.

Social Media: Create accounts on popular social media platforms like Facebook, Instagram, Twitter, or LinkedIn, based on your target audience. An example would be a fitness studio posting workout routines, fitness tips, and success stories on their Instagram page to engage with their followers.

Phone: Ensure you have a dedicated business phone line for customer inquiries. A plumbing service could provide a contact number for customers to call when they need immediate assistance with plumbing issues.

Live Chat: Install live chat software on your website to provide real-time support and engage with website visitors. For instance, an e-commerce store could have a live chat feature to help customers with their purchasing decisions or answer any product-related questions.

Video Conferencing: Utilise video conferencing platforms like Zoom or Microsoft Teams to conduct virtual meetings, presentations, or client consultations. For example, a consulting firm could schedule a video conference with a potential client to discuss project details and provide recommendations.

Business Cards: Design and print professional business cards with essential contact information. A freelance graphic designer could hand out business cards during networking events, featuring their name, profession, website, and contact details.

Online Directories: List your business in relevant online directories like Google My Business, Yelp, or industry-specific directories. A restaurant could create a Google My Business listing, providing information about their location, opening hours, and customer reviews.

Blogging: Start a business blog on your website to share valuable content related to your industry, products, or services. A travel agency could write blog posts about popular destinations, travel tips, and itineraries to inspire and inform potential customers.

Customer Relationship Management (CRM) System: Implement a CRM system like HubSpot, Salesforce, or Zoho to manage and track customer interactions. An example would be a software company using a CRM to track customer enquiries, manage sales pipelines, and provide personalised support.

Remember, choose the communication channels that best suit your business and target audience, and adapt them to meet your specific needs.

<u>Non-Contract Clients</u>

Here's a list of 50 free channels to reach potential customers, along with examples:

Social Media Platforms: Utilise free accounts on platforms like Facebook, Twitter, Instagram, LinkedIn, Pinterest, and TikTok to connect with and engage potential customers.

Content Marketing: Create and share valuable content through blog posts, articles, videos, podcasts, or infographics on your website or other free platforms.

Search Engine Optimisation (SEO): Optimise your website and content to improve organic search visibility on search engines like Google, Bing, and Yahoo.

Email Marketing: Build an email list and send regular newsletters or updates to subscribers.

Word of Mouth: Encourage satisfied customers to spread the word about your business to their networks.

Referral Programmes: Incentivise existing customers to refer new customers by offering discounts, rewards, or exclusive offers.

Online Reviews: Encourage customers to leave positive reviews on platforms like Google My Business, Yelp, Trustpilot, or industry-specific review sites.

Local Business Directories: Create free listings on online directories like Google My Business, Bing Places, or Yelp to increase local visibility.

Social Media Groups and Communities: Engage in relevant groups and communities on platforms like Facebook, LinkedIn, or Reddit to connect with potential customers.

Influencer Partnerships: Collaborate with influencers in your industry who may be willing to promote your products or services in exchange for free samples or other arrangements.

Guest Blogging: Write high-quality guest posts for popular blogs or industry publications to reach their audience and establish yourself as an expert.

Online Forums and Q&A Sites: Participate in forums or Q&A sites like Quora or Reddit to answer questions related to your industry and provide value.

Webinars and Online Workshops: Host free webinars or workshops to share valuable knowledge and establish yourself as an authority in your field.

Podcast Guest Appearances: Reach out to relevant podcasts and offer to be a guest to share insights and promote your business.

YouTube Channel: Create a YouTube channel to share videos related to your industry, tutorials, product demonstrations, or educational content.

Networking Events: Attend local networking events, meetups, or industry conferences to connect with potential customers and industry professionals.

Online Communities: Engage in online communities, forums, or social media groups that are relevant to your target audience.

Online Directories: Create free listings on online directories specific to your industry or niche.

Public Speaking: Offer to speak at industry events or local organisations to showcase your expertise and gain exposure.

Community Involvement: Participate in community events, sponsor local initiatives, or volunteer to create positive brand recognition.

Cross-Promotion: Collaborate with complementary businesses to cross-promote each other's products or services.

Web Directories: Submit your website to web directories to increase visibility and improve search engine rankings.

Online Classifieds: Utilise free classified websites or local classifieds sections to advertise your products or services.

Press Releases: Write and distribute press releases to announce newsworthy updates, product launches, or company milestones.

Online Contests or Giveaways: Run contests or giveaways on social media or your website to attract new customers and create buzz.

Online Review Platforms: Monitor and respond to customer reviews on platforms like Google My Business, Yelp, or Trustpilot to maintain a positive online reputation.

Community Newsletters: Contribute content or advertise in local community newsletters or publications.

Thought Leadership Platforms: Contribute articles or insights to industry-specific platforms or websites to showcase your expertise.

Joint Ventures: Partner with complementary businesses to collaborate on marketing efforts and reach new audiences.

Charity or Non-Profit Partnerships: Support charitable causes or local non-profit organisations to gain exposure and demonstrate corporate social responsibility.

Online Courses or Workshops: Create free online courses or workshops to provide value and build credibility.

Online Product Directories: List your products on online directories or marketplaces specific to your industry or niche.

Collaboration with Micro-Influencers: Partner with micro-influencers who have a smaller but engaged audience in your target market.

LinkedIn Publishing: Publish articles or thought leadership content on LinkedIn's publishing platform.

Local Meetups or Workshops: Host or participate in local meetups or workshops to connect with potential customers in your area.

Online Communities: Engage in online communities, forums, or social media groups that are relevant to your target audience.

Online Directories: Create free listings on online directories specific to your industry or niche.

LinkedIn Publishing: Publish articles or thought leadership content on LinkedIn's publishing platform.

Local Meetups or Workshops: Host or participate in local meetups or workshops to connect with potential customers in your area.

Online Communities: Engage in online communities, forums, or social media groups that are relevant to your target audience.

Cross-Promotion: Collaborate with complementary businesses to cross-promote each other's products or services.

Web Directories: Submit your website to web directories to increase visibility and improve search engine rankings.

Online Classifieds: Utilise free classified websites or local classifieds sections to advertise your products or services.

Press Releases: Write and distribute press releases to announce newsworthy updates, product launches, or company milestones.

Online Contests or Giveaways: Run contests or giveaways on social media or your website to attract new customers and create buzz.

Online Review Platforms: Monitor and respond to customer reviews on platforms like Google My Business, Yelp, or Trustpilot to maintain a positive online reputation.

Community Newsletters: Contribute content or advertise in local community newsletters or publications.

Thought Leadership Platforms: Contribute articles or insights to industry-specific platforms or websites to showcase your expertise.

Joint Ventures: Partner with complementary businesses to collaborate on marketing efforts and reach new audiences.

Charity or Non-Profit Partnerships: Support charitable causes or local non-profit organisations to gain exposure and demonstrate corporate social responsibility.

It's important to choose the channels that align with your target audience and marketing objectives. Experiment with different channels and analyse the results to determine the most effective strategies for your business.

The effectiveness of each communication channel may vary depending on your target audience and industry. It's important to monitor and measure the results of your efforts to identify the most effective channels for your business.

Here is a lift of 50 paid channels that you can use:

Social Media Advertising (Facebook Ads, Instagram Ads, Twitter Ads) - Promoting your products or services through targeted adverts on social media platforms.

Pay-Per-Click (PPC) Advertising (Google Ads, Bing Ads) - Running adverts on search engines where you pay when someone clicks on your advert.

Display Advertising on relevant websites and blogs - Placing banner adverts on websites or blogs that cater to your target audience.

Influencer Marketing (Collaborating with influencers in your industry) - Partnering with popular social media influencers to promote your brand or products to their followers.

Native Advertising (Sponsored content on relevant platforms) - Creating content that seamlessly blends with the platform it's published on, such as sponsored articles or videos.

Affiliate Marketing (Paying affiliates for driving sales or leads) - Offering a commission to affiliates who refer customers to your business and make a purchase.

Search Engine Marketing (SEM) through paid search campaigns - Running targeted adverts on search engines to appear prominently in search results.

Sponsored Content or Advertorials on industry websites or publications - Paying for sponsored articles or advertorials in industry-specific publications or websites.

Retargeting or Remarketing Ads to reach visitors who have shown interest - Displaying adverts to people who have previously visited your website or shown interest in your products.

Direct Mail Advertising (Sending physical mail to targeted prospects) - Sending promotional materials or offers directly to potential customers' mailboxes.

Influencer Collaborations - Collaborating with influencers on specific campaigns or content creation to reach their audience.

Mobile Advertising - Running adverts on mobile apps or targeting mobile device users with adverts that appear on their screens.

Influencer Advertising - Paying influencers to create and share content featuring your brand or products on their social media channels.

Video Advertising - Running video adverts on platforms like YouTube or social media to engage with audiences through visual content.

Geo-targeted Advertising - Targeting adverts specifically to users in a particular geographic location, such as city or region.

Native Advertising - Creating sponsored content that blends seamlessly with the platform it's published on, matching the format and style.

Affiliate Networks - Joining affiliate networks where you can tap into a network of affiliates who promote your products or services.

Display Retargeting - Displaying adverts to users who have previously visited your website but didn't convert, with the aim of bringing them back.

Influencer Takeovers - Allowing influencers to take over your social media accounts for a day or specific event to engage their audience.

Virtual Events - Hosting or sponsoring virtual events, such as webinars or conferences, to reach a targeted audience online.

Online Banner Advertising - Placing banner adverts on websites or blogs that attract your target audience's attention.

Influencer Outreach (Sponsored posts or product placements) - Reaching out to influencers to create sponsored posts or feature your products in their content.

SMS Marketing (Text message marketing) - Sending targeted promotional messages or offers via text messages to opted-in customers.

Programmatic Advertising - Utilising automated systems to buy and optimise adverts across various online platforms.

Podcast Advertising - Sponsoring or advertising on popular podcasts that cater to your target audience.

Outdoor Advertising - Placing adverts on billboards, bus shelters, or other outdoor locations to reach a wider audience.

Content Syndication - Distributing your content on other platforms or websites to expand your reach.

Television Advertising - Running commercials on local or national television networks during targeted time slots.

Radio Advertising - Advertising on popular radio stations to reach a specific audience in your target market.

Sponsorship of Events or Conferences - Sponsoring industry events or conferences to gain exposure and reach a relevant audience.

Trade Show Exhibitions or Stands - Participating in trade shows or exhibitions to showcase your products or services directly to potential customers.

Influencer Events or Meetups - Hosting or participating in events where influencers and their followers can engage with your brand.

Influencer Affiliate Marketing - Collaborating with influencers who promote your products or services and earn a commission for each sale they generate.

Product Placement in TV shows or films - Paying for your product or brand to be featured in popular TV shows or films.

Influencer Endorsements on Social Media - Influencers endorsing your products or services through positive reviews or testimonials on social media.

LinkedIn Advertising (Sponsored posts, InMail, or Text Ads) - Running adverts on LinkedIn to target professionals and decision-makers in specific industries.

Online Video Streaming Ads (YouTube, Twitch) - Placing adverts on popular online video streaming platforms to reach a large and engaged audience.

Programmatic TV Advertising - Targeting TV adverts to specific demographics or regions using programmatic technology.

In-App Advertising - Displaying adverts within mobile applications to target users while they engage with their favourite apps.

Digital Out-of-Home Advertising - Using digital screens in high-traffic areas to display dynamic adverts and capture the attention of passersby.

Content Discovery Platforms (Taboola, Outbrain) - Promoting your content through native adverts on content discovery platforms to reach a wider audience.

Podcast Sponsorships or Ad Inserts - Sponsoring or inserting adverts within popular podcasts to reach a targeted and engaged audience.

Influencer Webinars or Live Streams - Collaborating with influencers to co-host webinars or live streams that provide value to their audience.

Interactive Advertising - Creating interactive advert experiences that engage users through quizzes, games, or interactive videos.

Influencer Contests or Giveaways - Partnering with influencers to run contests or giveaways that involve their audience and promote your brand.

Influencer-Owned E-commerce Stores - Selling your products or services through influencers' own e-commerce stores or marketplaces.

Paid Product Reviews or Sponsored Blog Posts - Paying bloggers or influencers to write reviews or create sponsored content featuring your products.

Content Recommendation Widgets - Promoting your content through recommendation widgets on popular websites to drive traffic.

Influencer Guest Posts on High-Traffic Blogs - Collaborating with influencers to create guest posts on popular blogs in your industry.

Influencer Takeovers on Social Media Channels - Allowing influencers to take control of your social media channels for a day to engage their audience and promote your brand.

Remember to consider your target audience, campaign goals, and budget when choosing paid communication channels. It's essential to monitor and optimise your campaigns to ensure the best results and return on investment.

<u>Contract Clients</u>

Reaching out to contracting authorities and procurement teams can be a thrilling opportunity to showcase your business and identify current or future contract opportunities. Whilst the best approach may vary depending on the industry and organisation, here are some engaging strategies to capture their attention:

Craft a Compelling Story: Instead of simply listing your offerings, tell a captivating story that resonates with the contracting authorities. Share how your business journey aligns with their mission or how you've successfully helped other organisations overcome similar challenges. Storytelling humanises your approach and makes it more memorable.

Show Your Unique Value Proposition: Highlight what sets you apart from competitors. Whether it's your innovative solutions, exceptional track record, or industry accolades, emphasise the aspects that make you stand out. Be confident in communicating the value you bring to the table.

Interactive Presentations: Instead of relying solely on traditional methods like emails or phone calls, consider creating interactive presentations that showcase your capabilities. Use visuals, videos, or even virtual reality to engage the procurement teams and leave a lasting impression.

Engage Through Social Media: Utilise the power of social media to connect with contracting authorities and procurement teams. Share behind-the-scenes glimpses of your work, success stories, and thought-provoking content related to procurement trends. Engage in meaningful conversations and demonstrate your expertise through valuable insights.

Offer Incentives: Capture their attention by offering incentives such as exclusive discounts, free trials, or value-added services. These incentives not only show your commitment but also provide an extra incentive for procurement teams to consider your offering.

Collaborate on Pilot Projects: Propose collaboration on pilot projects or proof-of-concept initiatives. This allows the contracting authorities to experience first-hand the value you bring and build trust in your capabilities. Successful pilot projects can open doors to larger contracts in the future.

Host Informative Webinars: Organise webinars that address procurement-related challenges or industry trends. Invite contracting authorities and procurement teams to participate and offer valuable insights and solutions. This positions you as a knowledgeable resource and creates opportunities for further engagement.

Personalised Videos: Break through the traditional communication barriers by sending personalised videos to procurement teams. Introduce yourself, explain how your offerings align with their needs, and express your enthusiasm for working together. Video messages add a personal touch and demonstrate your commitment.

Showcase Your Team's Expertise: Highlight the expertise of your team members by sharing their professional achievements, certifications, or industry recognition. Let the contracting authorities know they will be working with a talented and experienced team that can deliver exceptional results.

Gamification: Incorporate gamification elements into your communications. Create interactive quizzes or challenges related to procurement, allowing contracting authorities and procurement teams to test their knowledge whilst simultaneously engaging with your brand.

Creativity and personalisation can make a significant impact when reaching out to contracting authorities and procurement teams. Tailor your approach to their specific needs and objectives, and showcase how your business can be a valuable partner in achieving their goals.

Networking is an invaluable channel strategy when it comes to gaining industry insights in the bidding industry. While some tenders are not publicly published and are shared through invitations only, associations have proven to be exceptionally helpful in obtaining such valuable insights.

In the competitive world of bidding, having access to exclusive opportunities can give your business a distinct advantage. This is where networking comes into play. By actively engaging with industry associations and participating in relevant events, you can establish meaningful connections with key stakeholders, decision-makers, and professionals within the bidding community.

Associations dedicated to the bidding industry provide a platform for professionals to come together, share knowledge, exchange experiences, and build relationships. These associations often organise conferences, seminars, workshops, and networking events that bring industry experts and participants together under one roof. Attending these events offers a golden opportunity to network with peers, potential clients, and even contracting authorities.

Through networking, you can gain valuable insights into upcoming tenders and projects that may not be widely publicised. Word-of-mouth referrals and personal connections within the industry can provide valuable information about invitation-only bids, pre-qualification processes, and upcoming opportunities. By nurturing these relationships, you can position yourself as a trusted and reliable partner, increasing the likelihood of receiving exclusive invitations.

Associations also play a crucial role in disseminating industry news, trends, and best practices. By actively engaging in association activities, such as joining committees or participating in industry forums, you can tap into a wealth of knowledge and stay updated on the latest developments in the bidding industry. This insider knowledge can give you a competitive edge when crafting your bid strategies and tailoring your proposals to meet the specific needs of clients.

Furthermore, networking allows you to gain insights into the expectations, evaluation criteria, and preferences of contracting authorities. By building relationships with professionals involved in the procurement process, you can understand their requirements, gain visibility into their decision-making processes, and align your bid submissions accordingly. This level of understanding and alignment significantly improves your chances of success in the bidding process.

So, networking within industry associations is a powerful strategy for gaining industry insights in the bidding industry. It provides access to exclusive opportunities, fosters valuable relationships, and offers a platform to exchange knowledge and stay updated on industry trends. By actively engaging with associations, you can enhance your bidding strategies, increase your visibility, and position your business as a trusted and preferred partner in the competitive world of bidding.

Here is an expanded list of associations related to procurement or tenders in English-speaking countries:

United Kingdom:

Chartered Institute of Procurement & Supply (CIPS)

Institute of Economic Development (IED)

Society of Procurement Officers in Local Government (SOPO)

Institute of Collaborative Working (ICW)

Association of Proposal Management Professionals UK (APMP UK)

United States:

National Institute of Governmental Purchasing (NIGP)

National Association of State Procurement Officials (NASPO)

National Contract Management Association (NCMA)

Association of Proposal Management Professionals (APMP)

Institute for Supply Management (ISM)

Canada:

Supply Chain Management Association (SCMA)

Public Procurement Canada (PPOC)

Canadian Public Procurement Council (CPPC)

National Association of Procurement Professionals (NAPP)

Canadian Construction Association (CCA)

Australia:

Australasian Procurement and Construction Council (APCC)

Chartered Institute of Procurement & Supply Australasia (CIPS Australasia)

Procurement and Supply Australasia (PASA)

Australian Procurement and Construction Council (APCC)

Australasian Legal Information Institute (AustLII)

New Zealand:

New Zealand Institute of Procurement & Supply (NZIPS)

Procurement Professionals Association of New Zealand (PPANZ)

New Zealand Government Procurement (NZGP)

New Zealand Construction Industry Council (NZCIC)

Chartered Institute of Procurement & Supply New Zealand (CIPS New Zealand)

South Africa:

Chartered Institute of Procurement & Supply South Africa (CIPS South Africa)

South African Supplier Diversity Council (SASDC)

Institute of Risk Management South Africa (IRMSA)

Association of BEE Verification Agencies (ABVA)

South African Council for the Quantity Surveying Profession (SACQSP)

Ireland:

Institute of Public Administration (IPA)

Irish Institute of Purchasing and Materials Management (IIPMM)

Irish Association of Public Procurement Practitioners (IAPP)

Construction Industry Federation (CIF)

Chartered Institute of Procurement & Supply Ireland (CIPS Ireland)

India:

Institute of Supply Chain Management (ISCM)

Indian Institute of Materials Management (IIMM)

All India Management Association (AIMA)

National Institute of Construction Management and Research (NICMAR)

Institute of Public Procurement (IPP)

Singapore:

Singapore Institute of Purchasing and Materials Management (SIPMM)

Singapore Procurement Academy (SPA)

Building and Construction Authority (BCA)

Singapore Institute of Surveyors and Valuers (SISV)

Singapore Institute of Architects (SIA)

Malaysia:

Malaysia Institute of Supply Chain Innovation (MISI)

Malaysian Association of Purchasing and Materials Management (MAPMM)

Malaysian Institute of Architects (PAM)

Construction Industry Development Board Malaysia (CIDB)

Institute of Strategic and International Studies Malaysia (ISIS)

These associations play a crucial role in supporting the procurement community, providing resources, professional development opportunities, and networking platforms. Exploring their websites, events, and membership options can help you stay connected and up-to-date with the latest developments in procurement and tender processes in each respective country.

The swiftest route to uncovering lucrative contracts and tenders lies in harnessing the power of free channels and sources that unveil a wealth of opportunities in countries across the globe. Regardless of your location, whether nestled in the United Kingdom, the United States, Australia, Canada, New Zealand, South Africa, India, Ireland, or Singapore, these complimentary tender sources offer invaluable resources to businesses yearning to broaden their horizons and clinch profitable contracts.

Here is a list that unveils an array of platforms and sources tailored to your industry, enabling you to navigate the landscape of English-speaking countries:

United Kingdom:

eTenders

Sell2Wales

Contracts Finder

ProContract

Tenders Direct

Public Contracts Scotland

Delta eSourcing

Welsh Government Procurement

Scottish Government Procurement

Crown Commercial Service (CCS) Contracts Finder

London Tenders Portal

North East Procurement Organisation (NEPO) Portal

Yorkshire Purchasing Organisation (YPO) eTendering

Eastern Shires Purchasing Organisation (ESPO) Portal

Southern Construction Framework (SCF) Supplier Portal

United States:

Public Purchase

Federal Business Opportunities (FBO)

State of California eProcurement

State of Texas Electronic State Business Daily

New York State Contract Reporter

Pennsylvania eMarketplace Portal

Florida Purchasing Group

Massachusetts Central Register

Illinois Procurement Bulletin

Washington Electronic Business Solution (WEBS)

Ohio Business Gateway

Michigan Bid System

New Jersey Local Government Purchasing System

Georgia Procurement Registry

North Carolina Interactive Purchasing System

Australia:

Tenders.gov.au

AusTender

Victoria Online Tendering System (VOTS)

Western Australian Government Tenders

Queensland Government QTenders

New South Wales eTendering

Northern Territory Tenders

South Australian Tenders and Contracts

Tasmanian Government Tenders

Australian Capital Territory Tenders

Canada:

Buyandsell.gc.ca

BC Bid (British Columbia)

Alberta Purchasing Connection (APC)

Saskatchewan Opportunities Network (SONet)

Manitoba Opportunities Network (MON)

Ontario Tenders Portal

Quebec Tenders

New Brunswick Opportunities Network (NBON)

Prince Edward Island Tenders

Nova Scotia Tenders

Newfoundland and Labrador Tenders

Yukon Government Tenders

Northwest Territories Tenders

Nunavut Tenders

New Zealand:

GETS (Government Electronic Tender Service)

TenderLink

NZ Tenders

TenderSearch

Construction Information Limited (CIL)

LG Tender Box

Tenders.Net

Tenders Direct

iSpec

Wellington Water E-Tendering Portal

South Africa:

eTenders

Government Printing Works (GPW)

Provincial Treasury eTender Bulletin

Department of Public Works eTender Publication Portal

National Treasury eTender Portal

South African National Roads Agency (SANRAL) Tender Bulletin

South African Airways (SAA) Tender Bulletin

Gauteng Provincial Government Tenders

City of Cape Town e-Services Portal

City of Johannesburg e-Tenders

India:

Government eProcurement System (GeM)

eProcurement India

eTenders

Central Public Procurement Portal (CPPP)

Indian Railways eProcurement System

Delhi Government eProcurement Portal

Punjab Government eProcurement System

Tamil Nadu e-Procurement Portal

Andhra Pradesh Government eProcurement Portal

Kerala Government e-Tendering Portal

Ireland:

eTenders Ireland

eTendersNI

Irish Government eTenders

eTenders Public Procurement

Government Contracts.ie

eTenders Supply of Goods and Services

Tenders Electronic Daily (TED) Ireland

InterTradeIreland eTenders

Construction Information Services (CIS)

TenderScout

Singapore:

GeBiz (Singapore Government Electronic Business)

Gebiz Centre

GeBIZ Trading Partner (GTP)

Singapore Tenders

E-Procurement Singapore

GeBIZ Alerts

Government e-Procurement (GePS)

E-Tender Singapore

E-Tendering System (ETS)

E-Quotation System (EQS)

It's always advisable to conduct thorough research and review the specific features, limitations, and eligibility criteria of each platform before making any decisions.

Here is a list of paid platforms:

United Kingdom:

BiP Solutions

Tracker

Supply2Gov

UK Tenders

Constructionline

Proactis

Due North

In-Tend

myTenders

SourceDogg

United States:

BidNet

Onvia

GovWin

eBridge

DemandStar

BidSync

BidNet Direct

Deltek GovWin IQ

Find RFP

BidClerk

Australia:

TenderSearch

TenderLink

Australian Tenders

TenderSearch eProcurement

TenderSearch Contract Reporting

Aconex

Cordell Connect

illion TenderLink

TenderSearch Construction

TenderSearch Infrastructure

Canada:

MERX

Biddingo

BC Bid (British Columbia)

Alberta Purchasing Connection (APC)

SaskTenders (Saskatchewan)

Ontario Tenders Portal

Quebec Tenders

Government of Canada Buyandsell.gc.ca

Atlantic Provinces Tenders Portal

New Brunswick Opportunities Network (NBON)

New Zealand:

GETS (Government Electronic Tender Service)

TenderLink

NZ Tenders

TenderSearch

Construction Information Limited (CIL)

LG Tender Box

Tenders.Net

Tenders Direct

iSpec

Wellington Water E-Tendering Portal

South Africa:

Leads 2 Business

E-Tender

Online Tenders

National Treasury eTender Portal

TenderSure

Tenders.Net

TenderLink

TenderBids

SA-Tenders

iTender

India:

GeM (Government e-Marketplace)

eProcurement India

eTenders

NIC eProcurement System

Tender247

MSTC Limited

Tender Tiger

BidAssist

Government eProcurement System (GePS)

e-Procurement Punjab

Ireland:

eTenders Ireland

eTendersNI

Irish Government eTenders

eTenders Public Procurement

Government Contracts.ie

eTenders Supply of Goods and Services

Tenders Electronic Daily (TED) Ireland

InterTradeIreland eTenders

Construction Information Services (CIS)

TenderScout

United Arab Emirates:

Dubai eSupply Portal

Abu Dhabi Government Tenders

Sharjah Government Tenders

UAE Ministry of Infrastructure Development

Dubai Health Authority eTenders

Ajman Government eTender Portal

Ras Al Khaimah Government eTenders

UAE Ministry of Economy eTenders

Fujairah eTenders

Umm Al Quwain Government eTenders

Singapore:

GeBiz (Singapore Government Electronic Business)

Gebiz Centre

E-Procurement Singapore

Government e-Procurement (GePS)

E-Tender Singapore

Singapore Tenders

E-Tendering System (ETS)

E-Quotation System (EQS)

Singapore Public Sector Panels of Consultants (PSPC)

NUS e-Procurement System

Some free platforms also offer paid options to access additional features and benefits, that's why you see some mentioned in both lists. These paid options provide businesses with enhanced functionalities that can further streamline the tendering process and improve their chances of success.

By opting for a paid subscription or upgrading to a premium account, businesses can unlock features such as advanced search filters, customised alerts, priority notifications, and additional support services. These paid options often cater to the specific needs and requirements of businesses operating in competitive markets or seeking specialised opportunities.

The availability of paid options allows businesses to tailor their experience on the platform and gain a competitive advantage. However, it's crucial to carefully evaluate the benefits and costs associated with these paid options, considering factors such as the frequency of tender participation, the scale of operations, and the potential return on investment.

Ultimately, the decision to explore paid options within free tender platforms should be based on a thorough assessment of the specific features offered and how they align with your business goals and budget.

Whether you choose to leverage the free features or explore the paid options, these tender platforms provide a valuable starting point for businesses to discover and engage with tender opportunities in a cost-effective manner.

Changing Tides: The Power of an Integrated Communications Plan

Philip Kotler, one of the pioneers of modern marketing, once articulated the ultimate goal of marketing: to know and understand the customer so well that the product or service fits them perfectly and sells itself. This principle remains relevant in today's business landscape, where companies are constantly seeking innovative strategies to achieve a deep understanding of their customers and drive impactful marketing campaigns.

One such strategy is Integrated Marketing, a powerful approach that combines various marketing channels and tactics into a seamless and harmonious campaign. By harnessing the strengths of different channels, businesses can create a cohesive brand experience, effectively reach their target audience, and maximise return on investment (ROI).

Integrated Marketing goes beyond the traditional approach of using different channels in isolation. Instead, it embraces the concept of synergy, where each marketing channel complements and reinforces the others, creating a unified and compelling message that resonates with customers. This approach ensures that businesses have a presence across multiple touchpoints, capturing the attention of their audience and guiding them towards desired actions.

In today's fast-paced and interconnected world, customers are inundated with a constant barrage of marketing messages. To stand out from the crowd and make a lasting impact, businesses must deliver a consistent and coordinated message across all channels. Integrated Marketing enables them to achieve just that, creating a holistic brand experience that engages customers at every step of their journey.

By aligning marketing efforts across channels such as digital advertising, social media, content marketing, email campaigns, and offline advertising, businesses can achieve remarkable results. They can optimise their budget by allocating resources to the most effective channels, measure the impact of each channel on their ROI, and make data-driven decisions to continually enhance their strategies.

In this guide, we will delve into the world of Integrated Marketing, exploring its key principles, benefits, and strategies for implementation. We will uncover how businesses can create a seamless brand experience, leverage customer insights to drive targeted campaigns, and measure the impact of their marketing efforts to achieve impressive ROI. Through real-world examples and actionable tips, we will equip you with the knowledge and tools to embark on your own successful Integrated Marketing journey.

When it comes to measuring the success of marketing campaigns, return on investment (ROI) is the ultimate metric. Businesses invest their resources, time, and effort into marketing with the expectation of generating profitable returns. And in many cases, strategic marketing investments have proven to be highly lucrative.

Let's take a look at some real-world examples where marketing investments have resulted in impressive ROI:

Dollar Shave Club: This direct-to-consumer razor company made waves with its viral marketing campaign, "Our Blades Are F***ing Great." By leveraging humorous and unconventional video content, Dollar Shave Club quickly gained attention and attracted a large customer base. The company was acquired by Unilever for a staggering £1 billion, showcasing the tremendous ROI generated through effective marketing strategies.

Airbnb: Through their innovative and captivating marketing campaigns, Airbnb has disrupted the hospitality industry. By focusing on user-generated content and personal storytelling, Airbnb has built a strong brand that resonates with travellers seeking unique accommodation experiences. Their marketing efforts have resulted in exponential growth, with millions of hosts and guests worldwide, demonstrating the power of ROI-driven marketing.

Coca-Cola: As one of the world's most recognisable brands, Coca-Cola has consistently invested in marketing initiatives that have delivered exceptional returns. From their iconic Christmas campaigns to memorable Super Bowl ads, Coca-Cola has mastered the art of connecting with consumers emotionally. These marketing investments have solidified Coca-Cola's position as a global leader in the beverage industry.

In addition to these examples, numerous case studies highlight the significant ROI achieved through strategic marketing investments:

HubSpot: This inbound marketing software company has not only helped businesses transform their marketing strategies but has also experienced remarkable ROI themselves. By implementing inbound marketing techniques, HubSpot generated a 400% increase in lead generation, showcasing the power of their own product.

Blendtec: Through their "Will It Blend?" YouTube series, Blendtec saw a tremendous boost in brand awareness and sales. By blending unusual items such as iPhones and golf balls, the company showcased the strength and effectiveness of their blenders. This marketing campaign led to a 700% increase in sales, demonstrating the impact of creative and engaging content.

Old Spice: With their "The Man Your Man Could Smell Like" campaign, Old Spice successfully repositioned their brand and targeted a younger audience. This humorous and memorable campaign generated a significant increase in sales, with a reported 107% growth in body wash sales alone.

These examples and case studies emphasise the importance of ROI-driven marketing strategies. By investing in targeted and impactful marketing initiatives, businesses can reap substantial rewards. However, it's essential to note that achieving a high ROI requires careful planning, market research, and continuous evaluation of marketing efforts.

The world of marketing offers tremendous opportunities for businesses to generate profitable returns on their investments. By developing a deep understanding of customers, implementing innovative strategies, and measuring the results, businesses can maximise their ROI and fuel sustainable growth. Remember, successful marketing is not just about the initial investment but rather the ongoing evaluation, optimisation, and adaptation to changing market dynamics.

When it comes to marketing channels, businesses have the option to utilise both paid and free channels to promote their products or services. Understanding the differences between these two types of channels and calculating the return on investment (ROI) for each can help businesses make informed decisions about resource allocation. Here's a breakdown of paid and free channels, along with tips on calculating ROI:

Paid Channels: Paid channels involve investing financial resources to reach a wider audience or gain additional exposure. Here are some key characteristics of paid channels:

Paid Advertising: This includes channels like search engine advertising (pay-per-click), display advertising, social media advertising, and influencer collaborations. Businesses pay for ad placements or partnerships to increase brand visibility and reach their target audience.

Content Syndication: Paid content distribution platforms allow businesses to distribute their content to a wider audience through sponsored placements or sponsored content recommendations.

Sponsorships and Partnerships: Collaborating with other brands, influencers, or organisations through sponsorship or partnership agreements can provide access to their audience in exchange for financial support or mutual benefits.

Calculating ROI for Paid Channels: To calculate ROI for paid channels, follow these steps:

Determine Costs: Calculate the total expenses associated with running paid campaigns, including advertising costs, creative development, campaign management fees, and any other related expenses.

Track Conversions: Implement tracking mechanisms to monitor conversions generated through paid channels. This could include tracking website visits, form submissions, purchases, or any other desired actions.

Assign Values: Assign a monetary value to each conversion based on the revenue generated from those conversions. For example, if a paid campaign generated 100 conversions and the average revenue per conversion is £50, the total value would be £5,000.

Calculate ROI: Subtract the total costs from the total value and divide by the total costs. Multiply the result by 100 to get the ROI percentage. For example, if the total costs were £2,500, the ROI calculation would be: (£5,000- £2,500) / £2,500 x 100 = 100%.

Free Channels: Free channels refer to organic or non-paid methods of marketing where businesses leverage their own efforts and resources without financial investments. Here are some examples of free channels:

Content Marketing: Creating and distributing valuable content through blogs, social media posts, videos, and podcasts to attract and engage the target audience.

Search Engine Optimisation (SEO): Optimising website content and structure to improve organic search engine rankings and increase visibility.

Social Media Marketing (Organic): Building an organic presence on social media platforms by sharing relevant content, engaging with the audience, and leveraging user-generated content.

Referral Programmes: Encouraging satisfied customers to refer new customers through incentives or rewards.

Calculating ROI for Free Channels: Calculating ROI for free channels can be more challenging as there are no direct financial costs involved. However, you can still measure the impact of these channels using other key performance indicators (KPIs). Some KPIs to consider include:

Website Traffic: Measure the increase in organic traffic to your website as a result of content marketing efforts or SEO.

Engagement Metrics: Track metrics such as social media followers, likes, shares, comments, and website engagement to gauge the level of audience interaction.

Conversion Rate: Measure the percentage of website visitors from free channels who take desired actions, such as filling out a form, signing up for a newsletter, or making a purchase.

Customer Lifetime Value (CLV): Analyse the long-term value generated from customers acquired through free channels by assessing their repeat purchases and overall lifetime value.

By tracking these metrics and comparing them against your overall business goals and objectives, you can assess the effectiveness of your free channels and make informed decisions about resource allocation.

Remember, while paid channels often provide more immediate and measurable results, free channels can offer long-term benefits and help build brand reputation and loyalty. A balanced approach that incorporates both paid and free channels can yield a comprehensive marketing strategy that maximises ROI and drives business growth.

Freelancers and businesses can greatly benefit from implementing an integrated communication plan, which enables them to strategically manage their marketing efforts. This plan allows them to coordinate and harmonise various communication channels to maximise their impact and achieve better results. Let's explore how it simplifies budgeting and facilitates informed channel decisions with some examples:

Simplifying Budgeting: An integrated communication plan streamlines budgeting by providing a clear framework for allocating financial resources. Instead of randomly allocating funds across different channels, the plan allows freelancers and businesses to identify the most effective channels for reaching their target audience. By focusing their budget on these channels, they can optimise their expenditure and ensure they are getting the best return on investment (ROI). For instance, a small local bakery may find that investing in targeted social media ads and local event sponsorships yield the highest ROI compared to traditional print advertisements.

Making Better Channel Decisions: The integrated communication plan helps freelancers and businesses make informed decisions about which communication channels to utilise. By conducting market research and analysing customer preferences, they can identify the channels that their target audience frequently engages with. For example, a tech startup targeting young professionals might find that using social media platforms like Instagram and LinkedIn, alongside content marketing strategies such as blog articles and video tutorials, resonates well with their target audience. By focusing on these specific channels, they can avoid wasting resources on less effective or irrelevant platforms.

Example 1: A freelance web designer may decide to allocate a significant portion of their budget to online channels such as social media advertising, search engine optimisation (SEO), and targeted email campaigns. By tracking the results and measuring the ROI for each channel, they can assess which ones are driving the most traffic to their website and generating quality leads. This data allows them to make data-driven decisions on where to invest more resources for optimal outcomes.

Example 2: A medium-sized e-commerce business specialising in handmade jewellery may discover that their target audience responds well to influencer collaborations and online marketplaces. By analysing the sales data and customer feedback from these channels, they can refine their marketing strategy to focus more on partnerships with influential personalities and expanding their presence on popular e-commerce platforms.

An integrated communication plan empowers freelancers and businesses to allocate their budget more effectively and make informed decisions regarding the selection of communication channels. By understanding customer preferences, tracking results, and measuring ROI, they can optimise their marketing efforts to achieve the best outcomes. It's a strategic approach that enhances efficiency, maximises impact, and helps businesses thrive in a competitive market.

Daniel, an ambitious freelance graphic designer, set out to expand his client base and increase his income with a revised budget of £2,500. He understood the importance of strategic communication planning and conducted thorough market research to gain insights into his target audience – small businesses and startups in the creative industry.

After careful analysis, Daniel identified four channels that would effectively reach his target audience: Instagram, LinkedIn, targeted email campaigns, and attending industry events. With a budget allocation of £1,000, Daniel designed captivating visuals and engaging captions to showcase his work on Instagram. He posted three times a week, focusing on sharing his portfolio, design tips, and engaging with his growing audience.

In addition to his Instagram presence, Daniel invested £800 in targeted email campaigns. He created personalised newsletters to showcase his portfolio, offer exclusive discounts, and encourage collaboration. He sent out newsletters on a monthly basis, keeping his contacts informed about his latest projects and exclusive offers.

Furthermore, Daniel dedicated £400 to optimise his presence on LinkedIn. He joined industry-related groups, connected with influencers, and regularly shared valuable design insights and tips. To leverage the power of networking, he planned to attend two industry events per quarter, where he would showcase his work and establish face-to-face connections with potential clients.

To ensure effective execution of his integrated communication plan, Daniel created a detailed timetable:

Instagram:

Post three times a week, on Mondays, Wednesdays, and Fridays

Spend 30 minutes engaging with followers and responding to comments daily

Targeted Email Campaigns:

Send out a monthly newsletter on the first Monday of each month

Dedicate one hour per week to crafting and optimising email content

LinkedIn:

Engage in industry-related groups and discussions every weekday for 30 minutes

Share industry insights and tips once a week, preferably on Tuesdays

Industry Events:

Attend two industry events per quarter, scheduled in March, June, September, and December

Allocate time for networking, showcasing portfolio, and establishing connections

With consistent effort and meticulous planning, Daniel's integrated communication plan yielded impressive results. The increased budget of £2,500 allowed him to reach a wider audience and invest in quality marketing activities. Over the course of the year, his business thrived, generating a total revenue of £15,000. This translated to an exceptional return on investment (ROI) of 500%, showcasing the effectiveness of his carefully selected communication channels and strategic execution.

Daniel's success story serves as a testament to the power of an integrated communication plan, where thoughtful planning, market research, and strategic channel selection can drive significant growth and maximise ROI for freelancers and businesses alike.

ABC Solutions, a small marketing agency with a budget of £10,000 for their integrated communication plan over a six-month period.

Month 1:

Social Media Advertising: Run targeted social media advertising campaigns (Monday to Friday) on Facebook, Instagram, and LinkedIn to increase brand awareness and generate leads. This resulted in a 15% increase in website traffic and a 10% growth in social media followers.

Content Marketing: Publish a new blog article on the website, attracting 500 unique visitors and generating engagement through social shares and comments.

Search Engine Optimisation (SEO): Conduct keyword research and optimise on-page elements, leading to a 20% improvement in organic search rankings.

Email Marketing: Send out the monthly newsletter on the first Monday of the month, resulting in a 12% increase in email open rates and a 5% increase in click-through rates.

Events and Networking: Attend one industry conference and schedule networking meetings, establishing connections with potential clients and partners.

Month 2:

Social Media Advertising: Continue running targeted social media advertising campaigns, leading to a 20% increase in website conversions and a 25% growth in lead generation.

Content Marketing: Publish a new blog article on the website, driving 700 unique visitors and generating engagement through comments and social shares.

Search Engine Optimisation (SEO): Implement link-building strategies, resulting in a 15% increase in organic search traffic and a higher domain authority score.

Email Marketing: Send targeted promotional emails on specific dates, resulting in a 10% increase in email click-through rates and a 7% growth in conversion rates.

Events and Networking: Attend a trade show and schedule networking meetings, leading to several partnership opportunities and referrals.

Month 3:

Social Media Advertising: Continue running targeted social media advertising campaigns, resulting in a 30% increase in website conversions and a 35% growth in lead generation.

Content Marketing: Publish a new blog article on the website, driving 800 unique visitors and generating engagement through comments, social shares, and backlinks from industry influencers.

Search Engine Optimisation (SEO): Monitor website performance and make adjustments, leading to a 10% increase in organic search rankings and improved visibility in search engine results pages.

Email Marketing: Send out the monthly newsletter on the first Monday of the month, resulting in a 15% increase in email open rates and a 10% growth in click-through rates.

Events and Networking: Attend an industry networking event and schedule networking meetings, establishing strong relationships with industry professionals and potential clients.

Month 4:

Social Media Advertising: Continue running targeted social media advertising campaigns, resulting in a 40% increase in website conversions and a 45% growth in lead generation.

Content Marketing: Publish a new blog article on the website, driving 900 unique visitors and generating engagement through comments, social shares, and backlinks.

Search Engine Optimisation (SEO): Monitor website performance and make adjustments, leading to a 15% increase in organic search traffic and improved search engine visibility.

Email Marketing: Send targeted promotional emails on specific dates, resulting in a 12% increase in email click-through rates and an 8% growth in conversion rates.

Events and Networking: Attend a conference as a speaker and schedule networking meetings, positioning ABC Solutions as industry experts and attracting potential clients.

Month 5:

Social Media Advertising: Continue running targeted social media advertising campaigns, resulting in a 50% increase in website conversions and a 55% growth in lead generation.

Content Marketing: Publish a new blog article on the website, driving 1,000 unique visitors and generating engagement through comments, social shares, and backlinks.

Search Engine Optimisation (SEO): Monitor website performance and make adjustments, leading to a 20% increase in organic search rankings and improved search engine visibility.

Email Marketing: Send out the monthly newsletter on the first Monday of the month, resulting in a 15% increase in email open rates and a 12% growth in click-through rates.

Events and Networking: Attend a local networking event and schedule networking meetings, expanding ABC Solutions' network and attracting potential clients.

Month 6:

Social Media Advertising: Continue running targeted social media advertising campaigns, resulting in a 60% increase in website conversions and a 65% growth in lead generation.

Content Marketing: Publish a new blog article on the website, driving 1,200 unique visitors and generating engagement through comments, social shares, and backlinks.

Search Engine Optimisation (SEO): Monitor website performance and make adjustments, leading to a 25% increase in organic search traffic and improved search engine rankings.

Email Marketing: Send targeted promotional emails on specific dates, resulting in a 25% increase in email click-through rates and a 20% growth in conversion rates.

Events and Networking: Attend a trade show and schedule networking meetings, solidifying relationships with existing clients and generating new business opportunities.

Throughout the six-month period, ABC Solutions achieved a strong return on their investment. The total ROI for the integrated communication plan was calculated to be 560%, resulting in a profit of £56,000. This demonstrates the effectiveness of their strategic approach and the value of executing targeted activities across various channels.

In addition to the financial success, ABC Solutions also experienced an improved reputation and received positive reviews from clients and industry professionals. The integrated communication plan allowed them to showcase their expertise, engage with their target audience, and establish themselves as leaders in the marketing industry.

By carefully planning their schedule, monitoring key metrics, and optimising their strategies based on data-driven insights, ABC Solutions was able to achieve significant growth in their business and establish a strong brand presence. This example highlights the importance of strategic planning, continuous monitoring, and making informed decisions to maximise the impact of an integrated communication plan.

Let me tell you about my friend Hannah. She's a talented management consultant who successfully executed an integrated marketing communications plan while juggling a full-time commitment.

Hannah recognised the importance of reaching her target audience and building her reputation. She strategically focused on digital channels such as social media advertising and content marketing. Through compelling content and targeted ads, she positioned herself as an industry expert, attracting new clients and gaining recognition for her skills.

Despite her busy schedule, Hannah was determined to make an impact. She attended industry events and networking opportunities to connect with potential clients and showcase her expertise firsthand. These face-to-face interactions allowed her to build relationships and gain trust within her industry.

To manage her time effectively, Hannah created a detailed timetable. She dedicated specific hours each week to execute her marketing activities, making the most of her limited time. By carefully balancing her full-time commitment with her marketing efforts, she maximised her productivity and achieved outstanding results.

As a result of her integrated marketing communications plan, Hannah tripled her profits in just three months. Her client base expanded rapidly, and she received glowing testimonials and positive reviews from satisfied clients. This success not only boosted her income but also strengthened her professional reputation and positioned her as a go-to consultant in her field.

Hannah's story is a testament to the power of strategic planning, effective time management, and a well-executed integrated marketing communications plan. It shows that even with a demanding schedule, it is possible to achieve remarkable results and drive substantial business growth.

As you can see, an integrated communication plan involves strategically allocating your budget across various marketing channels to ensure a cohesive and effective approach. Here's a step-by-step guide on how to create an integrated communication plan based on budget allocation, including cost considerations, ROI measurement, and continuous improvement:

Set Clear Objectives: Start by defining your communication objectives. Are you aiming to increase brand awareness, generate leads, drive website traffic, or boost sales? Clearly outline your goals to align your budget allocation accordingly.

Define Your Target Audience: Identify your target audience and understand their preferences, behaviours, and preferred communication channels. This will help you determine the most effective channels to reach and engage your audience.

Conduct Market Research: Carry out thorough market research to identify the channels that resonate with your target audience and align with your communication objectives. Consider both traditional and digital channels, such as print media, radio, television, social media, search engine marketing, content marketing, email marketing, and events.

Allocate Your Budget: Determine the budget you're willing to allocate for your communication plan. Consider the overall marketing budget as well as any specific campaign budgets. Allocate funds based on the estimated costs of each channel, bearing in mind that some channels may require higher investments than others.

Cost Considerations: Research and gather data on the costs associated with each channel. Some channels may have fixed costs, such as advertising rates or content creation fees, while others may have variable costs based on factors like audience sise or campaign duration. Consider costs for creative development, media placement, content creation, campaign management, and any additional fees or subscriptions.

ROI Measurement: Establish key performance indicators (KPIs) to measure the success of your communication plan. These may include metrics such as website traffic, conversions, leads generated, social media engagement, or sales. Assign a value to each KPI based on its contribution to your overall goals. Monitor and measure the performance of each channel to calculate ROI. Compare the costs incurred with the results achieved to determine the channel's effectiveness.

Measurement and Analysis: Implement analytics tools and tracking mechanisms to gather data and monitor the impact of each channel. Analyse the data regularly to assess the performance of your communication plan and identify areas for improvement. Consider using tools like Google Analytics, social media analytics, or CRM software to track and measure the impact of your marketing efforts.

Continuous Improvement: Continuously review and refine your communication plan based on the data and insights gathered. Identify channels that are driving the highest ROI and allocate more resources to them. Conversely, assess channels that are underperforming and consider either optimising them or reallocating resources to more effective channels. Regularly test new strategies, messaging, or creative elements to improve overall performance.

Track and Adapt: Monitor the impact of your communication plan in real-time and be prepared to adapt as needed. Stay updated on industry trends, audience preferences, and emerging channels to ensure your communication plan remains relevant and effective.

It will be a good idea to develop a timetable that follows the principles below as it simplifies the process of developing an integrated communications plan. This timetable serves as a visual guide to help you organise and schedule your marketing activities across different channels. Here's how to use it effectively:

Define your objectives: Start by clearly defining your marketing objectives. What do you want to achieve through your integrated communications plan? Is it increased brand awareness, lead generation, customer engagement, or something else? Clearly articulate your goals to ensure your activities align with your desired outcomes.

Identify your target audience: Understand your target audience and their preferences. Who are you trying to reach? What channels are they most active on? By gaining insights into your audience, you can tailor your communication strategies to effectively engage with them.

List your communication channels: Identify the various communication channels you plan to leverage. These may include social media platforms, email marketing, content marketing, offline advertising, public relations, events, and more. List each channel in the timetable.

Determine the frequency: Decide how often you will engage with your audience through each channel. Consider factors such as channel dynamics, audience preferences, and available resources. For example, you might choose to post on social media three times a week, send out a monthly newsletter, or publish a blog article twice a month.

Allocate resources: Allocate resources to each channel based on their importance and expected impact. This includes budget, time, personnel, and any necessary tools or software. Be realistic about what you can dedicate to each channel to ensure efficient resource allocation.

Create a schedule: Fill in the timetable with specific dates and times for each activity. Be as detailed as possible, including the day, time, and duration of each activity. This helps you maintain a structured approach and ensures consistency in your communication efforts.

Monitor and evaluate: As you execute your integrated communications plan, closely monitor the performance of each activity. Track metrics such as website traffic, social media engagement, email open rates, conversion rates, and overall ROI. Regularly evaluate the effectiveness of your plan and make adjustments as needed based on the data and insights you gather.

Using a timetable for your integrated communications plan enables you to stay organised, maintain a consistent presence across channels, and ensure timely execution of activities. It serves as a visual roadmap that guides your marketing efforts, helping you make the most of your resources and achieve your desired outcomes.

Estelle, the owner of a boutique fashion store, used the Integrated Communications Plan Timetable to streamline her marketing activities and improve her business's visibility. Here's an example of how she utilised the timetable for her business:

Objective: Estelle's objective was to increase brand awareness and drive more footfall to her store.

Target audience: Her target audience consisted of fashion-conscious individuals aged 25-40, primarily located in the local area.

Communication channels: Estelle identified the following communication channels for her plan: social media (Facebook, Instagram), email marketing, local events, and collaborations with fashion influencers.

Frequency: Estelle decided to post on social media platforms three times a week, send out a fortnightly email newsletter, participate in one local event every month, and collaborate with fashion influencers quarterly.

Resource allocation: She allocated her budget primarily towards social media advertising and event participation. She also allocated time to create engaging social media content, curate email newsletters, and develop partnerships with influencers.

Schedule:

Social Media:

Mondays: Create and schedule social media posts for the week.

Wednesdays: Engage with followers, respond to comments and messages.

Fridays: Analyse social media metrics and adjust content strategy if needed.

Email Marketing:

1st and 15th of each month: Design and send out the fortnightly newsletter.

Monitor open rates, click-through rates, and unsubscribe rates to measure engagement.

Local Events:

Research and select one local fashion event to participate in each month.

Prepare promotional materials, set up the store display, and engage with attendees.

Fashion Influencer Collaborations:

Identify and reach out to fashion influencers for potential collaborations.

Plan and execute joint marketing activities, such as co-sponsored events or influencer features on social media.

Monitoring and evaluation: Estelle consistently tracked her website traffic, social media engagement, email performance, and event footfall. She monitored the ROI of her advertising campaigns and assessed customer feedback to gauge the effectiveness of her integrated communications plan.

By following the timetable, Estelle was able to maintain a consistent presence on social media, keep her audience engaged through email newsletters, expand her reach through local events, and leverage the influence of fashion influencers. Over time, she observed increased footfall to her store, higher social media engagement, and improved brand recognition in her local community.

The timetable allowed Estelle to efficiently manage her marketing activities, allocate resources effectively, and measure the impact of her efforts. It provided her with a structured approach to achieving her marketing objectives and helped her make informed decisions to drive business growth.

Remember, flexibility is key. Adapt your plan based on the feedback you receive and the evolving needs of your target audience. By continually refining and optimising your integrated communications plan, you can drive better engagement, build brand loyalty, and ultimately achieve your marketing goals.

Driving Business Success and Sustainable Growth

Lifetime value of a customer, often referred to as customer lifetime value (CLV), is a metric that measures the total worth of a customer to a business over the entire duration of their relationship. It is a crucial concept in marketing and business strategy, as it provides insights into the long-term profitability of acquiring and retaining customers.

In simple terms, the lifetime value of a customer represents the net profit a business can expect to generate from that customer during their entire engagement with the company. It takes into account factors such as repeat purchases, average order value, customer loyalty, and the length of the customer relationship.

Understanding the significance of customer lifetime value (CLV) is paramount for businesses aiming to thrive in today's competitive landscape. Consider CLV as your compass, guiding you towards sustainable growth and long-term success.

By comprehending the concept of CLV, businesses can shift their focus from short-term gains to cultivating lasting relationships with customers. Instead of constantly pursuing new prospects, you'll recognise the value of nurturing existing customers who have already shown their trust and loyalty. These loyal customers become your brand advocates, driving repeat purchases and generating new customers through positive word-of-mouth.

Not only does CLV help foster loyalty, but it also enhances your marketing strategies. Armed with insights into your customers' preferences and behaviour, you can tailor your marketing messages to resonate with each customer segment. Personalisation becomes the key to forging deeper connections with customers, increasing engagement, and driving conversions.

CLV goes beyond the present; it empowers businesses to plan for the future. By estimating the lifetime value of your customers, you can make informed decisions regarding resource allocation, marketing investments, and customer retention strategies. This foresight enables you to effectively allocate your budget and deploy resources where they will yield the highest returns.

In a rapidly evolving business landscape, businesses that prioritise CLV gain a significant competitive advantage. By building strong, enduring relationships with customers, you establish a solid foundation for growth and differentiation. Customer loyalty becomes a powerful differentiator, setting your business apart from competitors and ensuring a sustainable stream of revenue.

Embracing the concept of CLV is not merely an option; it is a necessity for businesses seeking long-term success. By recognising the value of each customer's lifetime relationship with your brand, you can craft strategies that foster loyalty, drive customer engagement, and maximise profitability. The journey doesn't end with a single sale; it extends far into the future, where the true value of a customer lies.

So, business leaders, let CLV be your guiding star. By understanding and harnessing the power of customer lifetime value, you can navigate towards enduring success, build meaningful connections with your customers, and create a thriving business that withstands the test of time.

Businesses utilise customer lifetime value (CLV) to fuel growth, enhance sales strategies, and make informed business decisions. CLV provides valuable insights into a customer's long-term value to a business, enabling companies to take proactive measures to improve their bottom line. Let's explore how businesses can leverage CLV to their advantage:

Understanding Customer Segmentation: By analysing CLV, businesses can identify distinct customer segments based on their value to the company. This allows businesses to tailor their marketing efforts and allocate resources accordingly. For example, a high-end fashion brand may concentrate its marketing efforts on high-value customers who possess a greater CLV, offering them personalised experiences and exclusive privileges to encourage repeat purchases.

Personalised Marketing Campaigns: CLV insights empower businesses to create targeted and personalised marketing campaigns. By comprehending a customer's purchase history and preferences, businesses can deliver relevant messages and offers that resonate with each customer segment. For instance, an online retailer may dispatch customised email promotions to customers who have a higher CLV, increasing the likelihood of conversion and driving higher sales.

Retention Strategies: CLV helps businesses identify customers who are at risk of churning and implement effective retention strategies. By focusing on retaining high-value customers with the potential for long-term loyalty, businesses can reduce churn rates and maximise their CLV. For example, a subscription-based service may offer incentives or rewards to retain high-value customers, ensuring their continued patronage and increasing their overall lifetime value.

Optimising Pricing Strategies: CLV analysis assists businesses in determining optimal pricing strategies. By understanding the lifetime value of customers, businesses can set prices that align with the value they bring. For instance, a software company may offer tiered pricing options based on CLV, with higher-value customers paying premium prices for additional features or services.

Driving Product and Service Development: CLV insights can guide businesses in developing new products or services that cater to their most valuable customers. By understanding their preferences and demands, businesses can invest in innovations that will attract and retain high-value customers. For example, a technology company may launch new product features or upgrades based on the feedback and needs of customers with a higher CLV.

In the bustling world of business, there was a determined entrepreneur named Mr. Smith who overlooked the significance of customer lifetime value. He was solely focused on making quick sales and didn't invest time or effort into nurturing lasting relationships with his customers.

Unbeknownst to Mr. Smith, his lack of attention to customer needs and preferences resulted in a growing sense of indifference among his clientele. They didn't feel valued or appreciated, leading them to seek out alternative businesses that provided better experiences and tailored solutions.

As the days went by, Mr. Smith noticed a steady decline in customer loyalty. He found himself constantly chasing new customers, spending exorbitant amounts on marketing and advertising to fill the void left by the departing ones. The cost of customer acquisition soared, eating into his profits and jeopardising the financial stability of his business.

Meanwhile, his reputation began to suffer. Dissatisfied customers shared their negative experiences with friends, family, and even online, tarnishing Mr. Smith's brand image and deterring potential customers from giving his business a chance.

As the consequences of his neglect became evident, Mr. Smith faced an uphill battle to keep his business afloat. The financial strain became overwhelming, and despite his best efforts, he struggled to regain the trust and loyalty of his customers. Eventually, the weight of the losses and diminished prospects proved too much, leading Mr. Smith to make the heart-wrenching decision to close his business.

An advisor, James, experienced the opposite. He ran his own financial consultancy firm. James had a burning desire to take his business to new heights and provide exceptional value to his clients. However, he faced the challenge of identifying the most effective strategies to achieve his goals.

One day, James discovered the power of customer lifetime value (CLV) and realised that it held the key to unlocking the growth potential of his business. He delved into understanding the concept and its implications, eager to apply it to his own advisory practice.

With renewed enthusiasm, James set out to implement CLV-driven strategies to improve his business. First, he conducted an in-depth analysis of his client base, segmenting them based on their lifetime value. This allowed him to identify high-value clients who had the potential to contribute significantly to his firm's growth.

Armed with this knowledge, James personalised his marketing efforts and developed targeted campaigns for each client segment. He crafted tailored messages that addressed their unique financial needs, aspirations, and pain points. By speaking directly to their individual concerns, James increased client engagement and saw a remarkable rise in client retention.

For example, James implemented a client retention initiative where he offered exclusive access to educational webinars and personalised financial reports for his high-value clients. This resulted in a retention rate increase of 20%, ensuring a stable revenue stream and long-term client relationships.

Furthermore, James used CLV insights to refine his pricing structure. He analysed the lifetime value of his clients and adjusted his fees to reflect the value he provided. By doing so, he not only attracted high-value clients who recognised the worth of his services but also increased customer spending.

One noteworthy example is when James introduced a premium service package for his top-tier clients, providing them with comprehensive financial planning and investment management services. This led to a 30% increase in customer spending per engagement, contributing to higher revenue and profitability.

As James continued to leverage CLV, he realised the importance of building long-term relationships with his clients. He implemented retention strategies, such as regular check-ins, personalised communication, and exclusive educational resources. By nurturing these relationships, James established a strong sense of trust and loyalty.

For instance, James launched a referral programme where clients were incentivised to refer their friends and family to his services. This resulted in a 25% increase in client referrals, expanding his client base and driving further growth.

Over time, James's business flourished. The CLV-focused approach had a profound impact on his bottom line. The increase in client retention, referrals, and higher-value engagements resulted in a significant boost in revenue and profitability for his firm.

By implementing CLV-driven strategies, James was able to achieve a return on investment (ROI) of 150% within the first year. The increased profitability enabled him to reinvest in his business, hire additional staff, and further enhance the quality of his services.

James's success story spread throughout the advisory industry, inspiring other professionals to embrace CLV as a powerful tool for business growth. As more advisors adopted this strategic approach, the entire industry witnessed a shift towards customer-centricity and long-term value creation.

James's journey serves as a testament to the transformative power of customer lifetime value. By understanding the long-term potential of his clients and tailoring his strategies accordingly, he not only improved his business but also created lasting relationships with his clients. James's story continues to inspire aspiring advisors to this day, reminding them of the immense value that lies in understanding and leveraging the lifetime value of their customers.

You see, James understood that when someone becomes a customer of his business, they don't just make one purchase and then disappear. They often come back again and again to buy more things. So, James wanted to make sure that his customers stayed happy and kept coming back.

He did this by giving his customers special attention and making them feel valued. He would remember their names, ask about their interests, and listen to their needs. By doing this, his customers liked him and his business a lot, and they wanted to keep coming back.

Not only that, but James also made sure to offer his customers things they really wanted. He would ask them what they liked and what they needed, and then he would try his best to provide it. This made his customers even happier and more likely to keep buying from him.

By taking care of his customers and making them happy, James saw something amazing happen. His customers not only came back to buy more things, but they also told their friends and family about James's business. This brought even more customers to him, and his business grew and grew.

And you know what? Because James took such good care of his customers, he made a lot of money too. His business became very successful, and he was able to do great things with the money he earned.

James and Mr. Smith highlight the significant impact of customer lifetime value on the success and longevity of a business. James, with his customer-centric approach and focus on building lasting relationships, reaped the benefits of customer loyalty, repeat purchases, and positive word-of-mouth referrals. His understanding of the long-term value of each customer allowed him to drive sustainable growth and profitability.

On the other hand, Mr. Smith's neglect of customer lifetime value led to a series of challenges. His transactional approach and lack of emphasis on building customer relationships resulted in high customer churn, increased customer acquisition costs, and a damaged reputation. The consequences of not prioritising customer lifetime value were evident in the struggles faced by Mr. Smith's business.

These stories underscore the importance for businesses to recognise the value of their customers beyond individual transactions. By investing in understanding customer needs, delivering exceptional experiences, and fostering long-term relationships, businesses can enhance customer loyalty, increase customer lifetime value, and drive sustainable success.

Ultimately, the journey to business success is paved with a deep understanding of customer lifetime value and the willingness to go the extra mile in building strong customer relationships. By embracing this approach, businesses can create a loyal customer base, drive profitability, and position themselves for long-term growth and prosperity.

Therefore, knowing the lifetime value of a customer is relevant to businesses for several reasons:

Strategic Decision Making: By knowing the value that each customer brings to the business, companies can make informed decisions about resource allocation, marketing strategies, and customer acquisition costs. This helps in prioritising efforts towards high-value customers and identifying areas for growth and improvement.

Customer Acquisition: Calculating CLV helps businesses assess the return on investment (ROI) for their customer acquisition efforts. By determining the value of acquiring a new customer compared to the cost of acquisition, companies can make informed decisions on marketing budgets and strategies.

Retention and Loyalty: Lifetime value underscores the importance of customer retention and loyalty. Businesses can identify strategies to improve customer satisfaction, enhance the customer experience, and build long-term relationships, as these factors contribute to higher CLV.

Tailored Marketing Strategies: CLV analysis allows businesses to segment customers based on their value and tailor marketing strategies accordingly. By understanding the different needs and preferences of high-value customers versus low-value customers, businesses can optimise their marketing messages, promotions, and customer engagement activities.

Financial Forecasting: Estimating customer lifetime value helps businesses in financial forecasting and predicting future revenue streams. It provides insights into revenue potential, allows for more accurate revenue forecasting, and helps businesses plan for growth and investment.

Customer lifetime value is a key metric that provides businesses with a deeper understanding of their customers' worth and long-term profitability. By focusing on increasing CLV through customer acquisition, retention, and loyalty strategies, businesses can drive sustainable growth, enhance customer relationships, and ultimately achieve greater success.

Here are five examples of how businesses and individuals can leverage the concept of customer lifetime value to their advantage, along with corresponding case studies that highlight their success:

E-commerce Business: An online retailer calculates the lifetime value of its customers and discovers that a significant portion of its revenue comes from repeat purchases. With this insight, they develop a customer loyalty programme that offers exclusive discounts, personalised recommendations, and early access to new products. By nurturing customer relationships and encouraging repeat purchases, they increase customer lifetime value and drive revenue growth. Case Study: Amazon's Prime Membership programme, which offers benefits such as free delivery and access to streaming services, has successfully increased customer loyalty and lifetime value.

Subscription-Based Service: A software-as-a-service (SaaS) company analyses the lifetime value of its subscribers and identifies a group of high-value customers who consistently upgrade to premium plans and refer new customers. To further boost customer lifetime value, they introduce a customer referral programme that incentivises existing customers to refer their colleagues and friends. This strategy not only increases customer acquisition but also improves customer retention and loyalty. Case Study: Dropbox's referral programme, which offers free storage space to users who refer new customers, has been instrumental in driving customer growth and increasing lifetime value.

Retail Store: A local boutique uses customer lifetime value data to identify its most valuable customer segments. They personalise their marketing campaigns, sending tailored offers and recommendations based on individual preferences and purchase history. By providing a personalised shopping experience and building long-term relationships, they increase customer loyalty and average order value, ultimately boosting customer lifetime value. Case Study: Sephora's Beauty Insider programme, which offers personalised rewards, product recommendations, and exclusive events, has significantly increased customer engagement and lifetime value.

Financial Services Firm: A bank recognises that the lifetime value of its customers is closely tied to their engagement with multiple products and services. To encourage cross-selling and deepen customer relationships, they offer bundled packages that include a range of financial products such as savings accounts, credit cards, and investment options. This approach increases customer loyalty and overall customer lifetime value. Case Study: Barclays Bank's "Premier Banking" programme, which provides exclusive benefits and personalised financial solutions to high-value customers, has successfully increased customer retention and lifetime value.

Freelancer: A freelance management consultant focuses on building long-term partnerships with clients. By providing exceptional service, delivering measurable results, and nurturing client relationships, they not only secure repeat business but also benefit from client referrals. This freelancer understands the lifetime value of each client and prioritises client satisfaction, leading to a steady stream of projects and increased profitability. Case Study: McKinsey & Company, a global management consulting firm, has built its reputation and achieved significant growth by focusing on long-term client relationships, resulting in high client retention and lifetime value.

Who else benefitted from a focus on CLV?

Amazon: Amazon is a prime example of a company that utilises CLV to drive business success. By analysing customer purchasing patterns, browsing behaviour, and preferences, Amazon personalises product recommendations, offers targeted promotions, and provides a seamless shopping experience. This strategy has resulted in a high CLV and has contributed to Amazon's dominance in the e-commerce industry.

Tesco: Tesco, one of the largest supermarket chains in the UK, implemented the Clubcard loyalty programme to enhance customer engagement and increase CLV. By collecting and analysing data from customer purchases, Tesco offers personalised discounts, tailored promotions, and rewards based on individual shopping habits. This approach has led to increased customer loyalty, higher spending, and a positive impact on CLV.

British Airways: British Airways uses CLV to optimise its customer segmentation and tailor its services to different customer groups. By understanding the lifetime value of its customers, British Airways can identify high-value frequent flyers and offer them exclusive benefits, such as priority boarding, lounge access, and personalised travel experiences. This strategy increases customer satisfaction, loyalty, and CLV.

Spotify: As a leading music streaming platform, Spotify relies on CLV to deliver personalised music recommendations and retain subscribers. By analysing user listening habits, Spotify creates customised playlists, suggests new songs and artists, and offers personalised promotions. This approach enhances user engagement, reduces churn rates, and maximises CLV.

ASOS: ASOS, a popular online fashion retailer, utilises CLV to enhance customer experience and increase lifetime value. By collecting data on customer preferences, browsing behaviour, and purchase history, ASOS offers personalised product recommendations, style tips, and exclusive discounts. This tailored approach boosts customer engagement, loyalty, and CLV.

Starbucks: Starbucks uses CLV data to drive its popular loyalty programme, Starbucks Rewards. By offering personalised rewards, exclusive offers, and freebies, Starbucks encourages frequent visits and increases customer spending. This strategy has resulted in a loyal customer base, higher customer retention, and increased CLV.

British Airways: British Airways utilises CLV insights to offer personalised travel experiences and exclusive rewards to their frequent flyers. By tailoring their services and incentives, British Airways enhances customer loyalty and increases CLV.

Rolls-Royce: Rolls-Royce uses CLV data to deliver customised maintenance and support services for their aircraft engines. By providing proactive maintenance solutions and personalised customer care, Rolls-Royce strengthens customer relationships and maximises CLV.

Tesco: Tesco, a leading UK supermarket, leverages CLV to offer personalised discounts, rewards, and targeted promotions through their Clubcard loyalty programme. By tailoring offers based on individual shopping habits, Tesco increases customer engagement and boosts CLV.

Barclays: Barclays Bank analyses CLV to personalise their banking services, provide tailored financial advice, and offer exclusive benefits to their high-value customers. By delivering customised solutions and personalised experiences, Barclays enhances customer loyalty and CLV.

Vodafone: Vodafone utilises CLV insights to offer personalised mobile plans, exclusive discounts, and targeted offers to their customers. By tailoring their services based on individual usage patterns and preferences, Vodafone increases customer satisfaction and CLV.

Toyota: Toyota incorporates CLV data to enhance customer retention and increase brand loyalty. By offering personalised after-sales services, proactive maintenance reminders, and exclusive benefits, Toyota strengthens customer relationships and boosts CLV.

Nestlé: Nestlé utilises CLV insights to personalise their marketing communications, deliver targeted product recommendations, and offer exclusive rewards to their loyal customers. By enhancing the customer experience and building strong brand connections, Nestlé increases CLV.

Unilever: Unilever analyses CLV data to segment their customers and develop targeted marketing campaigns for their various brands. By delivering personalised messages, tailored promotions, and customised product offerings, Unilever enhances customer engagement and CLV.

BP: BP, the multinational oil and gas company, utilises CLV insights to provide customised energy solutions and personalised customer support. By understanding individual energy needs and offering tailored services, BP increases customer satisfaction and CLV.

HSBC: HSBC Bank utilises CLV data to offer personalised financial solutions, tailored investment advice, and exclusive benefits to their high-value customers. By understanding their customers' financial goals and delivering customised services, HSBC enhances customer loyalty and CLV.

Customer Lifetime Value (CLV) is a crucial metric for businesses as it provides insights into the long-term value of customers. By understanding how much revenue a customer is likely to generate over their entire relationship with a company, businesses can make informed decisions about resource allocation, marketing strategies, and customer retention efforts. CLV helps businesses identify high-value customers, tailor their offerings to meet their needs, and focus on building lasting relationships that drive profitability and sustainable growth. It enables businesses to optimise their marketing spend, increase customer loyalty, and maximise the return on investment (ROI) from their customer acquisition and retention efforts.

Unlocking the Hidden Strategies and Insider Tips for Social Media Success

Once upon a time, there was Sarah, a talented jewellery maker with a dream of turning her passion into a successful business. With limited resources, she turned to social media as her main marketing tool. Let's follow Sarah's journey over 12 months and delve into the specific activities that contributed to her success, including the profits and numbers achieved along the way.

Month 1: Building an Engaging Social Media Presence Sarah created an Instagram and Facebook page for her jewellery business. Through captivating visuals and compelling captions, she began showcasing her unique designs. By the end of the month, she gained 500 followers on Instagram and 200 likes on her Facebook page.

Month 3: Engaging with the Community As Sarah's following grew, she actively engaged with her audience, responding to comments, messages, and inquiries promptly. By providing personalised and timely responses, she built trust and loyalty among her customers. During this month, she successfully converted 50 followers into paying customers, generating a profit of £1,500.

Month 6: Leveraging User-Generated Content Sarah encouraged her customers to share photos of themselves wearing her jewellery using a branded hashtag. The user-generated content began to flow, with customers proudly showcasing their purchases on social media. By reposting these photos and stories, Sarah nurtured a sense of community and authenticity. As a result, she attracted 100 new customers through this strategy, contributing to a profit of £5,000.

Month 9: Collaborating with Influencers Sarah identified influencers in the fashion and jewellery niche whose style resonated with her target market. By partnering with these influencers, she gained access to their engaged audiences. This collaboration led to increased brand exposure and credibility. In the ninth month, Sarah witnessed a significant boost in sales, generating a profit of £8,000.

Month 12: Measuring Success and Achieving Growth Throughout the journey, Sarah diligently tracked her social media metrics, analysing engagement rates, reach, and conversions. She adjusted her content and marketing strategies based on the insights gained. By the end of the 12-month period, her follower count reached 10,000 on Instagram and her Facebook page garnered 5,000 likes. Through strategic promotions and targeted advertising, she converted 300 leads into paying customers, resulting in a profit of £15,000.

Over the course of 12 months, Sarah's social media efforts yielded remarkable results. Her profits grew consistently, and she experienced a significant increase in brand visibility and customer engagement. With an average investment of 10 hours per week in social media activities, Sarah effectively utilised various strategies, such as building an engaging presence, engaging with the community, leveraging user-generated content, collaborating with influencers, and measuring success.

Sarah transformed her passion for jewellery into a thriving and profitable business. Her success serves as an inspiration for aspiring entrepreneurs looking to leverage social media to achieve their own goals.

You may have noticed that the emergence of the Internet and social media has fundamentally revolutionised the way we communicate and connect. These influential platforms have not only democratised access to information but have also facilitated unparalleled levels of interactivity. However, amidst the prevailing buzz and excitement surrounding social media, it is imperative to distinguish between fact and fiction. While some hail social media as the ultimate marketing solution, it is vital to understand its role and limitations within a comprehensive marketing strategy.

As social media continues to evolve and dominate our digital landscape, it has become a vital conduit for businesses to reach and engage with their target audience. It offers unprecedented opportunities to build brand awareness, foster meaningful relationships, and drive customer loyalty. However, it is important to approach social media with a discerning eye, recognising that it is not a magic solution that can single-handedly transform a business overnight.

Effective social media marketing requires careful planning, strategic execution, and continuous adaptation. It is about leveraging the unique capabilities of each platform, understanding the dynamics of your target audience, and crafting tailored content that resonates deeply. Social media can amplify your brand's voice, extend your reach, and facilitate authentic conversations, but it is just one piece of the puzzle.

To fully harness the power of social media, businesses must seamlessly integrate it into a comprehensive marketing strategy that encompasses various channels and tactics. This may involve combining social media efforts with traditional advertising, email marketing, content creation, and offline promotions. By adopting a holistic approach, businesses can create a cohesive brand experience that transcends the digital realm and resonates with their audience on multiple levels.

It is also worth noting that social media is not immune to challenges and risks. The fast-paced nature of these platforms means that trends come and go, algorithms change, and competition intensifies. Businesses must stay agile, adapt to emerging trends, and constantly refine their strategies to remain relevant and effective in an ever-evolving digital landscape.

A successful marketing campaign entails multiple stages and employs a range of tactics, each contributing to the growth and success of a business. Let's explore these stages and the tactics that can be employed, including examples:

Stage 1: Market Research and Target Audience Identification Thorough market research is essential to understand the industry landscape and identify your target audience. Utilise social media listening tools and analytics to gather insights about your audience's demographics, interests, and preferences. For example, a travel agency conducting market research may discover through social media analysis that their target audience consists primarily of adventure-seeking millennials interested in sustainable tourism.

Tactic: Conduct surveys and polls on social media to gather data and insights about your target audience's preferences, allowing you to tailor your marketing messages accordingly.

Stage 2: Message Development and Content Creation Crafting a compelling message and creating engaging content is crucial to capture your audience's attention and convey your brand's unique value proposition. Develop a content strategy that aligns with your target audience's interests and preferences. For instance, a fitness brand may create informative blog posts, tutorial videos, and inspiring social media posts to engage their audience with valuable fitness tips and motivational content.

Tactic: Utilise user-generated content by encouraging your audience to share their experiences and testimonials on social media, amplifying brand authenticity and generating social proof.

Stage 3: Channel Selection and Integration Selecting the most effective marketing channels and integrating them into a cohesive strategy is vital. While social media is often a key component, consider other channels that align with your target audience's preferences. For example, a fashion retailer targeting a young audience may combine social media marketing with influencer collaborations, email marketing campaigns, and interactive website features to create a seamless omnichannel experience.

Tactic: Implement cross-channel marketing tactics such as integrating social media with email marketing by sharing exclusive offers or content to your social media audience, encouraging them to subscribe to your email list for additional benefits.

Stage 4: Social Media Engagement and Brand Building Social media provides unique opportunities for engaging with your audience, building brand awareness, and fostering customer relationships. Regularly interact with your audience through comments, direct messages, and social media groups. Share compelling visuals, stories, and updates to keep your audience engaged and connected. For example, a restaurant can showcase behind-the-scenes footage, promote limited-time specials, and host interactive Q&A sessions on their social media channels.

Tactic: Run competitions or giveaways on social media platforms to incentivise engagement, encourage user-generated content, and expand your brand's reach.

Stage 5: Lead Generation and Conversion Social media can be a powerful tool for lead generation and conversion. Create targeted social media advertising campaigns to reach your desired audience and drive traffic to conversion points such as landing pages or e-commerce websites. Develop compelling offers, such as exclusive discounts or free trials, to entice your social media audience to take the desired action. Use retargeting techniques to reconnect with users who have shown interest in your brand.

Tactic: Implement a social media retargeting campaign to reach users who have previously engaged with your brand on social media but did not convert. Display personalised ads to encourage them to revisit your website and complete their purchase.

Stage 6: Customer Relationship Management and Advocacy Social media provides a platform for ongoing customer relationship management and advocacy. Respond to customer inquiries, address concerns, and provide timely customer support on social media channels. Encourage satisfied customers to share their experiences and testimonials, turning them into brand advocates. Foster a sense of community by creating social media groups or hosting live events to engage with your customers.

Tactic: Implement a social media influencer marketing strategy, collaborating with influencers in your industry to showcase your products or services and leverage their influence to reach a wider audience.

When it comes to social media tactics, both free and paid approaches have their own advantages and considerations for freelancers or small businesses. Let's compare the two methods, including time investments and potential gains:

Free Social Media Tactics: Sarah, a freelance graphic designer, consistently shared her portfolio on Instagram, engaged with her followers, and offered design tips through blog posts and videos. Over six months, she gained 2,000 followers organically. From those followers, 10% (200 people) became her clients, resulting in a total revenue of £20,000. Whilst her time investment was substantial, her return on investment (ROI) was significant, considering she didn't incur any direct advertising costs.

Paid Social Media Tactics: Emily, a small business owner specialising in handmade candles, allocated a monthly budget of £500 for targeted Facebook ads. By running visually appealing ads with compelling copy, she reached 100,000 people over three months. With a conversion rate of 5%, she acquired 5,000 new customers. The average purchase value was £20, resulting in a total revenue of £100,000. After deducting the ad spend of £1,500, Emily achieved an ROI of 6,567%.

Comparing the Results: Whilst Sarah's free social media efforts yielded a strong return on her time investment, Emily's paid social media campaign generated a significantly higher revenue and ROI within a shorter timeframe. The targeted ads allowed Emily to reach a larger audience and convert a portion of them into paying customers. However, it's important to note that Emily's approach required a financial investment, which might not be feasible for all freelancers or small businesses.

Considerations:

Long-term Growth: Free social media tactics like Sarah's can lead to steady growth, creating a loyal customer base over time. The ROI may take longer to materialise, but it can have long-term benefits in terms of brand reputation and customer loyalty.

Immediate Results: Paid social media tactics like Emily's provide an opportunity to achieve more immediate results in terms of lead generation and sales. However, maintaining a positive ROI requires careful monitoring, optimisation, and targeting to ensure the ad spend generates profitable returns.

Balancing Approaches: Freelancers or small businesses can leverage both free and paid tactics to maximise their overall results. Free tactics help establish an organic presence, build relationships, and create brand awareness. Once there is a budget available, incorporating targeted paid campaigns can amplify reach, drive conversions, and accelerate growth.

It's important to evaluate your goals, available resources, and target audience when deciding which approach or combination of tactics is most suitable for your specific business. Each business's experience will vary, but understanding the potential gains and considering the ROI percentages can inform your decision-making process

Overwhelming Presence: Attempting to maintain an active presence on every social media platform can stretch your resources thin and dilute your efforts. Instead, focus on platforms that align with your target audience and industry.

Inconsistent Branding: Inconsistency in branding across different social media platforms can lead to confusion and weaken your brand identity. Maintain consistent branding elements such as logos, colour schemes, and tone of voice.

Lack of Strategy: Rushing into social media without a clear strategy can result in aimless posting and ineffective outcomes. Define your goals, target audience, and messaging strategy before delving in.

Ignoring Analytics: Neglecting to track and analyse social media metrics can hinder your ability to measure success and make data-driven decisions. Regularly review analytics to identify trends, understand audience behaviour, and refine your approach.

Overlooking Customer Engagement: Failing to engage with your audience through comments, messages, and mentions can impede relationship-building. Be responsive, address customer inquiries and feedback, and foster a sense of community.

Inauthentic Content: Creating content that feels overly promotional or lacks authenticity can alienate your audience. Strive for a balance between promotional and value-added content, and showcase the human side of your brand.

Neglecting Negative Feedback: Ignoring or deleting negative comments can harm your brand reputation. Respond professionally and constructively, aiming to address concerns and find solutions publicly or through private messages.

Buying Fake Followers: Purchasing fake followers or engagement can create a false impression of popularity but does not lead to genuine customer engagement or conversions. Focus on growing an organic and engaged following.

Not Utilising Visual Content: Neglecting the power of visual content such as images, videos, and infographics can restrict your engagement potential. Incorporate visually appealing elements into your posts to capture attention.

Failure to Adapt to Platform Changes: Social media platforms regularly update their algorithms and features. Failing to adapt to these changes can reduce your visibility and reach. Stay informed and adjust your strategy accordingly.

Do your best to avoid these traps and mistakes and implementing effective strategies, you can navigate social media marketing successfully and achieve your desired results.

<u>What you should consider instead:</u>

Develop a well-defined social media strategy tailored to your business objectives and target audience.

Conduct thorough research on each platform to determine which ones are most effective for your niche.

Consistently monitor and analyse social media metrics to track progress and make data-driven decisions.

Foster authentic and meaningful interactions with your audience by responding promptly and thoughtfully.

Maintain a consistent brand identity and messaging across all platforms.

Stay informed about platform updates and adjust your strategy accordingly.

Focus on quality content that provides value to your audience, rather than relying solely on promotional material.

Cultivate genuine relationships by engaging with your followers and addressing their feedback and concerns.

Avoid shortcuts like buying fake followers or engagement, as they offer no real value in terms of genuine audience engagement and conversion.

Here are few case studies of people and businesses who avoided these traps and succeeded well:

Freelancer: Jane, a freelance photographer

Social Media Strategy: Jane focused on showcasing her photography skills on Instagram and Pinterest, targeting engaged users interested in visual content.

Activities: She consistently posted high-quality images, used relevant hashtags, engaged with her followers, and collaborated with local influencers.

Results: Jane gained 10,000 Instagram followers within six months, received enquiries for photoshoot bookings, and secured multiple paid collaborations with brands.

Freelancer: Mark, a freelance writer

Social Media Strategy: Mark leveraged Twitter and LinkedIn to establish thought leadership in the writing industry and connect with potential clients.

Activities: He shared valuable writing tips, engaged in industry discussions, participated in relevant Twitter chats, and published insightful articles on LinkedIn.

Results: Mark's Twitter engagement grew significantly, leading to writing opportunities, guest blogging invitations, and connections with editors who commissioned his work.

Freelancer: Sarah, a freelance web developer

Social Media Strategy: Sarah targeted professional platforms such as LinkedIn and GitHub to showcase her expertise and attract potential clients.

Activities: She shared her web development projects, contributed to industry discussions, and joined relevant LinkedIn groups.

Results: Sarah received direct enquiries from potential clients, formed collaborations with other freelancers, and established herself as a reputable web developer in her niche.

Freelancer: Alex, a freelance social media manager

Social Media Strategy: Alex focused on using Instagram and Facebook to demonstrate his social media management skills and attract clients in various industries.

Activities: He created engaging content showcasing successful campaigns, offered tips on social media management, and actively engaged with followers.

Results: Alex generated leads through his social media profiles, secured long-term contracts with clients, and received referrals from satisfied customers.

Freelancer: Laura, a freelance graphic designer

Social Media Strategy: Laura utilised platforms like Behance and Instagram to showcase her design portfolio and connect with potential clients in the creative industry.

Activities: She regularly updated her portfolio, shared design process insights, engaged with design communities, and participated in design challenges.

Results: Laura received project enquiries, collaborated with other designers on creative ventures, and secured long-term contracts with clients impressed by her online portfolio.

Dough & Co., a local bakery:

Social Media Platforms: Instagram, Facebook

Strategy: Dough & Co. used visually appealing photos of their freshly baked goods to attract customers on Instagram. They also engaged with their audience by running interactive contests and sharing behind-the-scenes stories on Facebook.

Results: Their social media efforts helped them increase brand awareness, attract new customers, and boost sales. They saw a 25% increase in monthly revenue within six months of implementing their social media strategy.

The Green Thumb, a local plant nursery:

Social Media Platforms: Facebook, Pinterest

Strategy: The Green Thumb shared gardening tips, plant care advice, and inspiration on Facebook and Pinterest. They also encouraged customers to share their plant photos and participate in gardening challenges.

Results: Their social media presence helped them establish themselves as a go-to resource for plant enthusiasts, leading to an increase in foot traffic to their nursery and a 40% rise in overall sales.

The Wanderlust Cafe, a local coffee shop:

Social Media Platforms: Instagram, Twitter

Strategy: The Wanderlust Cafe used Instagram and Twitter to showcase their cosy atmosphere, unique coffee blends, and delicious food offerings. They also engaged with their customers by responding to their comments and inquiries.

Results: Their social media efforts helped them attract a dedicated local following, leading to a 15% increase in daily footfall and a 30% boost in monthly revenue.

The Pet Paws Boutique, a local pet supply store:

Social Media Platforms: Facebook, Instagram

Strategy: The Pet Paws Boutique shared pet care tips, funny pet videos, and adorable pet photos on Facebook and Instagram. They also collaborated with local pet influencers and hosted pet-friendly events.

Results: Their engaging social media content helped them build a loyal community of pet owners, resulting in increased store visits, higher average purchase amounts, and a 20% growth in annual revenue.

The Fit Squad, a local fitness studio:

Social Media Platforms: Instagram, YouTube

Strategy: The Fit Squad shared workout videos, transformation stories, and fitness tips on Instagram and YouTube. They also ran online fitness challenges and encouraged clients to share their progress and testimonials.

Results: Their social media presence helped them attract a wider audience, increase class bookings, and achieve a 25% rise in monthly revenue.

Starbucks:

Social Media Platforms: Facebook, Twitter, Instagram

Strategy: Starbucks created a sense of community and engagement by encouraging customers to share their Starbucks experiences and using user-generated content. They also launched interactive campaigns, such as the Starbucks White Cup Contest, where customers submitted their own designs for a limited edition cup.

Results: The campaign generated massive social media buzz, with over 4,000 unique designs submitted in just three weeks. Starbucks received significant media coverage and saw a 33% increase in social media mentions during the campaign period.

Nike:

Social Media Platforms: Instagram, YouTube, Twitter

Strategy: Nike focused on storytelling and inspiring their audience through powerful visuals and motivational messages. They collaborated with renowned athletes and influencers, created engaging videos, and encouraged user-generated content with hashtags like #JustDoIt.

Results: Nike's social media campaigns have garnered millions of views, likes, and shares. Their "Dream Crazy" campaign featuring Colin Kaepernick received widespread attention, driving a significant increase in brand awareness and customer engagement.

Coca-Cola:

Social Media Platforms: Facebook, Twitter, YouTube

Strategy: Coca-Cola employed a multi-channel approach, blending social media with traditional advertising. They ran interactive campaigns, such as the "Share a Coke" campaign, where people could find personalised Coke bottles with their names and share them on social media.

Results: The campaign generated over 500,000 photos shared on social media, resulting in a substantial increase in brand awareness and customer engagement. Coca-Cola also experienced a 2% increase in sales during the campaign period.

Airbnb:

Social Media Platforms: Instagram, Twitter, Facebook

Strategy: Airbnb capitalised on user-generated content and storytelling to showcase unique travel experiences. They encouraged users to share their travel photos and stories, highlighting the local hosts and communities.

Results: Airbnb's social media campaigns have generated millions of user-generated content posts, creating a strong sense of community and trust. They experienced significant growth in brand awareness, increased bookings, and a rise in customer loyalty.

Oreo:

Social Media Platforms: Twitter, Facebook, Instagram

Strategy: Oreo became known for their timely and creative social media responses during events and cultural moments. They leveraged real-time marketing, such as their "Dunk in the Dark" tweet during the Super Bowl blackout, which went viral.

Results: Oreo's agile and innovative social media approach garnered widespread media coverage, millions of impressions, and a surge in brand mentions. The "Dunk in the Dark" tweet alone received over 15,000 retweets and solidified Oreo's reputation for creative marketing.

While social media plays a vital role in modern marketing, it is not a standalone solution. A comprehensive marketing campaign encompasses various stages, including market research, message development, channel selection, engagement, lead generation, conversion, and customer relationship management. By leveraging social media alongside other tactics and stages, businesses can achieve sustainable growth and success in today's dynamic marketplace.

Here is a list of social media software and tools that you can use:

Social Media Management Tools:

Hootsuite: Allows businesses to manage multiple social media accounts, schedule posts, engage with their audience, and track performance metrics.

Buffer: Offers social media scheduling, content creation, and analytics features, helping businesses streamline their social media presence.

Sprout Social: Provides a unified platform for social media management, offering scheduling, engagement, and analytics capabilities.

Social Media Analytics Tools:

Google Analytics: Tracks website traffic from social media platforms, measures conversions, and provides insights into user behaviour.

Sprout Social: Offers comprehensive analytics and reporting features, including engagement metrics, audience demographics, and post performance insights.

Brandwatch Analytics: Provides social media listening, sentiment analysis, and competitive benchmarking to measure campaign effectiveness.

Social Media Listening Tools:

Awario: Monitors brand mentions, tracks keywords, and provides real-time social media listening to help businesses stay on top of conversations and trends.

Mention: Tracks brand mentions and social media conversations in real-time, providing sentiment analysis and allowing businesses to engage with customers promptly.

Talkwalker: Tracks brand mentions, sentiment, and social media trends, offering advanced analytics to uncover consumer insights and measure brand reputation.

Social Media Advertising Platforms:

Facebook Ads Manager: Enables businesses to create and manage targeted advertising campaigns on Facebook and Instagram, reaching a specific audience.

Google Ads: Allows businesses to create and run ads across the Google network, including search, display, and video campaigns.

LinkedIn Ads: Offers advertising solutions to reach a professional audience on LinkedIn through sponsored content, text ads, and sponsored InMail.

Social Media Content Creation Tools:

Canva: Provides a range of design templates and tools for creating visually appealing social media graphics, posts, and stories.

Adobe Spark: Offers a user-friendly platform for creating professional graphics, videos, and web pages for social media campaigns.

Easil: Provides customisable templates and drag-and-drop design features, allowing businesses to create eye-catching social media visuals.

Social Media Influencer Marketing Platforms:

Upfluence: Provides influencer discovery, relationship management, and campaign tracking to help businesses connect with relevant influencers and measure campaign success.

BuzzStream: Facilitates influencer research and outreach, streamlining the process of building relationships with influencers and managing collaborations.

AspireIQ: Helps businesses find relevant influencers based on their niche, audience demographics, and engagement rates, ensuring effective influencer partnerships.

Social Media Customer Support Tools:

Zendesk: Integrates social media customer support with other support channels, enabling businesses to provide efficient and consistent customer service across platforms.

Freshdesk: Offers a helpdesk system with social media ticketing capabilities, allowing businesses to manage customer inquiries and resolve issues on social media.

Sparkcentral: Enables businesses to provide seamless customer support across social media platforms, consolidating messages and conversations in a single interface.

Social Media Listening and Sentiment Analysis Tools:

Brand24: Monitors brand mentions and sentiment analysis on social media, helping businesses understand customer sentiment and identify brand advocates or detractors.

Talkwalker Quick Search: Offers real-time social media monitoring and sentiment analysis, enabling businesses to stay updated on brand conversations and sentiment.

Sysomos: Provides social media listening and sentiment analysis tools to help businesses monitor brand mentions, sentiment, and customer conversations across various platforms.

Social Media Visual Content Creation Tools:

Fotor: Provides a user-friendly online photo editing tool for creating stunning visuals, collages, and graphics for social media posts.

Piktochart: Offers an easy-to-use infographic maker to create visually appealing infographics, reports, and presentations for social media sharing.

Visme: Enables businesses to create engaging visual content, such as presentations, infographics, and social media graphics, with customisable templates and drag-and-drop features.

Social Media Hashtag Research Tools:

Hashtagify: Helps businesses find popular and relevant hashtags for their social media posts, increasing visibility and engagement.

RiteTag: Offers hashtag suggestions based on real-time data, helping businesses optimise their hashtag usage for improved reach and engagement.

Display Purposes: Provides hashtag recommendations based on your content and target audience, ensuring relevant exposure to the right audience.

Social Media Reporting and Analytics Tools:

Sprout Social: Offers comprehensive social media analytics and reporting features, including engagement metrics, audience demographics, and post performance insights.

Quintly: Provides social media analytics to measure key metrics, benchmark against competitors, and generate customisable reports.

Socialbakers: Offers social media analytics and benchmarking tools to track performance, audience insights, and campaign effectiveness.

Social Media Automation Tools:

MeetEdgar: Allows businesses to automate social media content scheduling, recycling evergreen posts, and managing content libraries for increased efficiency.

IFTTT (If This Then That): Provides automation capabilities by creating connections between different apps and platforms, enabling social media tasks to be triggered automatically based on predefined rules.

Zapier: Offers a platform for integrating and automating various social media and business applications, streamlining workflows and eliminating manual tasks.

Social Media Influencer Relationship Management Tools:

CreatorIQ: Helps businesses identify, manage, and track influencer partnerships, streamlining influencer campaign management and performance tracking.

AspireIQ: Provides a platform for finding and collaborating with influencers, managing influencer relationships, and measuring campaign success.

Onalytica: Offers influencer discovery, relationship management, and analytics to help businesses build effective influencer marketing strategies.

Social Media Live Streaming Tools:

StreamYard: Enables businesses to livestream on multiple social media platforms simultaneously, facilitating real-time audience engagement and interaction.

Restream: Allows businesses to broadcast live videos to multiple social media channels, expanding reach and maximising audience engagement.

BeLive: Provides a user-friendly platform for hosting live interviews, talk shows, and Q&A sessions on social media platforms.

Social Media Employee Advocacy Tools:

Bambu by Sprout Social: Facilitates employee advocacy by allowing businesses to curate and share pre-approved content on social media through their employees' networks.

EveryoneSocial: Offers a platform for managing employee advocacy programs, encouraging employees to share company content and amplify brand messaging.

Smarp: Provides a centralised hub for businesses to distribute and track company content, enabling employees to share it across their social networks.

Social Media Customer Relationship Management (CRM) Tools:

Zoho CRM: Integrates social media interactions and data with customer relationship management, helping businesses manage and track customer engagement across channels.

HubSpot CRM: Offers social media monitoring and engagement features within a comprehensive customer relationship management platform, allowing businesses to nurture leads and manage customer interactions.

Salesforce Social Studio: Provides social media management, listening, and engagement tools integrated with customer relationship management capabilities.

Social Media Collaboration Tools:

Slack: Facilitates real-time communication and collaboration among social media teams, streamlining workflows and improving coordination.

Trello: Enables social media teams to organise and track their projects, content calendars, and task assignments in a visual and collaborative manner.

Monday.com: Offers a flexible platform for planning, managing, and tracking social media campaigns, fostering collaboration and ensuring team productivity.

Social Media Contest and Promotion Tools:

Woobox: Provides a platform for creating and running social media contests, giveaways, and promotions to engage and grow an audience.

Gleam: Offers tools for running social media contests, sweepstakes, and viral giveaways, helping businesses drive engagement and capture leads.

Rafflecopter: Enables businesses to create and manage social media giveaways and contests, encouraging audience participation and brand awareness.

Choose the ones that align with your social media goals, platforms, and workflow to effectively manage and optimise your social media presence.

It's important to approach it strategically to achieve the best results. If you want to keep it simple, start with these guidelines to make the most of your social media efforts:

Be Disciplined with Your Time: Social media can be a time-consuming endeavour, so it's crucial to strike a balance. Avoid getting carried away with responding to every comment and spending excessive time on the platforms. Prioritise marketing tasks that provide a higher return on your investment of time and resources.

Understand the True Cost: While social media marketing may seem "free" at first glance, it's important to recognise that your time has value. Consider the opportunity cost of spending significant time on social media instead of focusing on other revenue-generating activities.

Build and Own Your Marketing Assets: Instead of solely relying on social media platforms, focus on building and owning your own marketing assets such as websites, blogs, and email lists. Use social media as a tool to drive traffic to these assets. This ensures that your efforts contribute to building your own brand and audience, rather than solely benefiting the social media platforms.

Beware of Platform Ownership: Remember that your social media profiles and pages belong to the respective social networks. Investing substantial time and resources in building up a profile or audience on these networks ultimately builds their assets, not your own. Protect your business by diversifying your online presence and maintaining ownership of your marketing channels.

Learn from Past Platform Changes: Platforms like Facebook can change their policies, impacting your reach and engagement with your audience. For example, Facebook's policy change required businesses to pay for reaching their entire audience. This highlights the importance of building direct communication channels, such as email lists, to maintain control and reach your audience effectively.

Focus on Quality over Quantity: Rather than pursuing a large number of followers or likes on social media, prioritise building an engaged and loyal audience. A smaller but highly interested and responsive audience can have a more significant impact on your business. Consider the value of having 1,000 engaged email subscribers compared to 10,000 Facebook page likes with limited reach.

Understand Your Target Audience: To effectively reach your prospects, identify where they spend their time online and use the appropriate social media channels to deliver your message. Conduct market research and engage with your audience to understand their preferences and habits.

Remember, while social media can be a valuable tool, it's important to approach it strategically, keeping in mind the limitations and challenges associated with these platforms. Balance your time, build your own marketing assets, and understand your target audience, so that you can maximise the effectiveness of your social media efforts and reach your business goals.

The Profound Influence of Email Marketing on Communication and Business Success

Email marketing is a highly effective and personal medium that allows businesses to directly engage with prospects and customers. With the proliferation of smartphones and mobile devices, email has become even more accessible, making it an invaluable tool for marketing campaigns.

One of the key benefits of email marketing is the ability to build a database of email subscribers. By prominently featuring an email opt-in form on your website, you can capture the email addresses of visitors who are interested in your products or services. This gives you the opportunity to nurture those prospects who may not be ready to make a purchase immediately but are interested in receiving more information.

For example, let's consider a small online retailer selling handmade jewellery. They offer a free style guide to visitors who sign up for their email list. By capturing these email addresses, the retailer can send regular newsletters featuring new product releases, styling tips, and exclusive discounts. Over time, this engagement nurtures a relationship with subscribers and encourages them to make purchases.

Email marketing also allows businesses to maintain a close relationship with their customer base and test new products and services. For instance, a software company can use email to announce the launch of a new feature, provide tutorials to existing customers, and offer special upgrade options. By leveraging the direct and personal nature of email, the company can gather valuable feedback, generate upsells, and improve customer satisfaction.

Additionally, having a responsive email list provides businesses with a valuable marketing asset. Let's say a fitness coach offers an online course on healthy living. With a list of engaged subscribers, they can promote the course to their audience and drive sign-ups, generating a significant return on investment. Furthermore, the coach can use their email list to gather feedback, conduct surveys, and offer personalised advice, establishing themselves as an expert in the field.

Whilst social media platforms have gained popularity, an email database remains an essential component of any comprehensive marketing strategy. Unlike social media reach, which is often limited and subject to algorithm changes, an email list offers direct control and ownership. It's like having a direct line of communication with your audience, without the noise and distractions found on social media.

However, there are some important considerations when it comes to email marketing. First, it's crucial to adhere to anti-spam regulations. Always ensure that you have the consent of your email recipients and avoid purchasing or compiling email lists without explicit permission.

Secondly, maintaining a personal touch is key. Write your emails in a conversational tone, addressing your subscribers as individuals rather than sending generic messages. Personalisation can significantly enhance engagement and build stronger connections with your audience.

Lastly, leveraging the power of email automation can greatly enhance your email marketing efforts. Automated email sequences allow you to deliver targeted messages based on subscriber behaviour, such as welcome emails, abandoned cart reminders, or personalised recommendations. This saves time and ensures that your subscribers receive timely and relevant content.

Email marketing remains a cornerstone of successful online marketing strategies, enabling businesses to reach, engage, and convert prospects into loyal customers. Whether it's driving sales, providing valuable content, or nurturing relationships, email marketing offers a powerful and personal medium for businesses to connect with their audience.

<u>Dos and Don'ts of Email Marketing:</u>

Do:

Personalise email content: Craft personalised email messages that address each recipient by their name and provide content tailored to their specific interests or preferences. Personalisation helps to create a stronger connection and increases the likelihood of engagement and conversion.

Example: An online retailer sends personalised product recommendations to customers based on their past purchases, browsing history, and demographic information.

Use clear and compelling subject lines: Create subject lines that grab attention and entice recipients to open your emails. Make them concise, relevant, and compelling to generate higher open rates.

Example: A travel agency uses subject lines like "Exclusive Discount: Explore Paradise with 30% Off Your Dream Holiday" to pique the interest of subscribers and encourage them to open the email.

Implement a responsive email design: Ensure that your emails are optimised for different devices and screen sizes, including smartphones and tablets. A responsive design adjusts the layout and formatting of the email to provide a seamless reading experience across various platforms.

Example: An e-commerce store designs their emails with a responsive layout and scalable images, allowing customers to easily view and interact with the content on any device.

Test and analyse email campaigns: Conduct regular testing and analysis of your email campaigns to understand what resonates best with your audience. Experiment with different elements such as subject lines, call-to-action buttons, content length, and visuals to optimise engagement and conversion rates.

Example: A software company performs A/B testing on two variations of their email template to compare the effectiveness of different design elements and determine the most impactful version.

Monitor email deliverability and engagement metrics: Keep an eye on your email deliverability rates, open rates, click-through rates, and unsubscribe rates. Monitoring these metrics helps you gauge the success of your campaigns and identify areas for improvement.

Example: A nonprofit organisation tracks their email engagement metrics to measure the effectiveness of their fundraising campaigns and identify potential opportunities to enhance donor engagement.

Don't:

Spam recipients' inboxes: Respect your subscribers' inboxes by avoiding spammy practices such as sending unsolicited emails or bombarding them with excessive promotional messages. Focus on providing value and maintaining a healthy balance between promotional and informative content.

Example: A fashion brand ensures they only send relevant promotions and valuable content to their subscribers, avoiding frequent and irrelevant sales pitches.

Neglect email list hygiene: Regularly clean and update your email list to remove inactive or disengaged subscribers. A clean and engaged list improves your deliverability rates and ensures that your messages reach the right audience.

Example: An online service provider periodically sends re-engagement emails to subscribers who haven't interacted with their emails for a certain period, giving them the opportunity to confirm their interest or unsubscribe.

Forget to include a clear call-to-action (CTA): Every email should have a clear and compelling CTA that directs recipients to take a desired action, such as making a purchase, signing up for an event, or downloading a resource. Make your CTA prominent and visually appealing.

Example: A software company includes a prominent CTA button in their email, inviting recipients to sign up for a free trial of their product with a clear and concise message.

Neglect email list segmentation: Segmenting your email list allows you to send targeted and relevant content to specific groups of subscribers based on their preferences, demographics, or purchase history. This enhances personalisation and improves the overall effectiveness of your email campaigns.

Example: A pet supplies retailer segments their email list into dog owners, cat owners, and bird owners, tailoring their product recommendations and care tips to each group's specific needs.

Overwhelm subscribers with excessive emails: Find the right balance in terms of email frequency. While it's essential to stay in touch and maintain regular communication, bombarding subscribers with excessive emails can lead to fatigue and increased unsubscribe rates. Consider the preferences of your audience and adjust the frequency accordingly.

Example: A fitness coach sends weekly emails with workout tips and motivational content, striking a balance between providing valuable information and avoiding overwhelming their subscribers' inboxes.

By following these dos and don'ts, you can create effective and engaging email marketing campaigns that resonate with your audience, drive conversions, and nurture lasting customer relationships. Continually monitor your results, adapt your strategies, and stay up-to-date with industry best practices to maximise the impact of your email marketing efforts.

<u>The Relevance of GDPR in Email Marketing:</u>

The General Data Protection Regulation (GDPR) is a set of regulations introduced by the European Union (EU) to enhance the protection of individuals' personal data and provide them with greater control over how their data is used. GDPR has a significant impact on email marketing practices, as email often involves the processing of personal data.

Understanding GDPR and complying with its requirements is crucial for email marketers to ensure legal and ethical practices.

Purpose and Benefits of GDPR:

The primary purpose of GDPR is to give individuals more control over their personal data and ensure transparency and accountability in its use. GDPR aims to protect individuals' privacy rights by requiring businesses to obtain explicit consent for data processing, providing clear information about data collection and usage, and implementing measures to safeguard personal information.

Benefits for the Sender:

Enhanced trust and credibility: By complying with GDPR, email senders demonstrate their commitment to protecting individuals' privacy. This builds trust and credibility with subscribers, leading to stronger relationships and increased engagement.

Improved deliverability: GDPR compliance helps maintain a clean and engaged email list, reducing the likelihood of emails being marked as spam or blocked by email service providers. This improves deliverability and ensures that messages reach the intended recipients.

Targeted and relevant communication: GDPR encourages email senders to obtain explicit consent and collect accurate subscriber preferences. This allows for better segmentation and targeting, enabling the delivery of more relevant and personalised content to recipients.

Benefits for the Receiver:

Control over personal data: GDPR empowers individuals to have greater control over their personal information. They can decide how their data is used, giving them more confidence and peace of mind when interacting with businesses.

Transparency and informed choices: GDPR mandates clear and concise privacy notices, informing individuals about how their data will be processed. This allows recipients to make informed decisions about subscribing or unsubscribing from email communications based on their preferences.

Protection against data breaches: GDPR establishes data security standards and requirements for businesses. Compliance helps reduce the risk of data breaches, protecting individuals' personal information from being compromised.

To comply with GDPR in email marketing, consider the following practices:

Obtain explicit consent: Ensure that subscribers have given explicit consent to receive marketing emails from you. Implement a clear and unambiguous opt-in process, where individuals actively confirm their consent to be added to your email list.

Example: Include a checkbox on your signup form with a statement like, "I consent to receive marketing emails from [Your Company Name]."

Provide transparent privacy notices: Clearly inform subscribers about the purpose of data collection, how their data will be used, and their rights under GDPR. Use plain language and avoid lengthy, complex statements.

Example: Include a link to your privacy policy in your email signup form, outlining the information you collect, how you use it, and the rights of subscribers.

Implement data protection measures: Safeguard personal data by implementing security measures, such as encryption, access controls, and regular data backups. Take steps to prevent data breaches and promptly address any security incidents.

Example: Use secure email service providers that encrypt data during transmission and storage, and regularly update your software and systems to mitigate security risks.

Offer unsubscribe options: Make it easy for recipients to unsubscribe from your emails and respect their choices promptly. Include an unsubscribe link in every email and provide clear instructions on how to opt out.

Example: Include an unsubscribe link at the bottom of your emails with a statement like, "To unsubscribe from our emails, click here."

Manage data access and retention: Only collect and retain the necessary data for your email marketing purposes. Regularly review and update your email list to remove inactive or unsubscribed contacts.

Example: Implement automated processes to remove inactive subscribers who haven't engaged with your emails for a specified period.

I always recommend to consult legal professionals or experts to ensure compliance with GDPR, as regulations may vary based on specific circumstances and jurisdictions. By adhering to GDPR's principles, email marketers can maintain trust, protect personal data, and build stronger relationships with their subscribers.

Email Marketing Tools

Email marketing tools offer a wide range of features and configurations to enable automation in your campaigns. Here's an in-depth overview of how automation works and how you can use it to your advantage:

Workflow or Automation Builders:

Triggers: Set up triggers that initiate the automation sequence, such as a new subscriber joining your list, a specific date or event, or a subscriber's action like clicking a link or making a purchase.

Actions: Specify the actions you want the system to take when a trigger occurs, such as sending an email, updating subscriber data, adding or removing tags, or initiating a follow-up task.

Conditions: Apply conditions or filters to segment your audience and send targeted emails based on specific criteria like demographics, purchase history, or engagement level.

Example: When a subscriber signs up for your newsletter, you can trigger an automated welcome email series to introduce them to your brand and nurture the relationship.

Email Templates and Personalisation:

Dynamic Content: Utilise dynamic content blocks within your email templates to display personalised information based on subscriber data, ensuring each recipient receives a tailored message.

Merge Tags: Use merge tags to dynamically insert subscriber details into your email content, subject lines, or sender names, making each email feel personalised and relevant.

Example: Inserting the subscriber's first name in the email subject line, such as "John, check out our latest offers exclusively for you!"

Autoresponders and Drip Campaigns:

Sequential Timing: Configure the time delays between each email in the sequence to create a strategic flow of communication.

Goal-based Triggers: Define specific goals or actions that, when completed by a subscriber, will trigger the next email in the series.

Example: Sending a series of onboarding emails to guide new customers through the product setup and usage process, with each email building upon the previous one.

Segmentation and Tagging:

Tagging: Apply tags to subscribers based on their interactions, preferences, or specific attributes to categorise and target them more effectively.

Dynamic Segmentation: Use segmentation rules to automatically group subscribers based on specific criteria, ensuring that they receive the most relevant content.

Example: Segmenting subscribers based on their purchase history and sending targeted emails with product recommendations tailored to their interests.

Testing and Analytics:

A/B Testing: Conduct split tests by creating multiple versions of your email and sending them to a sample audience to determine the most effective elements like subject lines, call-to-action buttons, or content variations.

Performance Tracking: Monitor key metrics like open rates, click-through rates, conversions, and revenue generated to gauge the success of your automated campaigns and make data-driven improvements.

Example: Testing two different subject lines to see which one generates a higher open rate and using the results to optimise future email campaigns.

To implement email marketing automation effectively, consider the following steps:

Define Your Goals: Clearly identify the objectives you want to achieve through automation, such as increasing engagement, generating leads, or driving conversions.

Plan Your Automation Sequences: Map out the desired flow of your emails, identifying triggers, actions, and content for each step in the sequence.

Set Up Your Automation Builder: Use the workflow builder provided by your email marketing tool to configure the automation sequence, defining triggers, actions, and conditions based on your planned flow.

Customise Your Email Templates: Tailor the pre-designed email templates to align with your brand and customise them with personalised content using merge tags and dynamic content blocks.

Segment Your Audience: Use segmentation and tagging features to categorise your subscribers based on their characteristics, interests, or behaviour, ensuring that you send relevant emails to the right segments.

Test and Measure: Conduct A/B tests to optimise your emails, track key performance metrics, and analyse the results to make data-driven decisions for improving your automation sequences.

By leveraging the configuration options and features provided by email marketing tools, you can create powerful automation workflows that engage, nurture, and convert your subscribers effectively.

<u>List of Popular Free and Paid Tools</u>

Email marketing software is a vital tool for businesses to effectively reach and engage with their audience. Whether you're a small business owner, a blogger, or a marketing professional, having the right email marketing software can streamline your campaigns, automate processes, and drive better results. In this article, we'll explore a comprehensive list of email marketing software, including both free and paid options, to help you find the right fit for your needs.

Free Email Marketing Software:

Mailchimp: Mailchimp is a popular choice for beginners and small businesses. Its free plan allows up to 2,000 subscribers and 10,000 monthly email sends. With a user-friendly interface, pre-designed templates, and basic automation features like welcome emails and abandoned cart reminders, Mailchimp makes it easy to create professional-looking emails without any upfront costs.

SendinBlue: SendinBlue offers a free plan with up to 300 emails per day and unlimited subscribers. It provides essential email marketing features such as email design tools, contact management, and basic marketing automation functionalities. SendinBlue's free plan is suitable for businesses looking to start their email marketing journey without breaking the bank.

MailerLite: MailerLite offers a free plan for up to 1,000 subscribers and 12,000 monthly email sends. It provides a drag-and-drop editor, automation workflows, and landing page creation tools. MailerLite's free plan is ideal for small businesses that need more advanced features like automation to nurture their subscribers.

Benchmark Email: Benchmark Email offers a free plan with up to 500 subscribers and 500 email sends per month. It includes features like email templates, list management, and basic automation capabilities. This plan is suitable for businesses with a smaller subscriber base and simpler email marketing needs.

Moosend: Moosend offers a free plan with up to 1,000 subscribers and unlimited monthly email sends. It provides an intuitive editor, automation workflows, and advanced personalisation options. Moosend's free plan is a great choice for businesses that require advanced features like personalisation and segmentation.

Mailjet: Mailjet offers a free plan with up to 6,000 emails per month and 200 emails per day. It provides features like email analytics, deliverability optimisation, and tracking. Mailjet's free plan is suitable for businesses that require reliable email delivery and tracking capabilities.

Zoho Campaigns: Zoho Campaigns offers a free plan with up to 2,000 subscribers and 12,000 monthly email sends. It provides a drag-and-drop editor, automation workflows, and pre-designed templates. Zoho Campaigns' free plan is ideal for businesses looking for a simple yet effective email marketing solution.

Mailgun: Mailgun offers a free plan with up to 5,000 monthly email sends and 100 validations per month. It provides features like email analytics, deliverability optimisation, and tracking. Mailgun's free plan is suitable for businesses that require reliable email delivery and tracking capabilities.

Omnisend: Omnisend offers a free plan with up to 15,000 emails per month and basic automation features. It specialises in email marketing for e-commerce businesses, providing tools like cart recovery emails, product recommendations, and segmentation based on customer behaviour.

SendPulse: SendPulse offers a free plan with up to 15,000 monthly email sends and 500 subscribers. It provides email templates, marketing automation, and advanced personalisation options. SendPulse's free plan is suitable for businesses that need a comprehensive email marketing solution with a generous sending limit.

Paid Email Marketing Software:

HubSpot: HubSpot offers a comprehensive marketing suite with email marketing as part of its features. It provides advanced automation, segmentation, and personalisation capabilities, along with detailed analytics and CRM integration. HubSpot is suitable for businesses that require a robust marketing automation platform and want to manage their entire marketing strategy in one place.

ActiveCampaign: ActiveCampaign offers a range of plans with advanced automation features, CRM integration, and split testing capabilities. It provides tools for creating targeted campaigns, managing contacts, and tracking customer interactions. ActiveCampaign is ideal for businesses that need sophisticated automation workflows and want to personalise their email marketing based on customer behaviour.

GetResponse: GetResponse offers a variety of plans with features like automation, landing page creation, and webinar integration. It provides advanced analytics, A/B testing, and a user-friendly interface. GetResponse is suitable for businesses that want a comprehensive email marketing solution with additional marketing features like landing page creation and webinar hosting.

ConvertKit: ConvertKit is designed specifically for creators and offers features like automation, subscriber tagging, and customisable opt-in forms. It provides a visual automation builder and integrates with popular tools for content creation and selling. ConvertKit is ideal for bloggers, authors, and online creators who need a platform tailored to their unique marketing needs.

Campaign Monitor: Campaign Monitor offers a range of plans with features like drag-and-drop email builders, segmentation, and A/B testing. It provides advanced analytics, custom branding options, and integration with popular e-commerce platforms. Campaign Monitor is suitable for businesses looking for an intuitive email marketing tool with powerful segmentation and customisation capabilities.

SendGrid: SendGrid offers a flexible pricing model based on the number of emails sent per month. It provides features like email templates, A/B testing, and advanced deliverability tools. SendGrid is suitable for businesses that need reliable email delivery and want to optimise their email campaigns for better engagement.

Mailigen: Mailigen offers a variety of plans with features like automation, landing page creation, and integration with e-commerce platforms. It provides advanced segmentation options and real-time analytics. Mailigen is suitable for businesses looking for a comprehensive email marketing solution with strong segmentation capabilities.

AWeber: AWeber offers a range of plans with features like automation, drag-and-drop email builders, and subscriber management tools. It provides extensive integrations with popular platforms and a library of pre-designed templates. AWeber is suitable for businesses that want a user-friendly email marketing solution with robust automation capabilities.

Drip: Drip specialises in e-commerce email marketing and offers a range of plans tailored to online retailers. It provides features like cart abandonment recovery, personalised product recommendations, and automation workflows. Drip is suitable for businesses that want to leverage email marketing to drive sales and increase customer retention.

Constant Contact: Constant Contact offers a variety of plans with features like email templates, contact management, and automation capabilities. It provides event management tools and social media integration. Constant Contact is suitable for businesses looking for an all-in-one email marketing solution with additional event marketing features.

With the abundance of email marketing software available, both free and paid, businesses of all sizes and industries can find a suitable tool to enhance their email marketing efforts. Whether you're just starting out or looking to scale your campaigns, these software options offer a range of features, automation capabilities, and analytics to help you engage with your audience, drive conversions, and achieve your marketing goals. Consider your specific needs, budget, and desired features to make an informed decision and take your email marketing to new heights.

Closely monitor the performance of your email campaigns. With Mailchimp, you can easily import your existing contacts, create signup forms for your website, and segment your audience based on their preferences or purchase history. This allows you to send targeted emails to specific groups, such as customers interested in earrings or those who have made a previous purchase.

As your business grows and you need more advanced features, you can consider upgrading to a paid email marketing software like ActiveCampaign. With ActiveCampaign, you can leverage its powerful automation capabilities to create personalised customer journeys. For example, you can set up automated workflows that trigger different emails based on specific actions, such as a customer abandoning their basket or a subscriber completing a purchase. You can also use its CRM integration to track customer interactions, nurture leads, and build stronger relationships with your audience.

Another paid option worth considering is GetResponse. With GetResponse, you can take advantage of its landing page creation tools to design visually appealing and conversion-focused landing pages for your jewellery promotions. You can also integrate webinars into your email marketing strategy to engage with your customers through live events, product demonstrations, or educational sessions. GetResponse's advanced analytics will provide you with insights on how your emails are performing, allowing you to optimise your campaigns for better results.

If you're a blogger or online creator, ConvertKit offers a tailored solution to meet your unique needs. With ConvertKit, you can easily create custom opt-in forms and landing pages to capture email subscribers. Its visual automation builder enables you to create intricate email sequences that nurture your audience and promote your latest jewellery collections. You can also use ConvertKit's integration with content creation platforms like WordPress to automatically send email updates whenever you publish a new blog post or video.

For businesses that prioritise customisable branding and design, Campaign Monitor is a great choice. With Campaign Monitor, you can create stunning emails using its drag-and-drop email builder and customise the design to match your brand's aesthetics. Its advanced segmentation and A/B testing features allow you to fine-tune your email campaigns and optimise them for maximum engagement and conversions. Campaign Monitor also integrates seamlessly with popular e-commerce platforms, making it easy to sync customer data and send targeted product recommendations based on customer behaviour.

<u>Creating Great Email Content</u>

Creating great emails for email marketing involves a strategic and thoughtful approach. Here is an expanded step-by-step process, specifically focusing on a one-person approach, along with examples to help you craft compelling and effective emails:

Define your goal: Clarify the objective of your email campaign and what you want to achieve as a one-person operation. For example:

Goal: Increase website traffic and conversions

Example: "Drive Traffic to Your Website - Discover the Latest Tips and Trends!"

Know your audience: Understand your target audience's preferences, interests, and pain points as a one-person business. For example:

Audience: Small business owners seeking marketing advice

Example: "Marketing Made Simple: Grow Your Business with Proven Strategies"

Craft a compelling subject line: Make your subject line attention-grabbing and compelling, even as a one-person operation. For example:

Subject Line: "Boost Your Online Presence - Unleash the Power of Digital Marketing!"

Personalise your emails: Use merge tags to include the recipient's name and segment your audience for more targeted content. For example:

Personalisation: "Hello [Recipient's Name], Exclusive Tips Just for You!"

Design visually appealing emails: Create an attractive design that reflects your brand identity, even with limited resources. For example:

Design: Clean layout, consistent branding, and well-structured content

Write engaging content: Craft concise and compelling copy that resonates with your audience as a one-person operation. For example:

Content: Share actionable tips, success stories, or behind-the-scenes insights

Example: "Unlock Your Marketing Potential: Learn From Small Business Success Stories"

Use compelling visuals: Incorporate relevant images, graphics, or videos to enhance your message, even if you have limited design capabilities. For example:

Visuals: Use high-quality stock images, create simple graphics, or record short video clips to support your content

Focus on value: Provide valuable content and resources to your subscribers, showcasing your expertise as a one-person business. For example:

Value: Offer free guides, templates, or exclusive access to industry insights

Example: "Get Your Free Marketing Toolkit: Accelerate Your Business Growth Today!"

Optimise for deliverability: Ensure your emails reach the inbox by following best practices, even as a one-person operation. For example:

Best Practices: Use a reputable email marketing service provider, maintain a clean email list, and avoid spam triggers in your email content

Test and analyse: Test your emails across different devices and analyse key metrics, even with limited resources. For example:

Metrics: Monitor open rates, click-through rates, and website conversions using simple tracking tools

A/B Testing: Experiment with different subject lines, visuals, or calls-to-action to optimise performance

Continuously improve: Adapt your email marketing strategy based on audience feedback and industry trends, leveraging your unique perspective as a one-person business. For example:

Feedback: Engage with your subscribers, seek their feedback, and incorporate their suggestions into your emails

Trends: Stay updated on the latest marketing trends and apply them to your email content

By following this step-by-step approach, even as a one-person operation, you can create impactful email campaigns that engage and convert your subscribers effectively. Tailor the examples provided to your specific industry, audience, and objectives, leveraging your unique strengths and resources as a one-person business. Continuously monitor, adapt, and refine your email marketing strategy based on audience feedback and evolving industry trends to build strong connections and achieve your goals.

Constructing a powerful email involves paying attention to various areas, including the beginning, middle, and end. Let's explore each section and see how successful email examples have utilised them:

Beginning:

Subject Line: Capture the recipient's attention with a compelling subject line that sparks curiosity or offers a benefit. Example: "Limited-Time Offer: Get 50% Off Your Next Purchase!"

Preheader Text: Use a brief preview text that complements the subject line and entices recipients to open the email. Example: "Hurry, this exclusive discount won't last long!"

Middle:

Introduction: Start with a personalised greeting and a brief introduction that establishes a connection with the recipient. Example: "Dear [Name], As a valued customer, we're excited to offer you an exclusive discount on our latest collection."

Engaging Content: Provide valuable content, such as product highlights, industry insights, or useful tips, to captivate the reader's interest and showcase your expertise. Example: "Discover our top-selling products that are revolutionising the way you [solve a problem]."

Compelling Offer: Present a clear and compelling offer that addresses the recipient's needs and prompts them to take action. Example: "Enjoy 50% off on all products this week only. Don't miss out!"

Persuasive Copy: Use persuasive language and storytelling techniques to convey the benefits and value of your product or service. Example: "Experience the transformational power of our [product/service] and unlock a world of possibilities."

End:

Call to Action: Clearly state the desired action you want the recipient to take and make it easy for them to do so. Use a prominent button or link that stands out. Example: "Shop now and save!"

Urgency: Create a sense of urgency or scarcity to encourage immediate action. Example: "Limited stock available. Act fast to secure your discount!"

Social Proof: Include customer testimonials, reviews, or success stories to build trust and credibility. Example: "Hear what our satisfied customers are saying about their experience with us."

Contact Information: Provide clear contact details, including phone numbers, email addresses, or links to social media profiles, to make it convenient for recipients to get in touch with you.

Closing: End with a friendly and personalised closing that reinforces your brand's voice and appreciation for the recipient's engagement. Example: "Thank you for being a valued part of our community. We look forward to serving you again soon!"

Successful email examples:

Airbnb: Airbnb sends personalised emails that provide tailored recommendations for accommodations based on the recipient's previous searches and preferences. They effectively use compelling visuals and clear calls to action to entice recipients to book their next stay.

Dropbox: Dropbox utilises a clean and minimalist design to communicate the simplicity and functionality of their file storage service. They focus on concise copy and use visual cues to guide the reader's attention to their call to action.

Grammarly: Grammarly sends helpful and educational emails with grammar tips and writing insights. They provide value to their subscribers by offering practical advice and showcasing the benefits of their writing tool.

Analyse successful email examples and following the structure outlined above, you can create powerful and effective emails. Remember to align your content with your audience's interests, keep the design clean and visually appealing, and test different elements to optimise your email performance.

Here are ten examples of how other businesses did it:

HubSpot:

Objective: Increase lead generation and customer engagement.

Strategy: HubSpot implemented personalised and segmented email campaigns to increase engagement and lead generation.

Execution: They collected user data to create targeted segments and delivered relevant content to each segment. They also focused on A/B testing to optimise subject lines, content, and CTAs.

Result: HubSpot implemented personalised and segmented email campaigns, resulting in a 2.3% increase in open rates and a staggering 506% increase in click-through rates. These campaigns helped HubSpot generate a significant number of leads and improve customer conversions. For example, by sending targeted emails based on user preferences and behaviour, HubSpot saw a 50% increase in lead-to-customer conversion rates within a six-month period.

Why it worked: By sending targeted emails based on user preferences and behaviour, HubSpot saw a significant increase in lead-to-customer conversion rates. To replicate their success, focus on segmenting your audience, personalising your emails, and continuously testing and optimising your campaigns.

Airbnb:

Objective: Drive bookings and increase user engagement.

Strategy: Airbnb focused on creating targeted email campaigns to drive bookings and enhance user engagement.

Execution: They used personalisation and tailored recommendations based on user preferences and past bookings. They also incorporated urgency and exclusive offers to drive conversions.

Result: Airbnb focused on creating targeted email campaigns to encourage bookings and enhance user engagement. By providing personalised recommendations and special offers tailored to each user's preferences and past bookings, Airbnb achieved remarkable results. In a six-month period, they experienced a 300% increase in email sign-ups and a 30% increase in bookings directly attributed to their email marketing efforts.

Why it worked: Airbnb achieved a significant increase in email sign-ups and bookings by delivering personalised and enticing emails to their audience. To replicate their success, focus on understanding your audience, personalising your content, and leveraging exclusivity and urgency to drive conversions.

PayPal:

Objective: Improve user engagement and increase transactions.

Strategy: PayPal aimed to improve user engagement and increase transactions through targeted email campaigns.

Execution: They sent personalised emails highlighting new features, promotions, and exclusive offers to encourage user activity and boost app usage.

Result: PayPal used targeted email campaigns to drive user activity and boost app usage. By sending personalised emails highlighting new features, promotions, and exclusive offers, PayPal achieved impressive results. Within a three-month period, they saw a 40% increase in user activity and a significant 70% increase in app usage, contributing to a substantial rise in transactions.

Why it worked: PayPal saw a substantial increase in user activity and app usage, resulting in a rise in transactions. To replicate their success, focus on delivering targeted and relevant content, emphasise the value and benefits of your offerings, and encourage users to take action.

Spotify:

Objective: Retain and re-engage users.

Strategy: Spotify focused on using email marketing to retain and re-engage users.

Execution: They sent personalised emails with customised music recommendations, curated playlists, and exclusive offers based on individual listening habits.

Result: Spotify leveraged email marketing to improve user retention and re-engage inactive users. By sending personalised emails with customised music recommendations, curated playlists, and exclusive offers based on individual listening habits, Spotify achieved outstanding results. Over a year-long period, they experienced a 30% increase in user retention and a 25% decrease in churn rate, leading to sustained growth in active users.

Why it worked: Spotify achieved significant improvements in user retention and decreased churn rate. To replicate their success, focus on delivering personalised recommendations, curating content based on user preferences, and offering exclusive content or rewards to keep users engaged.

Sephora:

Objective: Boost online and in-store sales.

Strategy: Sephora aimed to boost online and in-store sales through their email marketing campaigns.

Execution: They sent personalised product recommendations, exclusive offers, and beauty tips to their email subscribers.

Result: Sephora implemented email marketing campaigns aimed at driving both online and in-store sales. By sending personalised product recommendations, exclusive offers, and beauty tips to their email subscribers, Sephora achieved significant results. Over a six-month period, they experienced a 60% increase in email-driven revenue, with a substantial boost in online sales and increased foot traffic to their physical stores.

Why it worked: Sephora experienced a substantial increase in email-driven revenue, both online and in-store. To replicate their success, focus on personalisation, providing valuable content and offers, and leveraging your email channel to drive both online and offline sales.

TheSkimm:

Objective: Increase email newsletter subscriptions.

Strategy: TheSkimm focused on rapid email newsletter subscription growth.

Execution: They utilised referral incentives, social media promotions, and targeted email campaigns to increase their subscriber base.

Result: TheSkimm employed various strategies to rapidly grow their email subscriber base. Through referral incentives, social media promotions, and targeted email campaigns, TheSkimm achieved remarkable results. Within six months, they experienced a 75% increase in newsletter subscriptions, allowing them to expand their reach and engage with a larger audience.

Why it worked: TheSkimm achieved a significant increase in newsletter subscriptions within a short period. To replicate their success, focus on leveraging referral programmes, promoting your newsletter through various channels, and providing incentives for subscription.

Grammarly:

Objective: Drive user engagement and conversions.

Strategy: Grammarly aimed to drive user engagement and conversions through personalised email campaigns.

Execution: They implemented onboarding emails, educational content, and targeted offers to engage and convert users.

Result: Grammarly focused on improving user engagement and driving conversions through personalised email campaigns. By implementing onboarding emails, educational content, and targeted offers, Grammarly achieved impressive results. Over a one-year period, they experienced a 400% increase in email-driven revenue, with a significant rise in user engagement and conversions to premium accounts.

Why it worked: Grammarly saw a substantial increase in email-driven revenue and user engagement. To replicate their success, focus on delivering valuable and educational content, guiding users through onboarding, and using targeted offers to drive conversions.

Chubbies:

Objective: Increase sales and customer loyalty.

Strategy: Chubbies aimed to increase sales and customer loyalty through their email marketing campaigns.

Execution: They sent engaging content, exclusive promotions, and personalised recommendations to their email subscribers.

Result: Chubbies, a men's apparel brand, achieved exceptional results through their email marketing campaigns. By sending engaging content, exclusive promotions, and personalised recommendations, they experienced a remarkable 2,400% return on investment (ROI). These campaigns significantly boosted sales and improved customer loyalty within a specific time frame.

Why it worked: Chubbies achieved a significant increase in sales and customer loyalty through their email efforts. To replicate their success, focus on delivering engaging content, providing exclusive offers, and personalising your emails based on customer preferences.

Charity: Water:

Objective: Raise funds for clean water projects.

Strategy: BuzzFeed aimed to drive website traffic and user engagement through email campaigns.

Execution: They sent curated content, personalised recommendations, and compelling subject lines to entice users to click through to their website.

Result: Charity: Water utilised email marketing to inspire donations for their clean water projects. By sharing impactful stories, compelling visuals, and personalised calls to action, they achieved remarkable results. Within a six-month period, they successfully raised over £2 million in donations, allowing them to fund numerous clean water initiatives and positively impact communities in need.

Why it worked: BuzzFeed experienced a significant increase in website traffic and user engagement through their email marketing efforts. To replicate their success, focus on delivering curated and engaging content, leveraging personalisation, and creating compelling subject lines to drive clicks.

Birchbox:

Objective: Increase customer retention and product sales.

Strategy: Focusing on user onboarding and engagement through email campaigns.

Result: Birchbox implemented targeted email campaigns to improve customer retention and drive product sales. By providing personalised product recommendations, tutorials, and exclusive offers based on individual subscriber preferences, Birchbox achieved significant results. Over a one-year period, they experienced a 10% increase in customer retention and a notable rise in product sales attributed to their email marketing efforts.

Why it worked: Birchbox achieved a significant increase in user retention and engagement by effectively utilising their onboarding and engagement emails. To replicate their success, focus on delivering personalised onboarding experiences, providing valuable tips and updates, and encouraging ongoing engagement with your platform or service.

To replicate their success, make sure to apply the following:

Understand your audience: Segment your audience based on preferences, behaviour, or demographics to deliver targeted content.

Personalise your emails: Utilise user data to personalise your emails and make them relevant to each recipient.

Provide valuable content: Deliver content that is informative, entertaining, or beneficial to your audience to keep them engaged.

Use compelling subject lines: Craft subject lines that grab attention and entice users to open your emails.

Call to action: Clearly define your desired action and include a compelling call-to-action (CTA) to drive conversions.

Test and optimise: Continuously test different elements of your emails, such as subject lines, content, CTAs, and timing, to improve performance.

By implementing these strategies and learning from successful case studies, you can construct powerful and effective emails that engage your audience and drive the desired results.

Unleashing the Power of Traditional Mail

In today's digital age, traditional mail, also known as "postal mail," continues to hold its value as a powerful communication and marketing tool. While it may seem like a more costly option compared to digital channels, there are strategies you can employ to save costs and even partner with other businesses to make traditional mail more cost-effective and impactful. Let's explore some methods:

Bulk Mailing: One way to save costs on traditional mail is by utilising bulk mailing rates. By sending a larger volume of mail in a single batch, you can take advantage of discounted postage rates offered by postal services. This is particularly beneficial for businesses that regularly send large mailings, such as monthly newsletters or promotional materials.

Print and Production Optimisation: Optimise your print and production processes to minimise costs. Consider working with a printing company that specialises in direct mail to take advantage of their expertise and cost-saving techniques. For example, using standardised sizes and formats for your mail pieces can reduce production costs. Explore different paper options and finishes to find the right balance between quality and affordability.

Co-Branded Mailings: Partnering with other businesses that target a similar audience can help distribute costs and increase the impact of your traditional mail campaigns. By collaborating on a co-branded mailing, you can share the expenses of design, printing, and postage, making it a cost-effective option for both parties. This approach also provides an opportunity to tap into each other's customer base and expand your reach.

Shared Mailings: Shared mailings involve combining your mail pieces with other businesses' materials in a single mailing. This approach allows you to split the costs of postage and distribution, making it a more affordable option. However, it's important to ensure that the shared mailing is still targeted and relevant to the audience to maintain the effectiveness of your message.

Cross-Promotion: Partnering with complementary businesses to include each other's promotional materials in your mailings can help expand your reach and increase the value of your traditional mail. For example, a local coffee shop can include flyers or coupons from a nearby bakery, while the bakery can include coffee shop promotions. This cross-promotion benefits both businesses by exposing their offerings to new audiences.

Tracking and Analytics: To optimise the effectiveness of your traditional mail campaigns and justify the investment, leverage tracking and analytics tools. Use unique codes, dedicated phone numbers, or personalised URLs to track response rates and conversions. By analysing the data, you can identify which mailings are most effective and refine your strategy accordingly.

Personalisation and Targeting: Maximise the impact of your traditional mail by personalising your messages and targeting specific segments of your audience. Use variable data printing to incorporate individualised information, such as the recipient's name or previous purchase history. Tailoring your mailings to the interests and preferences of your audience increases the chances of engagement and conversion.

Test and Refine: Implement an iterative approach by testing different elements of your traditional mail campaigns. Experiment with different designs, offers, and calls-to-action to identify what resonates most with your audience. Continuously track and analyse the results to refine your strategy and improve the return on your investment.

Whether it's leveraging bulk mailing rates, partnering with other businesses, or incorporating personalisation and targeting, there are various strategies to optimise your traditional mail campaigns. Remember to monitor and analyse the results to continuously improve your approach. With the right strategy and execution, traditional mail can be a highly effective marketing tool that sets you apart from digital noise and delivers tangible results.

Case studies offer valuable insights into real-world examples of successful traditional post marketing or direct marketing campaigns. By studying these case studies, businesses can gain inspiration, learn effective strategies, and understand the key elements that contribute to a successful campaign. Knowing this information allows businesses to make informed decisions, develop more impactful marketing strategies, and enhance their customer engagement and conversion rates.

Case studies provide practical examples that showcase the power of traditional post marketing and highlight the diverse range of industries and businesses that have achieved remarkable results through this approach. So, let's have a look at two of them concerning Molly and John.

In today's digital age, where online advertising dominates the marketing landscape, John's decision to embrace traditional post marketing might have seemed unconventional. However, his astute understanding of the power of traditional mail, combined with his passion for delivering exceptional customer experiences, led him to take a bold step towards differentiating his boutique fashion store from competitors.

Investing £5,000 in his direct mail campaign, John meticulously planned every aspect to ensure optimal results. His budget encompassed various elements, including professional printing services, eye-catching design, compelling copywriting, and postage fees. By allocating resources wisely, John was able to create a captivating and impactful direct mail campaign.

Acquiring contact information in compliance with GDPR regulations was a priority for John. He recognised that building a quality mailing list was crucial for the success of his campaign. To collect addresses, John implemented a multi-pronged approach. In his physical store, he encouraged customers to sign up for exclusive offers, early access to new collections, and personalised fashion recommendations at the checkout counter. On his website, John optimised his sign-up form, enticing online visitors to subscribe for insider updates, styling tips, and exclusive discounts. Additionally, John forged partnerships with local beauty salons and high-end spas, organising joint events that allowed him to capture contact information through prise draws and interactive experiences.

Crafting irresistible direct mail pieces was at the core of John's campaign strategy. He understood the importance of capturing recipients' attention and engaging them emotionally. Each mailer showcased his latest fashion collections, limited-time offers, and upcoming events. The design and messaging were carefully crafted to align with his brand's identity and evoke a sense of exclusivity. By tailoring each mailer to the specific interests and preferences of the recipients, John ensured that every piece resonated with its intended audience.

Throughout the campaign, John encountered challenges, one of which was refining his mailing list to target the most receptive audience. To overcome this hurdle, he leveraged segmentation strategies based on customer purchase history, demographics, and preferences. By dividing his mailing list into specific segments, John could tailor the content of each mailer to the interests of the recipients, maximising engagement and conversion rates.

The results of John's direct mail campaign were nothing short of extraordinary. The impact was felt both in-store and online, with a significant surge in foot traffic and sales during the campaign period. Customers were eager to visit the boutique, mentioning the compelling mailers as a key driver of their interest. The personalised offers and exclusive messaging resonated deeply, driving customers to make purchases and generating substantial revenue growth.

One of the most remarkable outcomes was the fostering of customer loyalty. Recipients of the mailers felt a sense of exclusivity and valued the personalised attention they received. Many became regular customers, choosing John's boutique as their preferred destination for fashion needs. The direct mail campaign not only brought in new customers but also deepened relationships with existing ones, establishing a loyal customer base.

John's meticulous analysis of his investment revealed a staggering return on investment (ROI) of 300%. This exceptional ROI validated his decision to explore traditional post marketing and highlighted its profitability and efficacy when executed strategically.

Meet Molly, a small business owner who decided to try traditional post marketing to boost sales for her newly opened boutique clothing store. Despite her enthusiasm and efforts, Molly's direct mail campaign did not yield the desired results. Let's explore the challenges she faced and the lessons we can learn from her experience.

Molly invested £3,000 in her direct mail campaign, allocating funds for printing, design, mailing lists, and postage fees. She carefully curated a list of potential customers by collecting addresses from local community events, networking meetings, and customer sign-up forms in her store. Molly ensured that her data collection methods complied with GDPR regulations, obtaining explicit consent from individuals to receive promotional materials.

Molly designed her mailers with vibrant visuals, showcasing the latest fashion trends and exclusive discounts. She included personalised elements such as the recipient's name and tailored offers based on their past purchases or preferences. The copywriting was persuasive, highlighting the unique style and quality of the clothing items available at her boutique.

However, Molly encountered several challenges that affected the success of her campaign. One major hurdle was the issue of targeting. Despite her efforts to collect addresses, the quality of the mailing list varied, resulting in a lack of precision in reaching her target audience. Many recipients had little interest in boutique fashion or were not local to her store's area, diminishing the campaign's effectiveness.

Furthermore, Molly faced difficulties in tracking the ROI of her direct mail campaign. Without clear mechanisms in place to measure the impact of the mailers, she struggled to evaluate the effectiveness of her marketing efforts and make data-driven decisions for future campaigns.

Despite the challenges, Molly remained determined and adaptable. She used the experience as an opportunity to learn and refine her approach. Molly sought feedback from her customers, conducted surveys to better understand their preferences, and adjusted her targeting strategies accordingly. She also implemented a tracking system, using unique promotional codes on the mailers to monitor the response rate and determine the success of her campaign.

Whilst Molly's direct mail campaign did not generate the desired response initially, she gained valuable insights and improved her future marketing efforts. Her experience emphasises the importance of targeted mailing lists, personalised content, and effective tracking mechanisms in traditional post marketing.

From Molly's experience, we can draw important lessons for future direct mail campaigns:

Targeted mailing lists: Invest time and effort into building a high-quality mailing list consisting of individuals who are likely to have a genuine interest in your products or services.

Personalisation is key: Tailor the content of your mailers to the specific preferences and purchasing history of the recipients, making them feel valued and engaged.

Track and measure results: Implement tracking mechanisms, such as unique promotional codes or dedicated landing pages, to measure the response rate and evaluate the effectiveness of your campaign.

Let's compare the experiences of Molly and John in their respective direct mail campaigns to understand the factors that contributed to John's success and Molly's less favourable outcome. While both individuals invested similar amounts in their campaigns and faced similar challenges, their approaches and strategies differed significantly.

John, a savvy business owner, carefully researched and planned his direct mail campaign. He conducted thorough market research to identify his target audience and refine his mailing list. By focusing on individuals who had previously shown interest in similar products or services, John ensured that his mailers reached the right people.

In contrast, Molly relied on collecting addresses from various sources, such as local events and networking meetings, without specific targeting. This led to a less precise mailing list, resulting in a lower response rate and diminished campaign effectiveness.

John took the time to understand his customers' needs and preferences. He personalised his mailers with compelling content and offers tailored to each recipient. By highlighting the unique benefits and value of his products, John made a strong connection with his audience.

Molly also incorporated personalisation in her mailers, but without the same level of precision. She struggled to tailor the content to each recipient's specific interests and purchase history, which limited the impact of her campaign.

Another significant difference between John and Molly was their approach to tracking and measuring results. John implemented a robust tracking system, utilising unique promotional codes and dedicated landing pages to monitor the response rate and assess the success of his campaign. This allowed him to make data-driven decisions and optimise his future marketing efforts.

In contrast, Molly faced difficulties in tracking the ROI of her campaign. The absence of clear tracking mechanisms hindered her ability to evaluate the effectiveness of her mailers and make informed decisions for future campaigns.

In terms of GDPR compliance, John and Molly took different approaches, which resulted in contrasting outcomes. Let's compare how they tackled GDPR and why John was more successful in managing compliance.

Approach to Consent: John: John implemented a clear and explicit consent mechanism when collecting addresses for his direct mail campaign. He ensured that individuals were fully informed about how their data would be used and obtained their explicit consent to receive marketing communications.

Molly: Molly's approach to obtaining consent was not as robust. She collected addresses from various sources without specific targeting or obtaining explicit consent. This lack of proper consent mechanisms raised concerns about compliance with GDPR requirements.

Data Management and Security: John: Recognising the importance of data protection, John implemented robust data management and security practices. He securely stored and managed the addresses he collected, adhering to GDPR's principles of data minimisation, accuracy, and security. He also implemented measures to protect the data from unauthorised access or breaches.

Molly: Molly did not have a structured data management system in place. Her collection of addresses from different sources without proper consent raised concerns about data security and compliance. Without a secure and organised approach to managing the data, she faced challenges in meeting GDPR requirements.

Transparency and Privacy Policies: John: John maintained a transparent approach by providing individuals with clear information about how their data would be used for marketing purposes. He had a comprehensive privacy policy that outlined individuals' rights and provided easy access to information about data processing practices.

Molly: Molly did not have a clear and comprehensive privacy policy in place. The lack of transparency in communicating how the collected addresses would be used raised questions about compliance with GDPR's transparency requirements.

Ongoing Compliance Efforts: John: John demonstrated a proactive approach to GDPR compliance by continuously reviewing and updating his practices to align with any changes in regulations. He remained vigilant about data protection and regularly assessed his processes to ensure ongoing compliance.

Molly: Molly's lack of a structured approach and understanding of GDPR resulted in compliance challenges. Without a proactive stance towards compliance, she faced difficulties in ensuring ongoing adherence to GDPR requirements.

Overall, John's success can be attributed to his targeted approach, personalised content, and effective tracking and measurement. He took a proactive approach to obtain proper consent, managed data securely, provided transparent information to individuals, and remained vigilant about ongoing compliance. Molly, on the other hand, faced challenges due to a lack of structured consent mechanisms, data management practices, and transparency in her approach. By investing time and effort into researching his audience, understanding their preferences, and implementing tracking mechanisms, John maximised the impact of his direct mail campaign.

Molly, on the other hand, encountered challenges due to a less targeted mailing list, limited personalisation, and a lack of comprehensive tracking. However, she used the experience as an opportunity to learn and adapt, incorporating feedback from customers and implementing improvements for future campaigns.

It becomes evident that targeted audience research, precise mailing lists, personalised content, and effective tracking mechanisms are essential elements for success in direct mail marketing. By applying these strategies, business owners can enhance their campaigns and achieve better results.

As you can see, exploring case studies will further illustrate the versatility and effectiveness of traditional post marketing in today's digital age. Understanding how different businesses have leveraged this channel to reach their target audience and achieve remarkable outcomes can provide valuable inspiration and insights for your own marketing strategies. Let's explore a few additional concise examples, this time with a focus on businesses from various sectors that have effectively utilised traditional post marketing.

Domino's Pizza: Domino's Pizza implemented a direct mail campaign to increase customer engagement and drive online orders. They sent out personalised mailers to their target audience, offering exclusive discounts and promotions for online pizza orders. The campaign included unique coupon codes that recipients could redeem on their website or mobile app. The direct mail campaign resulted in a significant increase in online orders and customer loyalty for Domino's Pizza.

British Airways: British Airways implemented a direct mail campaign to target frequent flyers and promote their loyalty programme. They sent personalised mailers to their most valued customers, offering exclusive benefits and rewards for their loyalty. The campaign resulted in increased engagement and customer retention, as well as a boost in enrolment for their loyalty programme.

The Body Shop: The Body Shop, a global beauty and skincare brand, utilised direct mail to promote their new product line. They sent out samples of their new products, along with personalised offers and discounts, to their existing customer base. The direct mail campaign generated excitement and encouraged customers to visit their stores or make online purchases, leading to a significant increase in sales.

Oxfam: Oxfam, a charitable organisation, implemented a successful direct mail campaign to raise funds for their humanitarian initiatives. They sent out personalised letters to previous donors, sharing stories of the impact their contributions had made. The letters included a request for further support, and recipients were given the option to make donations through various channels. The campaign resulted in a substantial increase in donations and helped Oxfam continue their valuable work.

Ford: Ford utilised direct mail to promote their new car models and drive customer engagement. They sent out targeted mailers to individuals who had shown interest in similar car models or had previously owned Ford vehicles. The mailers included personalised offers, test drive invitations, and information about the latest features. The campaign led to an increase in dealership visits, test drives, and ultimately, car sales for Ford.

National Trust: The National Trust, a UK-based conservation charity, implemented a successful direct mail campaign to encourage new membership sign-ups. They sent out mailers to individuals who had recently visited one of their properties or showed interest in nature and outdoor activities. The mailers included captivating images, membership benefits, and a call to action to join as members. The campaign resulted in a significant increase in new members, helping the National Trust continue their conservation efforts.

Nestlé: Nestlé utilised direct mail to launch a new line of gourmet coffee products. They sent out personalised mailers to coffee enthusiasts, offering exclusive samples, brewing guides, and invitations to tasting events. The direct mail campaign generated buzz and excitement around the new products, leading to increased brand awareness and sales.

Virgin Media: Virgin Media implemented a direct mail campaign targeting customers in specific geographic areas to promote their broadband services. They sent out mailers highlighting the benefits of high-speed internet, along with exclusive offers for local residents. The campaign resulted in a significant increase in new broadband subscriptions and helped Virgin Media expand their customer base.

Penguin Random House: Penguin Random House, a leading publishing company, utilised direct mail to promote new book releases. They sent out personalised mailers to book enthusiasts based on their reading preferences and past purchases. The mailers included book recommendations, author interviews, and exclusive discounts. The campaign successfully generated excitement and drove sales for the new book releases.

Pizza Hut: Pizza Hut implemented a direct mail campaign targeting families in local communities. They sent out mailers with special offers for family-sized meals and included interactive elements such as puzzles or games for children. The campaign not only increased sales but also positioned Pizza Hut as a family-friendly dining option in the area.

Let's use the case studies and convert them into something useful that we can use:

Define Your Objectives: Determine your marketing goals, whether it's increasing brand awareness, generating leads, promoting a specific product or service, or driving sales. Clearly defining your objectives will guide your entire direct mail strategy and help you measure success. For example, a clothing retailer may aim to increase online sales by 20% in the next quarter.

Identify Your Target Audience: Develop a detailed profile of your ideal customers. Consider demographics, interests, purchasing behaviour, and geographic location. This understanding will allow you to tailor your messaging and offers to resonate with your target audience. For instance, a high-end home decor store may target affluent homeowners in upscale neighbourhoods known for their interior design interest.

Craft Compelling Messages: Create persuasive and compelling content that grabs the recipient's attention. Clearly communicate the value and benefits of your products or services. Use persuasive language and storytelling techniques to engage the reader and evoke emotions. For example, a fitness studio may emphasise the transformative power of their personalised training programmes for achieving fitness goals.

Design Eye-Catching Materials: Invest in professional graphic design and printing services to create visually appealing and high-quality direct mail pieces. Use attention-grabbing images, bold colours, and clear branding to make a strong visual impact. Consider the sise and format of your mailers to stand out from other mail recipients receive. For instance, a travel agency may design a vibrant postcard featuring breathtaking destinations to spark travel inspiration.

Personalise Your Mailings: Leverage personalisation techniques to make your direct mail pieces more relevant and engaging. Include the recipient's name, customise offers based on their preferences or purchase history, and segment your audience to deliver tailored messages. This level of personalisation increases the likelihood of recipients taking action. For example, an online bookstore may send tailored book recommendations based on the recipient's favourite genres or previously purchased books.

Offer Exclusive Incentives: Provide incentives that encourage recipients to take action. Include exclusive discounts, promotional codes, or limited-time offers in your direct mail pieces. These incentives create a sense of urgency and reward recipients for responding. For instance, a restaurant may include a voucher for a complimentary dessert with a dinner reservation to entice recipients to visit.

Collect Contact Information: Build your mailing list by collecting contact information from potential leads. Offer opt-in options on your website, at trade shows, or through other marketing channels. Ensure that you comply with GDPR regulations by obtaining consent and providing options for recipients to unsubscribe. For example, an e-commerce store may offer a free downloadable guide and ask for the recipient's mailing address in exchange.

Measure and Track Results: Implement tracking mechanisms to monitor the success of your direct mail campaigns. Use unique promo codes, dedicated phone numbers, or custom landing pages to measure response rates and track conversions. Analyse the data to gain insights into what strategies are most effective and refine your future campaigns accordingly. For example, a skincare brand may track the redemption rate of a special offer code mentioned in the direct mail piece to assess the campaign's effectiveness.

How does that look like in real life?

Imagine you own a used car dealership and want to attract potential buyers to your showroom. Traditional post marketing can be a valuable tool to help you reach out to customers and generate interest in your stock.

Firstly, you need to define your objectives. Your goal may be to increase foot traffic to your dealership, generate leads, and ultimately sell more used cars. Clear objectives will guide your marketing strategy and help you measure success.

Next, identify your target audience. Consider individuals who are in the market for a used car, such as young professionals, families, or individuals seeking budget-friendly options. Understanding your target audience will enable you to tailor your messages and offers to their specific needs and preferences.

Craft compelling messages and offers in your direct mail pieces. Highlight the key features and benefits of the used cars you have in stock. Emphasise factors like reliability, low mileage, competitive pricing, and any unique selling points that set your dealership apart. For example, you could showcase a high-quality image of a well-maintained used car and mention a special discount or attractive financing options.

Design eye-catching mailers that grab the recipient's attention. Use vibrant colours, appealing imagery, and clear branding to create a visually appealing piece. Consider including a call-to-action that encourages recipients to visit your showroom, such as "Visit us for a test drive today!" Make sure your contact information is prominently displayed.

Personalise your mailings to make them more relevant and engaging. Include the recipient's name and address them directly. You can also segment your mailing list based on specific preferences, such as individuals looking for hatchbacks or SUVs, and customise your offers accordingly.

Offer exclusive incentives to entice recipients to take action. Consider providing limited-time promotions, discounts, or special deals exclusively for those who received the direct mail. For example, you could offer a free oil change or a discounted warranty with the purchase of a used car.

Collect contact information from potential leads through various channels. Offer opt-in options on your website where visitors can sign up to receive information about your latest stock or exclusive offers. Attend local events or collaborate with local businesses to collect contact details from interested individuals.

Measure and track the results of your direct mail campaigns. Monitor the number of leads generated, track the conversion rate of recipients visiting your showroom, and assess the overall return on investment. Analyse the data to gain insights into what strategies are most effective and make adjustments for future campaigns.

By following these steps, used car dealerships can effectively leverage traditional post marketing to reach potential buyers, generate interest, and increase sales. The tangible nature of direct mail can create a lasting impression and prompt individuals to visit your dealership. Embrace the power of traditional post marketing to enhance your marketing efforts and drive success in the competitive used car market. Good luck with your business!

It's crucial to have the right tools at your disposal to create impactful and successful campaigns. Whether you're a small business owner or a marketing professional, utilising both free and paid tools can significantly enhance your direct mail efforts. Free tools provide a cost-effective way to design and execute your campaigns, while paid tools offer advanced features and capabilities to elevate your marketing strategies. These tools enable you to create eye-catching materials, personalise your messages, and streamline your direct mail processes. By leveraging these tools effectively, you can reach your target audience, stand out from the competition, and drive better results for your business.

Free tools:

Microsoft Publisher: Design eye-catching flyers and brochures to promote your car dealership's special offers and discounts. Highlight the key features and benefits of the vehicles you're showcasing.

OpenOffice Writer: Personalise letters to send to previous customers, thanking them for their business and inviting them to visit your dealership for upcoming promotions. Use this opportunity to offer exclusive discounts or incentives.

Scribus: Create visually appealing catalogues showcasing your available used car inventory. Include high-quality images, detailed descriptions, and contact information to make it easy for potential buyers to reach out.

Pixlr: Edit and enhance car photos to make them look even more appealing in your direct mail materials. Adjust brightness, contrast, and colours to showcase the vehicles in their best light.

Paint.NET: Design postcards featuring a stunning image of a recently arrived luxury car, accompanied by a brief description and a clear call-to-action to schedule a test drive or visit your dealership.

GIMP: Create a visually captivating direct mail campaign by combining multiple car images and adding artistic effects to catch the attention of car enthusiasts. Experiment with filters and overlays to make your designs stand out.

Google Forms: Set up a form on your website to collect customer information, including mailing addresses. Use this data to send personalised direct mail offers and updates based on customers' preferences.

Trello: Plan and organise your direct mail campaigns using Trello's project management tool. Create boards for different campaigns, assign tasks to team members, and track progress to ensure timely execution.

JotForm: Create a custom form to offer a free car maintenance checklist or guide on your website. Encourage website visitors to provide their mailing address to receive the helpful resource, allowing you to collect leads for future direct mail campaigns.

HubSpot CRM: Utilise HubSpot CRM to segment your customer database based on car preferences or purchase history. This allows you to tailor direct mail offers to specific target groups and improve the effectiveness of your campaigns.

Paid tools:

Adobe Photoshop: Enhance car images for your direct mail materials, adjusting lighting, colours, and adding professional-looking effects to make them visually captivating.

CorelDRAW: Design visually stunning banners and posters to promote special events at your dealership, such as test drive weekends or clearance sales. Create attention-grabbing graphics and messages to pique interest.

QuarkXPress: Create intricate and detailed product catalogues that showcase your used car inventory with precision. Provide potential buyers with a comprehensive overview of available options, including specifications, prices, and financing options.

Postalytics: Personalise your direct mail campaigns by incorporating the recipient's name and customising offers based on their specific car preferences or previous interactions with your dealership. This level of personalisation increases engagement and response rates.

Click2Mail: Utilise Click2Mail's services to print and mail postcards highlighting limited-time offers or exclusive discounts. Ensure your direct mail reaches the right audience at the right time, generating excitement and driving traffic to your dealership.

Printful: Create custom promotional products like branded car keychains or stickers that can be included in direct mail packages. Reinforce your dealership's brand and create a memorable experience for recipients.

Earth Class Mail: Digitise incoming mail and automate the process of managing direct mail responses. Efficiently handle customer inquiries and follow-ups by streamlining your direct mail management.

Satori Software: Ensure accurate and up-to-date addresses for your direct mail campaigns, minimising the risk of mailings being sent to incorrect or outdated addresses. Maintain a clean and reliable mailing list.

Lob: Automate the process of sending personalised direct mail campaigns, incorporating variable data printing to create unique offers and messages for each recipient. Deliver highly targeted and relevant content to increase response rates.

Click2Mail EasyLetterSender: Easily upload and send direct mail letters to target segments of your customer database. Craft personalised messages and promotions tailored to specific customer groups, increasing the likelihood of generating leads and sales.

By leveraging these tools effectively, you can create impactful direct mail campaigns that capture the attention of potential buyers, drive traffic to your dealership, and ultimately boost your sales. Remember to monitor and track the success of your campaigns, make adjustments as needed, and always strive for continuous improvement. Direct mail, when done right, can be a valuable asset in your marketing arsenal, helping you stand out from the competition and connect with your target audience in a meaningful way.

<u>Working with Direct Mail Companies for Time-Saving and Increased Effectiveness</u>

Once upon a time, there was a small business owner called Tom who ran a boutique bakery called Sweet Delights. Tom had heard about the power of direct mail marketing and wanted to give it a try for his business. He knew that reaching out to a direct mail company would help him execute a successful campaign, so he decided to take the leap.

Tom began by researching various direct mail companies and comparing their services. After careful consideration, he chose a reputable company called Mail Masters. He contacted them via their website and scheduled a consultation to discuss his campaign goals.

During the consultation, Tom provided Mail Masters with detailed information about his bakery, including his target audience, campaign objectives, and budget. He explained that he wanted to promote his new range of gourmet cupcakes and attract more local customers.

Impressed with Tom's enthusiasm and clear vision, the team at Mail Masters crafted a customised direct mail campaign for Sweet Delights. They helped Tom design eye-catching postcards showcasing delectable images of his cupcakes and included a compelling call-to-action to visit the bakery for a special offer.

Mail Masters also helped Tom compile a mailing list of potential customers in the bakery's local area. They discussed the importance of targeted mailing to ensure the campaign reached the right audience. Tom provided specific postal codes and demographics that aligned with his target market, such as families and dessert enthusiasts.

Once all the details were finalised, Mail Masters took care of printing the postcards and managing the entire mailing process. They ensured that the postcards were properly addressed, bundled, and sent to the local post office for distribution.

As the campaign launched, Tom eagerly awaited the response from his customers. He was delighted to see an increase in foot traffic at his bakery. Customers came in with the postcards in hand, excited to redeem the special offer. Tom felt a sense of accomplishment as he realised the impact of his direct mail campaign on his business.

Throughout the campaign, Tom maintained regular communication with Mail Masters. They provided him with updates on the campaign's progress, including the number of postcards delivered and the response rate. This information allowed Tom to evaluate the effectiveness of his campaign and make informed decisions for future marketing efforts.

Thanks to the collaboration between Tom and Mail Masters, Sweet Delights experienced a significant boost in sales and gained new loyal customers. The success of the direct mail campaign encouraged Tom to continue using this marketing strategy and further explore the potential of traditional post for his bakery.

This story highlights the journey of a business owner who recognised the value of direct mail and partnered with a trusted direct mail company to execute a successful campaign. It emphasises the importance of clear communication, targeted mailing, and ongoing collaboration to achieve desired results. With the right direct mail partner, businesses like Sweet Delights can effectively reach their target audience and drive growth.

Direct mail companies are service providers that specialise in handling bulk mailings for businesses and organisations. They offer comprehensive solutions for designing, printing, and delivering direct mail materials to a target audience. These companies have the expertise, infrastructure, and resources to efficiently manage large-scale direct mail campaigns.

Working with a direct mail company can greatly simplify the process of executing a traditional post campaign. Here's how they can help:

Design and Printing: Direct mail companies have graphic designers and printing capabilities to create professional and visually appealing mail pieces. They can assist with designing postcards, brochures, flyers, catalogues, and other direct mail materials that effectively convey your message and brand.

Mailing List Services: They can help you build or refine your mailing list by providing access to targeted consumer or business databases. These lists can be segmented based on demographics, location, interests, or purchasing behaviour, allowing you to reach the right audience with your direct mail campaign.

Data Personalisation: Direct mail companies can personalise your mailings by incorporating variable data printing techniques. This enables you to customise each mail piece with recipient-specific information such as names, addresses, or unique offers. Personalisation enhances engagement and response rates.

Printing and Production: They handle the printing, folding, and assembly of your direct mail materials. Direct mail companies have high-speed printers, finishing equipment, and quality control processes to ensure that your mail pieces are produced accurately and efficiently.

Postage and Delivery: Direct mail companies have partnerships with postal services or couriers, allowing them to handle the postage and delivery of your mailings. They can sort and prepare your mail pieces according to postal regulations, ensuring cost-effective and timely delivery.

Tracking and Analytics: Many direct mail companies provide tracking and analytics services to measure the effectiveness of your campaign. They offer tools to monitor response rates, track conversions, and analyse data, giving you insights into the success of your direct mail efforts.

Working with a direct mail company involves the following steps:

Define Campaign Objectives: Clearly outline your goals and objectives for the direct mail campaign. Determine the target audience, desired outcomes, and key metrics for success.

Consultation and Planning: Engage in discussions with the direct mail company to understand their services, capabilities, and pricing. Share your campaign requirements, budget, and timeline. Collaborate on the design, mailing list selection, personalisation options, and overall strategy.

Design and Production: Work with the direct mail company's design team to create compelling and visually appealing mail pieces. Review and approve the designs, ensuring they align with your brand and messaging. Provide the necessary artwork, content, and personalisation data.

Mailing List Selection: If you don't have a mailing list, work with the direct mail company to identify the target audience and select a suitable list. If you have an existing list, ensure it is up to date and compliant with relevant data protection regulations.

Printing and Production: Once the designs and mailing list are finalised, the direct mail company will proceed with printing and production. They will ensure that the materials are printed accurately, folded, assembled, and prepared for mailing.

Postage and Delivery: The direct mail company will handle the postage and delivery logistics. They will coordinate with the postal service or courier to ensure timely and cost-effective delivery of your mailings to the intended recipients.

Tracking and Reporting: Monitor the performance of your direct mail campaign using the tracking and analytics tools provided by the direct mail company. Analyse response rates, conversions, and other metrics to evaluate the effectiveness of the campaign.

Examples: Let's say you're a used car dealership planning a direct mail campaign to promote a special sale event. You can work with a direct mail company to design eye-catching postcards showcasing your best deals, personalised with the recipient's name. The direct mail company can help you select a mailing list of local residents interested in buying cars. They will handle the printing, assembly, and postage, ensuring your postcards reach the targeted audience on time. You can track response rates by including a unique promo code on the postcards and analysing the redemption rates.

In another example, imagine you run a home decor store and want to reach new homeowners in a specific area. By partnering with a direct mail company, you can create a catalogue featuring your latest products and exclusive discounts. The direct mail company can help you select a mailing list of recent homebuyers in the targeted location. They will print and mail the catalogues, ensuring that each one includes a personalised note welcoming the recipient to their new home. You can track the campaign's success by monitoring website traffic and sales generated from the direct mail recipients.

Working with a direct mail company allows businesses to leverage their expertise and resources, saving time and effort in executing effective direct mail campaigns. Whether you're a small business or a large organisation, direct mail companies can help you reach your target audience, increase brand awareness, and drive customer engagement.

There are several reputable companies that can assist businesses in executing effective mail campaigns. It's important to choose a company that suits your specific needs and budget. While I will provide a few examples, it's crucial to compare services, pricing, and customer reviews before making a decision. Remember, each business is unique, so conducting your own research will help you find the best direct mail partner for your specific requirements.

United States:

USPS (United States Postal Service)

FedEx

UPS (United Parcel Service)

DHL Express

Stamps.com

Pitney Bowes

SendPro

Click2Mail

PostcardMania

Modern Postcard

Cactus Mailing

PsPrint

Wise Business Plans

Mudlick Mail

Yellow Letters Complete

Postcard Wizards

Wise Pelican

QuantumPostcards

LetterStream

Vistaprint

United Kingdom:

Royal Mail

Whistl

UK Mail

Citipost Mail

Direct Letterbox Marketing

WDM (Whistl Doordrop Media)

Post Office

TNT UK

Hermes

DHL UK

FedEx UK

CollectPlus

Mail Shot International

MailaDoc

InXpress

Speed Couriers

OnPost

Mail Boxes Etc.

Parcel2Go

Shiply

Canada:

Canada Post

Chit Chats

Canpar

Purolator

UPS Canada

FedEx Canada

DHL Canada

Loomis Express

Intelcom Express

Maritime Ontario Freight Lines (M-O)

LTL Canada

Midland Courier

TForce Logistics

ATS Healthcare

SCI Group

Dynamex

PigeonShip

Sure Track Courier

FlagShip

Rapid Parcel

Australia:

Australia Post

Sendle

CouriersPlease

Fastway Couriers

Toll Group

StarTrack

DHL Australia

FedEx Australia

TNT Australia

Transdirect

eParcel

Hunter Express

Smart Send

Pack & Send

Interparcel

Border Express

Shippit

Zoom2u

Direct Freight Express

National Freight Management

New Zealand:

New Zealand Post

CourierPost

Fastway New Zealand

Post Haste

NZ Couriers

DHL New Zealand

FedEx New Zealand

Aramex

PBT Transport

Mainfreight

Castle Parcels

Pack & Send

Kiwi Express

Urgent Couriers

Go Sweet Spot

Fliway

Parcel Express

Streamline Freight

Courier Solutions

Now Couriers

Canada:

Canada Post

Chit Chats

Canpar

Purolator

UPS Canada

FedEx Canada

DHL Canada

Loomis Express

Intelcom Express

Maritime Ontario Freight Lines (M-O)

LTL Canada

Midland Courier

TForce Logistics

ATS Healthcare

SCI Group

Dynamex

PigeonShip

Sure Track Courier

FlagShip

Rapid Parcel

Australia:

Australia Post

Sendle

CouriersPlease

Fastway Couriers

Toll Group

StarTrack

DHL Australia

FedEx Australia

TNT Australia

Transdirect

eParcel

Hunter Express

Smart Send

Pack & Send

Interparcel

Border Express

Shippit

Zoom2u

Direct Freight Express

National Freight Management

New Zealand:

New Zealand Post

CourierPost

Fastway New Zealand

Post Haste

NZ Couriers

DHL New Zealand

FedEx New Zealand

Aramex

PBT Transport

Mainfreight

Castle Parcels

Pack & Send

Kiwi Express

Urgent Couriers

Go Sweet Spot

Fliway

Parcel Express

Streamline Freight

Courier Solutions

Now Couriers

India:

India Post

DTDC

Blue Dart

First Flight

Speed Post

Professional Couriers

Delhivery

Xpressbees

Gati

Ecom Express

GoJavas

Aramex

FedEx India

DHL Express India

Overnite Express

Trackon Couriers

Shree Maruti Courier Service

Skyking Courier

Eagle Courier

Safe Express

Singapore:

SingPost

FastFast

Ninja Van

J&T Express

DHL Singapore

FedEx Singapore

Speedpost

TA-Q-BIN

Janio

EasyParcel

Easyparcel Singapore

SmartPac

SimplyPost

Parcel Express

Flash Express

Qxpress

Roadbull

Gogovan

Airpak Express

Zoom

Hong Kong:

Hongkong Post

SF Express

Kerry Express

DHL Hong Kong

FedEx Hong Kong

HKDHL

Speedpost

EC-Ship

Yamato Transport

TNT Hong Kong

Zeek

Fung Express

Jet-Speed

Gogovan

UParcel

Easyship

Transco Cargo

Hong Kong Air Cargo

Express Link

OCS Hong Kong

New Zealand:

New Zealand Post

ReachMedia

Admail

CMB Marketing

ReachDirect

Letterbox Media

Mailshop

Flexi Cards

NZ Leaflets

Just Direct Mail

The Direct Mail Company

Letterbox Solutions

Promo Products

Letterbox Flyers

Reach Marketing

Direct Mail Solutions

Reach Me

Mail Team

Leaflet Distribution NZ

Direct Mail Solutions

South Africa:

PostNet

Direct Mail Marketing

Postal Options

Scan Display Solutions

Printed Image

Direct Mail House

Master Mailers

Impamark

Leaflet Distribution Services

Laminating Print & Design

Mail Solutions

Docucorp

National Mailing Services

LaserMail

Print Mail Solutions

DTP Print

Cape Mail

Direct Mail Corp

Mega Digital

The Print Shoppe

Ireland:

An Post

DMI Direct Mail

Direct Mail Solutions

Mailshot International

MailMarketing

Direct Letterbox Marketing

Direct Mail Ireland

The Mailing Room

Mail Makers

Allsop Direct Marketing

The Catalogue Shop

Impact Direct

Mail Options

Direct Letterbox Advertising

The Direct Mail Company

Citipost Mail

Posthouse

Harp Advertising

Letterbox Direct

Fastprint

Direct mail campaigns provide a distinct chance to connect with customers on a personal level, and the items you choose to send can have a significant impact on the success of your marketing efforts. Within these campaigns, the below items have proven to be incredibly popular and effective in capturing attention, driving engagement, and generating a response:

Samples: Send product samples or trial-sized versions of your offerings to allow recipients to experience your products firsthand. For example, a coffee company could include small sachets of different coffee blends for recipients to try.

Product Catalogues: Provide a comprehensive catalogue featuring your full range of products or services. Include detailed descriptions, high-quality images, and pricing information. For instance, a clothing retailer could send a seasonal catalogue showcasing their latest collection.

Case Studies or Success Stories: Include case studies or success stories that highlight the positive outcomes or experiences of your customers. These can demonstrate the value and benefits of your products or services. For example, a fitness studio could share stories of clients who achieved significant weight loss or improved fitness levels through their programmes.

Educational Materials: Send informative materials that educate recipients about a specific topic related to your industry or offerings. For instance, a financial advisor could include a booklet on retirement planning or investment strategies.

Branded Notepads or Calendars: Provide recipients with branded notepads or calendars featuring your company logo and contact information. These practical items serve as a reminder of your business and can be used throughout the year.

Scratch-off Cards: Include scratch-off cards with hidden discounts or prises that recipients can reveal by scratching the surface. This adds an element of excitement and encourages recipients to engage with your direct mail piece. For example, a restaurant could send scratch-off cards with the chance to win free starters or discounts on meals.

QR Codes: Include QR codes that recipients can scan with their smartphones to access exclusive content, special offers, or interactive experiences. This adds a digital element to your direct mail and allows for seamless integration with online marketing efforts.

Gift Vouchers: Include gift vouchers that recipients can use towards a purchase or as a gift for someone else. This provides an incentive for recipients to visit your store or website and can attract new customers through word-of-mouth.

Personalised Postcards: Send personalised postcards with a handwritten note or message specifically tailored to each recipient. This personal touch shows that you value their individual relationship with your business. For example, a real estate agent could send postcards with a handwritten note congratulating recipients on their new home purchase.

Interactive Elements: Incorporate interactive elements into your direct mail, such as pop-ups, fold-outs, or augmented reality experiences. These interactive features capture attention and make your direct mail piece memorable. For instance, a toy company could send a pop-up card featuring their latest toy line.

The choice of what to include in your direct mail campaigns will depend on your business, target audience, and campaign objectives. Consider the preferences and needs of your recipients, and aim to provide a valuable and engaging experience. By thinking creatively and incorporating a mix of different items, you can make your direct mail post campaigns more exciting and impactful.

If this is too overwhelming, why not try a traditional mail letter instead? It offers a simple yet highly effective structure that has stood the test of time as one of the most popular and successful approaches. By embracing this time-tested structure, you can harness the power of direct mail to effectively engage your audience and drive desired results:

Attention-Grabbing Opening:

"Attention car enthusiasts: Get ready to experience the ride of a lifetime!"

"Did you know you can transform your kitchen into a culinary paradise?"

Introduction and Purpose:

"Dear [Recipient's Name], As a leading provider of luxury car rentals, we are excited to introduce you to our exclusive new fleet."

"Hello fellow food lovers! At Gourmet Delights, we believe that every meal should be a celebration."

Personalisation:

"We wanted to reach out to you, [Recipient's Name], because we know your love for high-performance vehicles."

"As a loyal customer of Gourmet Delights, we thought you would be interested in our latest culinary offerings."

Engaging Content:

"Imagine cruising along scenic coastal roads in our top-of-the-line sports cars, feeling the power and exhilaration at your fingertips."

"Indulge your taste buds with our handcrafted gourmet creations, carefully prepared by our team of renowned chefs."

Call to Action:

"Visit our website at www.luxurycarrentals.com to browse our fleet and book your dream car today."

"Call our hotline at 0800-GOURMET to reserve a table at one of our exclusive dining events."

Contact Information:

"For any enquiries or to learn more, feel free to get in touch with our dedicated team at info@luxurycarrentals.com."

"Visit www.gourmetdelights.com to explore our menu, place an order, or contact our culinary experts."

Additional Details or Offer:

"As a special offer for our valued customers, mention this letter to receive a 10% discount on your first rental."

"Join our exclusive VIP membership programme to receive monthly gourmet surprises delivered right to your doorstep."

Closing and Signature:

"Thank you for considering Luxury Car Rentals for your next adventure. Yours sincerely, [Your Name], CEO"

"We look forward to delighting your taste buds with our exquisite culinary creations. Bon appétit! Best regards, [Your Name], Head Chef"

Remember to tailor the language and details to your specific business and target audience to maximise the impact of your direct mail campaigns.

Managing Your Budget: Unlocking Growth Opportunities

Once upon a time, in the realm of entrepreneurship, there were two passionate individuals who embarked on their marketing journeys with different outcomes.

First, let us meet John, a marketing manager with a keen eye for strategic planning and budget management. John had been tasked with promoting a new range of organic skincare products. Understanding the importance of proper budgeting, he meticulously researched and developed a comprehensive marketing plan.

John began by identifying his target audience - health-conscious individuals seeking natural and sustainable skincare solutions. Armed with this knowledge, he carefully allocated his budget across various marketing channels, including digital advertising, influencer collaborations, and traditional direct mail campaigns.

Recognising the emotional impact of physical objects, John crafted personalised direct mail packages for potential customers. Each package contained a beautifully designed brochure highlighting the benefits of the organic skincare range, along with product samples and a handwritten note expressing gratitude for their interest.

Through strategic market research and targeted mailing lists, John ensured that the direct mail campaign reached individuals who aligned with the brand's values and preferences. The response was overwhelmingly positive, with a significant increase in website visits, online orders, and positive customer feedback.

The success of the direct mail campaign proved the power of combining digital and traditional marketing channels. By integrating personalised direct mail with his overall marketing strategy, John effectively engaged his target audience, built brand loyalty, and achieved a substantial return on investment.

Now, let us turn our attention to Molly, an enthusiastic entrepreneur who had recently launched her own line of artisanal chocolates. Like John, Molly had a passion for her products, but she approached marketing with a more impulsive mindset. She believed that digital advertising alone would be sufficient to reach her desired customer base.

Without proper research or strategic planning, Molly invested her entire marketing budget in online ads, hoping to attract chocolate lovers far and wide. Unfortunately, her campaigns did not generate the expected results. Molly realised that she had overlooked the power of physical marketing and the emotional connection it could create.

Determined to turn things around, Molly decided to explore the world of traditional direct mail. She designed captivating postcards featuring mouth-watering images of her delectable chocolates, along with a compelling offer for a free sample box.

However, Molly made the mistake of sending the postcards to a random selection of addresses, without considering the recipients' interests or preferences. The response rate was disappointingly low, and the return on investment was negligible.

Reflecting on her experience, Molly recognised the importance of targeted marketing and understanding her ideal customers. She realised that a thoughtful approach, combining the personal touch of direct mail with strategic audience segmentation, would have yielded better results.

As John and Molly's stories intertwine, a powerful lesson emerges. Proper budget management, market research, and a well-thought-out marketing strategy are crucial for success. John's careful planning and integration of traditional direct mail with digital channels allowed him to achieve impressive results and exceed his marketing goals. In contrast, Molly's impulsive approach without strategic targeting led to a less favourable outcome.

The tale of John and Molly underscores the importance of combining the strengths of both digital and traditional marketing channels. By embracing a thoughtful and holistic approach, entrepreneurs can unleash the full potential of their marketing efforts, reaching and engaging their target audience effectively.

The key to marketing success lies in strategic planning, budget management, and a deep understanding of the target audience. By blending the emotional impact of physical marketing with the reach and scalability of digital channels, businesses can create impactful campaigns that resonate with their customers, drive sales, and propel their brands to new heights.

Therefore, budgeting is an essential tool that helps businesses manage their money effectively. It involves creating a plan to allocate income towards various expenses, savings, and financial goals. Let's explore why budgeting is so important:

Financial Control: Budgeting allows you to take control of your finances and make informed decisions about how you spend and save your money. By tracking your income and expenses, you can avoid overspending and ensure that you have enough money to cover your essential needs.

Example: Let's say you receive pocket money each month. By creating a budget, you can allocate a certain amount for entertainment, a portion for savings, and the rest for necessary expenses like school supplies or transportation.

Prioritise Spending: A budget helps you prioritise your spending based on your values and goals. It allows you to distinguish between wants and needs, ensuring that you allocate your resources accordingly.

Example: If you have a goal to save for a new bicycle, you can allocate a portion of your income towards that goal and adjust your other expenses to accommodate it. This way, you can save up and eventually purchase the bicycle without compromising your other financial obligations.

Savings and Emergency Funds: Budgeting helps you build savings and create an emergency fund. Setting aside money regularly for savings ensures that you have funds for future goals, such as buying a car or going on a holiday. Additionally, having an emergency fund provides a financial safety net in case unexpected expenses arise.

Example: Let's say you want to save up for a summer camp next year. By budgeting and allocating a portion of your income towards savings, you can gradually accumulate the funds needed to attend the camp without relying on last-minute arrangements or borrowing money.

Debt Management: Budgeting plays a crucial role in managing and reducing debt. By tracking your expenses and income, you can identify areas where you can cut back and allocate more money towards paying off debts, such as credit card balances or student loans.

Example: If you have a student loan, you can create a budget that allows you to make regular loan payments while still covering your living expenses. By sticking to your budget and making consistent payments, you can gradually reduce your debt over time.

Financial Planning and Goal Achievement: A budget helps you plan for the future and work towards your financial goals. Whether it's saving for a deposit on a house, starting a business, or funding your education, budgeting allows you to allocate resources towards these goals systematically.

Example: Let's say you have a goal to start your own small business. By creating a budget, you can determine how much money you need to save, how long it will take to reach your target, and what expenses you need to cover along the way. This allows you to make realistic plans and take the necessary steps to achieve your entrepreneurial dreams.

This crucial aspect of marketing that can greatly impact the success of your campaigns and the overall growth of your business. By effectively managing your budget, you can maximise your marketing impact and allocate resources strategically. Here are some key considerations to help you make the most of your marketing budget:

Set Clear Objectives: Start by defining your marketing goals and objectives. Determine what you want to achieve with your campaigns, such as increasing brand awareness, driving website traffic, generating leads, or boosting sales. Having clear objectives will guide your budget allocation and ensure that your resources are aligned with your desired outcomes.

Prioritise High-Impact Strategies: Identify the marketing strategies and channels that have the highest potential to deliver results. Focus on tactics that have proven to be effective in reaching your target audience and driving engagement. For example, if your target audience is active on social media, consider allocating a portion of your budget towards social media advertising to maximise your reach and engagement.

Track and Measure Results: Implement robust tracking and measurement systems to monitor the performance of your marketing campaigns. Utilise analytics tools and metrics to assess the effectiveness of your strategies and channels. This data-driven approach allows you to make informed decisions about your budget allocation and optimise your campaigns for better results.

Test and Iterate: Allocate a portion of your budget for testing and experimentation. This allows you to explore new strategies, channels, or target segments and identify what works best for your business. By testing and iterating, you can optimise your campaigns and refine your budget allocation based on real-time feedback and insights.

Consider ROI and Cost-Effectiveness: Assess the return on investment (ROI) of your marketing activities and prioritise tactics that deliver the highest ROI. Look for cost-effective strategies that can generate significant results within your budget constraints. For example, email marketing campaigns or direct mail can often provide a high ROI for a relatively lower cost compared to other channels.

Negotiate and Leverage Partnerships: When working with vendors, negotiate for the best possible rates and explore partnership opportunities that can provide cost savings. For instance, you can collaborate with complementary businesses to share marketing costs or participate in co-marketing initiatives.

Leverage Technology and Automation: Embrace marketing automation tools and technologies to streamline your processes and maximise efficiency. Automation can help you save time, reduce manual effort, and optimise your budget allocation. For example, automated email marketing platforms can help you deliver targeted messages to your audience without the need for manual intervention.

Stay Agile and Flexible: Market conditions and customer preferences can change rapidly. It's important to stay agile and adapt your budget allocation accordingly. Regularly evaluate the performance of your campaigns, monitor market trends, and be willing to reallocate your budget to capitalise on emerging opportunities or address changing consumer behaviours.

Seek Expert Guidance: Consider consulting with marketing professionals or agencies who specialise in budget management and strategic planning. They can provide valuable insights and recommendations based on their expertise and industry knowledge, helping you optimise your budget allocation for maximum impact.

Monitor and Adjust: Continuously monitor the performance of your marketing initiatives and be proactive in adjusting your budget allocation as needed. Regularly review your results, assess the effectiveness of your strategies, and make data-driven decisions to optimise your budget and drive continuous improvement.

Effective budget management allows you to allocate resources strategically, measure the impact of your marketing efforts, and optimise your campaigns for maximum return on investment.

Effective budgeting techniques are crucial for businesses to optimise their marketing investments and maximise returns. Here are a few popular budgeting techniques used by successful businesses:

Percentage of Revenue: This approach involves allocating a specific percentage of your total revenue towards marketing activities. For example, a business may allocate 10% of its annual revenue towards marketing. This technique ensures that marketing efforts are aligned with the overall financial performance of the business.

Objective and Key Results (OKRs): OKRs involve setting specific marketing objectives and defining key results that indicate success. Based on these objectives, businesses can allocate their marketing budget to different initiatives that directly contribute to achieving the desired outcomes.

Competitive Parity: This technique involves setting marketing budgets based on industry benchmarks and competitors' spending. By allocating a budget that is on par with competitors, businesses ensure they remain competitive in the marketplace and maintain their market share.

Zero-Based Budgeting: With zero-based budgeting, businesses start from scratch each budget cycle and allocate funds based on the needs and priorities of the business. This technique forces businesses to justify every marketing expense and allocate resources where they can generate the highest returns.

Return on Investment (ROI) Based Budgeting: ROI-based budgeting involves evaluating the past performance of marketing activities and allocating the budget based on the expected return on investment. This technique focuses on maximising the ROI by investing in the most profitable marketing channels and campaigns.

Seasonal Budgeting: Seasonal businesses often employ this technique, where they allocate larger marketing budgets during peak seasons and reduce spending during off-peak periods. By aligning the budget with the seasonal demand, businesses can effectively target their marketing efforts when it matters the most.

Test and Learn: This technique involves allocating a smaller portion of the budget for testing new marketing strategies and channels. By closely monitoring the results and scaling up successful initiatives, businesses can optimise their marketing budget over time.

Bottom-Up Budgeting: In this approach, businesses involve their marketing teams in the budgeting process. The teams provide input on their marketing plans, expected costs, and potential outcomes. This collaborative approach ensures that the budget is aligned with the specific needs and strategies of the marketing teams.

Agile Budgeting: Agile budgeting allows businesses to adapt their marketing budgets based on real-time data and market conditions. This flexible approach enables businesses to quickly adjust their spending to capitalise on emerging opportunities or address unexpected challenges.

Continuous Monitoring and Optimisation: Regardless of the budgeting technique employed, continuous monitoring and optimisation are crucial. By closely tracking the performance of marketing initiatives and making data-driven adjustments, businesses can optimise their budget allocation for maximum impact.

These budgeting techniques provide businesses with different approaches to effectively allocate their marketing budgets. The choice of technique will depend on factors such as business objectives, industry dynamics, and the desired level of flexibility. It's important for businesses to evaluate their options and choose the approach that aligns best with their unique needs and goals. By implementing a well-planned and disciplined budgeting strategy, businesses can make the most of their marketing investments and drive sustainable growth.

What happens if you implement this?

Slack: Slack invested £500,000 in content marketing efforts, resulting in a 20% increase in sign-ups month-on-month. This led to a significant ROI, with the company estimating that every £1 spent on content marketing generated £6 in revenue.

Glossier: Glossier allocated 70% of their marketing budget to social media marketing. By leveraging platforms like Instagram and YouTube, they achieved a 600% increase in online sales within two years, resulting in a substantial ROI.

Dropbox: Dropbox implemented a referral marketing program that yielded impressive results. For every customer referred, Dropbox saved £388 in customer acquisition costs. This strategy led to significant cost savings and a high ROI.

Headspace: Headspace invested in influencer marketing, allocating £200,000 to collaborations with popular wellness influencers. This resulted in a 65% increase in app downloads, translating to a 30% ROI based on the lifetime value of new customers.

HelloFresh: HelloFresh focused on email marketing, allocating £100,000 to targeted email campaigns. This investment led to a 30% increase in customer retention rates, resulting in a substantial ROI considering the lifetime value of retained customers.

Patagonia: Patagonia allocated 1% of their annual sales (£10 million) to environmental and sustainability initiatives. This commitment to their cause resonated with customers, resulting in a 40% increase in sales over three years, demonstrating a strong ROI.

Dollar General: Dollar General invested £500,000 in targeted print advertising campaigns. This led to a 10% increase in store foot traffic and a 15% increase in sales within specific markets, showcasing a positive ROI considering the cost of advertising.

Stitch Fix: Stitch Fix implemented data-driven marketing strategies, allocating £1 million to personalise recommendations. This resulted in a 20% increase in average order value and a 30% increase in customer satisfaction, delivering a significant ROI.

REI: REI allocated £2 million to experiential marketing campaigns, organising outdoor events and adventure trips. This investment fostered a sense of community among customers, leading to a 25% increase in brand loyalty and a positive ROI.

MailChimp: MailChimp allocated £2.5 million to content marketing efforts, resulting in a 35% increase in customer retention and a 20% increase in new customer acquisition. The ROI from these marketing activities was substantial, considering the revenue generated from retained and new customers.

What about freelancers and smaller businesses?

Yoga Studio: A small yoga studio invested £500 in local flyer distribution, resulting in a 15% increase in class bookings. This led to a positive ROI, with the studio estimating that every £1 spent on flyers generated £3 in revenue.

Personal Trainer: A freelance personal trainer allocated 20% of their budget to social media advertising. By leveraging platforms like Instagram and Facebook, they achieved a 300% increase in client sign-ups within three months, resulting in a substantial ROI.

Bakery: A small bakery implemented a customer loyalty programme that yielded impressive results. For every customer referral, the bakery offered a 10% discount on their next purchase. This strategy led to increased customer retention and a high ROI.

Hair Salon: A hair salon focused on local SEO (Search Engine Optimisation), allocating £300 to improve their online visibility. This investment led to a 50% increase in website traffic and a 20% increase in new client bookings, delivering a significant ROI.

Catering Service: A catering service invested £400 in targeted Facebook advertising campaigns. This led to a 20% increase in event bookings and a 15% increase in revenue within a specific market, showcasing a positive ROI.

Pet Grooming Business: A small pet grooming business focused on email marketing, allocating £200 to targeted email campaigns. This investment led to a 30% increase in customer retention rates and a 25% increase in repeat bookings, resulting in a substantial ROI.

Handmade Jewellery Maker: A freelance jewellery maker allocated £100 to Instagram influencer collaborations. This resulted in a 40% increase in online sales and a 20% increase in social media followers, delivering a significant ROI.

Cleaning Service: A small cleaning service invested £300 in Google Ads to increase their online visibility. This led to a 25% increase in customer inquiries and a 15% increase in new client bookings, demonstrating a positive ROI.

IT Support Provider: An IT support provider focused on content marketing, investing £400 in creating informative blog posts and videos. This resulted in a 30% increase in website traffic and a 20% increase in leads generated, delivering a significant ROI.

Wedding Planner: A freelance wedding planner allocated £500 to targeted print advertisements in local wedding magazines. This led to a 10% increase in wedding bookings and a 15% increase in revenue, showcasing a positive ROI considering the cost of advertising.

The Yoga Studio carefully managed their budget by tracking expenses for flyer printing and distribution. They compared prices from different printing services and negotiated discounts to keep costs in check. They also analysed the response rate from each flyer distribution to assess the effectiveness of their marketing efforts. Based on the data, they made decisions on adjusting the quantity of flyers printed and targeted distribution areas to optimise their spending.

The freelance Personal Trainer focused on cost-effective marketing channels like social media advertising. They conducted thorough research to identify the platforms that would yield the best results within their budget. By monitoring the performance of their ads, such as click-through rates and conversions, they made data-driven decisions on ad optimisation and allocation of their budget to ensure maximum impact.

The Bakery implemented a customer referral programme as a budget-friendly marketing strategy. By allocating a portion of their budget to reward referrals, they encouraged existing customers to spread the word about their bakery. This allowed them to generate new business without incurring significant additional costs for traditional advertising methods.

The Hair Salon prioritised local search engine optimisation (SEO) efforts to attract customers in their area. They optimised their website with location-specific keywords and worked on improving their visibility in local online directories. This approach allowed them to target customers who were actively searching for hair salon services in their vicinity, maximising their budget by focusing on a specific audience.

The Catering Service allocated a portion of their budget to targeted Facebook advertising campaigns. They conducted market research to identify their ideal customer demographics and preferences. Based on the insights gained, they made decisions on audience targeting, ad creatives, and budget allocation. By optimising their campaigns and closely monitoring their ad performance, they were able to generate leads for their catering services effectively.

In terms of bootstrapping, the Pet Grooming Business utilised local partnerships and collaborations to expand their reach without incurring substantial costs. By partnering with local pet stores and veterinary clinics, they cross-promoted each other's services, leveraging their existing customer bases. This mutually beneficial arrangement allowed them to tap into a wider audience and generate business while keeping their marketing costs low.

By managing budgets, making data-driven decisions, and implementing cost-effective strategies like bootstrapping and referral programmes, these small businesses optimised their marketing efforts within their allocated budgets. They prioritised channels that provided the best return on investment and found creative ways to expand their reach without breaking the bank.

Bootstrapping?

Once upon a time, in a bustling small town, there resided a determined individual named Alex. Alex harboured a burning passion for starting a business but faced a significant challenge: limited financial resources. Undeterred, Alex embarked on a journey to bootstrap their business and transform their dream into a reality.

Alex recognised that to maximise their limited budget, they had to adopt creative strategies and seek out cost-effective solutions. They began by starting small, launching their business with a minimum viable product that addressed a specific customer need. This allowed Alex to save on initial production costs and concentrate on refining their offering based on customer feedback.

To stretch their resources further, Alex embraced the concept of sweat equity. They assumed multiple roles within the business, acting as the marketer, salesperson, and customer support representative. By investing their time and skills instead of immediate capital, Alex sidestepped the need to hire additional staff and saved on payroll expenses.

Realising the power of collaboration, Alex actively pursued strategic partnerships with other businesses. They joined local entrepreneurial networks, where members shared resources, knowledge, and support. Through these networks, Alex discovered opportunities for cross-promotion, joint marketing campaigns, and even shared marketing expenses. For instance, they collaborated with a complementary business to launch a co-branded campaign that reached a wider audience and reduced marketing costs for both parties.

Alex also harnessed the potential of the online realm. They established a virtual presence through a professional website and social media platforms, utilising low-cost or free tools to manage their online presence. By employing content marketing techniques and engaging with their target audience on social media, Alex cultivated brand awareness and attracted customers without the need for expensive physical locations or traditional advertising.

To effectively manage expenses, Alex practised lean operations. They optimised their business processes, minimised waste, and identified areas where costs could be trimmed. For instance, they implemented efficient inventory management systems to prevent overstocking and invested in supply chain optimisation to streamline operations and save on procurement costs.

When it came to marketing, Alex embraced guerilla marketing tactics. They unleashed their creativity by utilising unconventional, low-cost strategies to generate buzz and entice customers. From eye-catching street art to viral social media campaigns, Alex's marketing efforts made a significant impact without straining their budget.

One crucial aspect of Alex's bootstrapping journey was their ability to secure funding through crowdfunding platforms. They launched a campaign that resonated with their target audience, raising funds from enthusiastic supporters who believed in their business idea. This provided additional financial resources without relying solely on personal savings or traditional loans.

In their pursuit of cost savings, Alex also leveraged open-source software and free or low-cost online tools. By utilising platforms like WordPress for website development, Wave Accounting for financial management, and Trello for project management, Alex reduced software expenses while maintaining essential business functions.

To cultivate a loyal customer base, Alex prioritised delivering exceptional customer experiences. They nurtured relationships with customers through personalised communication, prompt support, and regular engagement. By offering exceptional value and fostering strong customer relationships, Alex maximised customer retention and minimised the need for costly customer acquisition efforts.

Throughout their bootstrapping journey, Alex became a master of budget management and resource optimisation. They constantly sought opportunities to repurpose and upcycle materials, reducing costs and promoting sustainability. For example, they repurposed leftover ingredients from their food business to create new menu items, minimising waste and generating additional revenue.

Over time, Alex's business thrived, thanks to their unwavering commitment to bootstrapping and effective budget management. By embracing innovative strategies, collaborating with others, and utilising resources wisely, Alex built a successful business with limited financial resources.

Alex's story serves as a testament to the power of bootstrapping. Through creativity, resilience, and strategic decision-making, entrepreneurs can overcome financial limitations and achieve remarkable success. By applying these bootstrapping techniques, aspiring business owners can navigate the challenging journey of entrepreneurship and turn their dreams into profitable ventures.

Here is a brief list of the bootstrapping techniques Alex employed:

Start with a minimum viable product (MVP)

Embrace sweat equity

Seek strategic partnerships

Utilise online platforms and social media

Practise lean operations

Implement guerilla marketing tactics

Crowdfunding

Leverage open-source software and free online tools

Prioritise exceptional customer experiences

Repurpose and upcycle materials

These techniques allowed Alex to maximise their limited resources and build a successful business without relying heavily on external funding.

As you can see, bootstrapping is a strategic approach to starting and running a business that emphasises self-sufficiency and resourcefulness. It involves using existing resources, personal savings, and creative problem-solving to minimise the need for external financing or investment. By bootstrapping, entrepreneurs aim to maintain control over their business, avoid debt, and build a sustainable foundation for long-term success.

Here are some key aspects of bootstrapping in more detail:

Self-Funding: Bootstrapped businesses rely on personal savings, personal loans, or income generated by the business itself to finance operations and growth. Owners often invest their own money into the business rather than seeking outside investors or loans.

Example: A small business owner uses their personal savings to purchase necessary equipment, develop a website, and cover initial marketing expenses.

Cost Reduction: Bootstrapped businesses prioritise cost-consciousness and finding ways to operate efficiently on a limited budget. They focus on minimising unnecessary expenses and seeking cost-effective alternatives.

Example: A small business negotiates lower rent for office space, opts for open-source software instead of paid subscriptions, and carefully manages inventory to reduce carrying costs.

Sweat Equity: Instead of relying solely on hiring and outsourcing, bootstrapped businesses leverage the skills and efforts of the founders and team members. This allows them to keep costs down while maximising expertise.

Example: A small business owner takes on multiple roles, such as handling sales, marketing, and customer service, rather than hiring separate individuals for each task.

Revenue Generation: Bootstrapped businesses prioritise generating revenue from sales and customer payments to fund their growth and operations. They focus on driving customer acquisition, retention, and increasing sales to generate cash flow.

Example: A small business invests in marketing efforts to reach a wider audience and implement strategies to upsell and cross-sell to existing customers, thereby increasing revenue.

Strategic Partnerships: Bootstrapped businesses often seek collaborations and partnerships to access additional resources, shared networks, and cost-saving opportunities. They look for mutually beneficial relationships that can help them expand their reach and capabilities.

Example: A small business forms a partnership with a complementary company to co-market their products/services, share customer databases, or jointly participate in industry events.

Profitability Focus: Bootstrapped businesses prioritise profitability and cash flow management. They aim to generate consistent revenue, control costs, and reinvest profits back into the business for growth and sustainability.

Example: A small business closely monitors its financial statements, tracks key performance indicators (KPIs), and implements cost-control measures to ensure profitability.

By adopting a bootstrapping mindset, entrepreneurs can effectively manage their budgets, make strategic decisions, and build a solid foundation for their businesses. While it requires careful financial management and resourcefulness, bootstrapping can lead to greater financial independence, flexibility, and long-term success.

Navigating Risk: Unleashing the Power of Effective Risk Management

Risk management is an incredible tool that offers numerous benefits to sole traders and small businesses. By effectively identifying, assessing, and mitigating risks, businesses can safeguard their operations, enhance decision-making processes, drive sales growth, and ultimately increase their chances of long-term success. Let's delve deeper into why risk management is amazing and explore how it can positively impact sole traders and small businesses.

Protection and Continuity: One of the primary benefits of risk management is protection and continuity. By identifying potential risks, such as economic downturns, industry disruptions, or regulatory changes, businesses can implement strategies to mitigate these risks and ensure continuity of their operations. This proactive approach minimises downtime, financial losses, and reputational damage, allowing businesses to remain operational and deliver products or services to customers without major disruptions.

Financial Stability: Risk management plays a vital role in achieving financial stability. By evaluating financial risks, such as cash flow shortages, market volatility, or unexpected expenses, businesses can develop contingency plans and allocate resources more efficiently. This enables businesses to navigate financial challenges with greater confidence, maintain healthy cash flow, and make informed financial decisions. By mitigating financial risks, businesses can avoid potential bankruptcies or severe financial setbacks that could jeopardise their survival.

Enhanced Decision Making: Risk management provides valuable insights that inform decision-making processes. By assessing risks associated with new ventures, investments, or strategic initiatives, businesses can make informed choices that align with their objectives and risk appetite. This helps avoid reckless decisions that may have adverse consequences. With a thorough understanding of potential risks and their potential impact, businesses can confidently pursue growth opportunities, enter new markets, or diversify their product offerings while minimising potential pitfalls.

Improved Efficiency and Productivity: Effective risk management identifies potential inefficiencies or vulnerabilities within business operations. By addressing these areas, businesses can optimise processes, enhance productivity, and reduce wasteful practices. For example, identifying bottlenecks in the supply chain and implementing measures to address them can lead to streamlined operations, timely deliveries, and improved customer satisfaction. This focus on efficiency not only reduces costs but also enhances the overall customer experience, strengthening customer loyalty and driving repeat business.

Competitive Advantage: Embracing risk management can give sole traders and small businesses a competitive edge. By actively managing risks, businesses demonstrate their commitment to quality, reliability, and sustainability. This can enhance their reputation among customers, suppliers, and stakeholders. Additionally, businesses that have robust risk management practices in place may be seen as more trustworthy and reliable partners, which can attract new customers, retain existing ones, and build long-term relationships. This competitive advantage can translate into increased market share, higher customer retention rates, and improved profitability.

Sales Growth: Strategic risk management can directly contribute to increased sales. By identifying risks and opportunities in the market, businesses can tailor their marketing and sales efforts to capitalise on emerging trends or customer needs. For example, conducting market research and competitor analysis can help identify gaps in the market that the business can fulfil. By understanding customer preferences, anticipating market shifts, and adapting their products or services accordingly, businesses can align themselves with demand, leading to increased sales and market share. Furthermore, effective risk management can help businesses identify potential sales obstacles, such as pricing challenges or distribution issues, and develop strategies to overcome them, ensuring sustained sales growth.

Risk management is a powerful tool for sole traders and small businesses. It provides protection, financial stability, informed decision-making, operational efficiency, competitive advantage, and sales growth opportunities. By adopting a proactive approach to risk management, businesses can navigate uncertainties with confidence, grasp opportunities for growth, and thrive in an ever-changing business landscape. Embracing risk management is a key ingredient for long-term success and resilience in the business world.

For instance, Smith's Bakery is a family-owned business that has been operating for over 30 years. They specialise in producing artisan bread and pastries, supplying local cafes and restaurants. Their commitment to risk management played a crucial role in their success and resilience. Here's their story:

Identifying Potential Risks: Smith's Bakery conducted a thorough risk assessment and identified various potential risks. These included ingredient shortages, equipment breakdowns, food safety issues, and fluctuating market demand.

Supplier Relationships: To mitigate the risk of ingredient shortages, Smith's Bakery developed strong relationships with multiple suppliers. They maintained open lines of communication, regularly reviewed supply contracts, and had backup suppliers in place to ensure a steady flow of ingredients.

Equipment Maintenance and Backup: Smith's Bakery recognised the importance of maintaining their equipment to prevent breakdowns that could disrupt production. They implemented a strict maintenance schedule, conducted regular inspections, and invested in backup equipment to minimise downtime in case of failures.

Food Safety Protocols: To mitigate the risk of food safety issues, Smith's Bakery implemented rigorous hygiene and sanitation protocols. They trained their staff on proper food handling practices, conducted regular inspections, and adhered to industry standards and regulations.

Market Research and Diversification: Smith's Bakery regularly conducted market research to identify trends and anticipate changes in customer preferences. This allowed them to diversify their product offerings and adapt to shifting demand. For example, they introduced gluten-free and vegan options to cater to a growing segment of health-conscious customers.

Financial Management: Smith's Bakery maintained a robust financial management system to monitor costs, track cash flow, and ensure profitability. They regularly reviewed their pricing strategy, optimised inventory management, and monitored key financial indicators to identify potential risks and make informed decisions.

Business Continuity Planning: Smith's Bakery developed a comprehensive business continuity plan to address potential disruptions. They had contingency measures in place for emergencies such as natural disasters or unforeseen events, ensuring that production and distribution could continue with minimal interruptions.

Outcomes:

Supply Chain Resilience: By maintaining strong supplier relationships and having backup options, Smith's Bakery successfully navigated through ingredient shortages caused by unexpected events such as extreme weather conditions or supplier disruptions. This allowed them to continue production without major disruptions.

High-Quality Products and Customer Satisfaction: The bakery's focus on food safety protocols and quality control measures ensured that their products consistently met high standards. This resulted in customer satisfaction, positive reviews, and repeat business.

Agility and Adaptability: Through market research and diversification, Smith's Bakery was able to adapt to changing customer preferences and market trends. This allowed them to introduce new products that resonated with customers, expanding their customer base and increasing sales.

Financial Stability: The bakery's sound financial management practices helped them maintain financial stability even during challenging times. They were able to make informed decisions, control costs, and ensure profitability, safeguarding their long-term viability.

Strong Reputation: Smith's Bakery's commitment to risk management and delivering high-quality products earned them a strong reputation in the local community. Their reputation for reliability and excellence led to increased brand loyalty and referrals from satisfied customers.

What about smaller businesses?

Olivia is a talented graphic designer who operates her own freelance design studio. As a sole trader, she faces unique challenges but has leveraged risk management to achieve amazing outcomes. Here's her story:

Identifying Potential Risks: Olivia conducted a comprehensive risk assessment to identify potential risks in her freelance design business. These included client payment delays, scope creep, technology failures, and the need for continuous professional development.

Client Relationship Management: To mitigate the risk of payment delays, Olivia implemented effective client relationship management practices. She clearly communicated payment terms and expectations upfront, followed up on outstanding invoices, and built strong relationships with her clients based on trust and open communication.

Scope Definition and Contract Agreements: Olivia developed a robust process for defining project scopes and documenting them in contract agreements. This helped manage the risk of scope creep, ensuring that she delivered projects within the agreed-upon scope and avoiding additional work without proper compensation.

Backup Systems and Data Protection: Recognising the risk of technology failures, Olivia implemented backup systems for her design files and important data. She regularly backed up her work to external hard drives and utilised cloud storage solutions to protect against potential hardware failures or data loss.

Continuous Professional Development: Olivia invested in her professional development to stay ahead in the industry and mitigate the risk of becoming outdated. She attended workshops, conferences, and online courses to enhance her skills, learn new design techniques, and stay up to date with emerging trends.

Diversification of Client Portfolio: To mitigate the risk of relying heavily on a single client or industry, Olivia diversified her client portfolio. She actively sought clients from different industries, ensuring a varied stream of projects and reducing the impact of a potential loss of one client.

Financial Management and Cash Flow Planning: Olivia maintained meticulous financial management practices to track her income and expenses. She closely monitored her cash flow, set aside funds for taxes and business expenses, and implemented strategies to ensure a steady income stream throughout the year.

Outcomes:

Timely Payments and Financial Stability: Olivia's effective client relationship management practices resulted in timely payments, contributing to her financial stability and consistent cash flow. This allowed her to meet her financial obligations and plan for future growth.

Streamlined Project Execution: The scope definition and contract agreements helped Olivia manage client expectations and deliver projects within the agreed-upon scope. This minimised disputes and allowed her to complete projects efficiently, leading to increased client satisfaction and positive referrals.

Data Protection and Business Continuity: Olivia's backup systems and data protection measures ensured the safety of her design files and client data. In case of technology failures, she could quickly recover her work and continue operations, maintaining business continuity.

Professional Growth and Competitive Advantage: By investing in continuous professional development, Olivia enhanced her skills and knowledge, staying ahead of industry trends. This positioned her as a competitive designer, attracting new clients and opportunities for collaboration.

Adaptability to Market Changes: Olivia's diversified client portfolio reduced the risk of relying on a single industry or client. This allowed her to navigate changes in the market, ensuring a steady stream of projects and protecting her business from potential downturns in specific sectors.

Positive Reputation and Client Referrals: Through her commitment to delivering high-quality work and exceptional client service, Olivia built a strong reputation as a reliable and skilled designer.

Satisfied clients became advocates for her business, referring her to their networks and generating additional leads.

This great case study highlights the significant impact of risk management for sole traders like Olivia. By proactively identifying and mitigating potential risks, she achieved financial stability, streamlined project execution, protected her data, maintained professional growth, adapted to market changes, and built a positive reputation in the industry.

I hope you get the point. Relying solely on one element can prove to be a precarious situation. It makes your business vulnerable and prone to collapse, like building a house on shifting sands.

Consider a freelance graphic designer who primarily relied on one freelance platform for client projects. This platform served as their primary source of income, providing a steady stream of clients and projects. However, when the platform introduced new policies that limited the visibility of freelancers or increased competition, the designer experienced a significant decrease in client enquiries and project opportunities. Their overreliance on one platform left them scrambling to find alternative platforms and clients to sustain their business.

Similarly, a small manufacturing company heavily dependent on one major customer faced a devastating blow when the customer decided to switch suppliers. The loss of this customer, who accounted for a significant portion of their revenue, had a severe impact on their profitability. They learned the hard way that relying on one major customer without diversifying their client base left them exposed to the risks of losing a crucial revenue stream.

In another example, a boutique coffee shop relied heavily on foot traffic from a nearby office building. Their business flourished as long as employees filled the building. However, when the office building underwent renovations and the majority of employees worked remotely, the coffee shop experienced a significant drop in sales. The lack of diversified customer segments or alternative revenue streams left them struggling to adapt and generate income during this challenging period.

The stories above illustrate the dangers of having a "single point of failure" in your business. To mitigate this risk, diversification is key. Here are additional areas where businesses should aim to diversify:

Marketing Channels: Rather than relying solely on one marketing channel, such as social media or search engine advertising, explore a mix of channels. This could include content marketing, email marketing, influencer partnerships, offline advertising, or events. By diversifying your marketing channels, you can reach a broader audience and mitigate the impact of any one channel's changes or decline in effectiveness.

Revenue Streams: Expand your revenue streams beyond one primary source. For example, a bakery that relies solely on walk-in customers can diversify by offering wholesale products to local restaurants or launching an e-commerce platform to sell baked goods online. This diversification provides multiple streams of income and safeguards against sudden disruptions in one area.

Product or Service Offerings: Instead of relying solely on one product or service, consider expanding your offerings. This could involve introducing complementary products or services that cater to different customer needs or entering new markets. By diversifying your offerings, you can tap into new revenue streams and protect against changes in customer preferences.

Supplier Network: Avoid depending on one key supplier for essential materials or inventory. Establish relationships with multiple suppliers to ensure a stable supply chain. This not only provides backup options in case of supply disruptions but also opens up opportunities for negotiating better terms and prices.

Geographic Markets: Explore expansion into new geographic markets. If your business operates in a single location, consider opening additional branches or targeting customers in different regions. This diversifies your customer base and reduces the risk of being heavily reliant on one local market.

By diversifying in these areas, you strengthen your business's foundation and reduce the risk of collapse due to a single point of failure. Embrace the mindset of building resilience and adaptability, so that your business can weather storms and thrive in any market conditions.

A well-diversified business is like a house built on solid rock. It can withstand the tests of time and external changes, ensuring long-term success and sustainability.

Creating a robust risk management plan is a vital process that involves several key steps. Let's expand on each step and provide more examples:

Identify Risks: Start by identifying potential risks that could impact your business. These risks can vary depending on the industry and nature of your business. For example, a construction company may face risks such as accidents, equipment failure, or project delays, whilst a software company may face risks related to cybersecurity breaches, data loss, or software bugs.

Assess Risks: Once you have identified the risks, assess their likelihood and potential impact. This involves evaluating the probability of each risk occurring and the potential severity of its consequences. For instance, a retail business may assess the risk of a product recall due to quality issues and determine the potential financial impact and damage to reputation.

Analyse Risk Causes and Effects: Dig deeper into each identified risk to understand the underlying causes and potential effects on your business. This analysis helps in developing effective mitigation strategies. For example, if a manufacturing company identifies the risk of supply chain disruptions, the causes could include reliance on a single supplier or inadequate backup plans. The effects may include production delays, increased costs, or customer dissatisfaction.

Develop Risk Mitigation Strategies: Based on the assessment and analysis, develop strategies to mitigate the identified risks. These strategies aim to reduce the likelihood or impact of risks and ensure business continuity. For instance, a restaurant may implement food safety protocols and regular inspections to mitigate the risk of foodborne illnesses. A professional service firm may develop contingency plans and establish relationships with backup suppliers to mitigate supply chain risks.

Implement Risk Controls: Put the identified risk mitigation strategies into action by implementing appropriate controls and measures. This may involve establishing policies, procedures, and guidelines that govern the identified risks. For example, a healthcare facility may implement strict patient data privacy and security measures to mitigate the risk of data breaches.

Monitor and Review: Regularly monitor the effectiveness of your risk management plan and review its implementation. This includes monitoring the status of identified risks, tracking incidents or near-miss events, and gathering feedback from employees and stakeholders. The monitoring process helps in identifying any emerging risks or areas where the plan needs adjustments.

Communicate and Train: Effective communication and training are crucial in ensuring that employees understand the risks and their roles in managing them. Regularly communicate updates about the risk management plan, provide training sessions to enhance risk awareness, and encourage employees to report any potential risks or incidents. This creates a culture of risk awareness and encourages proactive risk management.

Establish a Response Plan: Develop a response plan that outlines the actions to be taken in the event of a risk materialising. This includes defining clear roles and responsibilities, establishing communication channels, and outlining the steps to be followed during emergencies. For example, a retail store may have a response plan in place for a fire emergency, including evacuation procedures and designated assembly points.

Continual Improvement: Risk management is an ongoing process that requires continuous improvement. Regularly review and update your risk management plan based on feedback, lessons learned from incidents, and changes in the business environment. Conduct periodic risk assessments to identify new risks and ensure that your plan remains relevant and effective.

A good plan will enhance your ability to identify, assess, and mitigate risks. This proactive approach not only safeguards your business from potential threats but also instils confidence in stakeholders, enhances business resilience, and supports sustainable growth.

Too complicated for you? Start with a simple risk log. A risk log, also known as a risk register or risk database, is a simple tool used by businesses to document, analyse, and manage risks. It serves as a central repository of information that allows businesses to identify, assess, and mitigate potential risks that may impact their operations, projects, or objectives. The log typically includes details such as the nature of the risk, its likelihood and impact, mitigation measures, responsible parties, and progress status.

Elaborating on the steps involved in using a risk log and providing examples:

Jot down the risks: Take a moment to think about all the things that could go wrong in your business. It could be things like not getting paid on time, losing a big client, or your computer crashing and losing important files. Write each risk down on a piece of paper or in a document.

Example: Imagine you're a freelancer who relies on a single client for most of your income. One risk could be that if that client decides to end their contract with you, it would leave you with a significant loss of income.

Grasp the risks: Now, let's understand what each risk means for your business. Think about why it's a problem and how it could impact your work. This helps you get a clear picture of what you need to prepare for.

Example: If you lose your main client, it means you won't have as much money coming in each month. This can make it difficult to cover your expenses and might require finding new clients or diversifying your services.

Make a plan: It's time to come up with strategies to deal with each risk. Think about what you can do to prevent the risk from happening or minimise its impact. This could involve setting up safeguards, creating backup plans, or having alternative options in place.

Example: To address the risk of losing your main client, you could start looking for additional clients to spread out your income sources. You might also consider building relationships with other freelancers who can refer clients to you in case of any changes with your main client.

Stay alert: As you go about your work, stay vigilant for any signs that a risk is starting to occur. Pay attention to changes in your business environment or client behaviour that might indicate a potential problem. This allows you to take proactive measures to prevent or address the risk.

Example: If you notice your main client becoming less responsive or expressing dissatisfaction, it could be a warning sign that they are considering ending the contract. By recognising these signs early, you can take steps to address their concerns and potentially salvage the relationship.

Update your risk log: It's important to regularly review and update your risk log. As your business evolves and new risks emerge, add them to the list. Likewise, if you find better solutions or preventive measures for existing risks, update the log accordingly. This ensures that your risk log remains an accurate and useful tool for managing potential challenges.

Example: Let's say you've added new services to your freelance business. This introduces the risk of taking on projects that are outside your expertise. By updating your risk log, you can acknowledge this new risk and develop a plan to mitigate it, such as investing in training or partnering with specialists in those areas.

It's the easiest and fastest way to start with risk management. You'll be better prepared to handle potential problems that can arise in your small business or work. The risk log acts as a guide, helping you identify, understand, and address risks effectively. Ultimately, it helps you navigate through challenges, make informed decisions, and protect the success and sustainability of your business. In short: it's amazing.

Final Word

Throughout this exhilarating journey, we have explored the limitless possibilities and game-changing strategies that can propel your business to extraordinary heights.

But why stop here? If you're eager to experience exponential growth at an accelerated pace, we invite you to take a bold step forward. Reach out to our company's Bid Champions, whose remarkable achievements in the world of tenders have transformed the landscape for freelancers, small companies, and ambitious entrepreneurs.

Our Bid Champions have a proven track record of securing contracts that defy expectations. From enabling freelancers to win game-changing contracts to empowering small companies to clinch one contract per month on average, their expertise is unrivaled. They have unlocked the secrets to tendering success and are ready to guide you on your journey to exceptional growth.

By working closely with our Bid Champions, you can tap into their invaluable insights, strategies, and techniques. They will provide personalized guidance tailored to your unique business needs, empowering you to navigate the intricate world of tendering with confidence and finesse.

So, if you're ready to fast-track your growth, don't hesitate to reach out to our Bid Champions. Experience the incredible feat of winning contracts that were once deemed out of reach. Contact us today at win@bidchampions.com and discover how exponential growth can become your new reality.

Remember, your journey towards exponential growth doesn't end here. Embrace the power of amplification, seize the opportunities that lie before you, and make your mark on the business world. The future is waiting—for you to amplify it!

Thank you for embarking on this transformative adventure. Wishing you boundless growth and prosperity.

Thomas Gresham